T0292817

Twitch

Digital Media and Society Series

Twitch

Mark R. Johnson

polity

First published in 2024 by Polity Press

Polity Press
65 Bridge Street
Cambridge CB2 1UR, UK

Polity Press
111 River Street
Hoboken, NJ 07030, USA

ISBN-13: 978-1-5095-5858-2
ISBN-13: 978-1-5095-5859-9(pb)

A catalogue record for this book is available from the British Library.

Library of Congress Control Number: 2023951445

Typeset in 10.25 on 13pt Scala
by Fakenham Prepress Solutions, Fakenham, Norfolk NR21 8NL
Printed and bound in Great Britain by TJ Books Ltd, Padstow, Cornwall

The publisher has used its best endeavours to ensure that the URLs for external websites referred to in this book are correct and active at the time of going to press. However, the publisher has no responsibility for the websites and can make no guarantee that a site will remain live or that the content is or will remain appropriate.

Every effort has been made to trace all copyright holders, but if any have been overlooked the publisher will be pleased to include any necessary credits in any subsequent reprint or edition.

For further information on Polity, visit our website:
politybooks.com

Contents

Acknowledgements

My two main expressions of gratitude go to my father – for his tireless support and love and protection – and to my girlfriend – for bringing long-forgotten laughter and joy to my life.

I'd also like to thank Chanel Larche for her constant and loving warmth in keeping me company digitally for a hard two years of lockdown and travel restrictions; Nathan Jackson for his friendship, often lending a listening ear, and the courage to meet the challenge of actually *playing* La-Mulana; Fiona Nicoll for supporting me on securing a Killam Postdoctoral Fellowship in Canada and giving me the time and space to pursue my research interests; Tom Brock, Brett Abarbanel, Gregory Blomquist and Dan Merriman for their friendship (and in the first two cases, collaboration) during times when I have not always been as responsive or accessible as I would like; and all the roguelike fans on the internet who make my day every time they take a moment to tell me the creative efforts of my decade of hobbyist game design work have not gone unnoticed. I am also very grateful to Tom Apperley for recommending me for this book project, and Tom Apperley (again), Benjamin Burroughs, Mahli-Ann Butt, Chris Chesher, Brandon Harris, Maxwell Foxman, Gerard Goggin, Nathan Jackson (again), and Polity's manuscript reviewers, for the generosity of their time in providing such detailed feedback and insights to strengthen the final manuscript. My editor Mary Savigar has always been highly positive about this project, supportive and responsive and helpful throughout, and for all these things I am also extremely grateful.

Introduction

What is Twitch?

Twitch is the dominant global platform for the 'live streaming' (live video broadcasting over the internet) of digital gaming – and much else besides. Examining how and why this happened, how Twitch and game streaming have evolved together, and the position we have arrived at, are among the principal objectives of this book. To understand contemporary game streaming, 'gamers', gaming as a public event, gaming as a newfound vehicle for aspiration and entrepreneurialism, gamers as celebrities and as friends, and the diversity and attitudes and behaviours in live-streaming communities and cultures both within gaming and beyond it, we need to understand Twitch. Yet Twitch is not solely a digital infrastructure and architecture for playing games: it is also now a keystone public location for debating, commenting, and disputing who gamers are, what gaming is, what the current issues are, what it should be, and where it's going. Twitch users now individually and collectively help to determine *what matters* in gaming. Twitch is also, however, not only about gaming, and throughout this work the challenges posed to the once-unquestioned association between Twitch and gaming are key. New forms of live stream continue to emerge which demand our attention, and are becoming just as important as gaming if we wish to understand the wider Twitch picture.

As with all major internet platforms Twitch increasingly exhibits a size and complexity that makes comprehensive appraisal, let alone analysis, a daunting task. I therefore begin with one of Twitch's very own slogans, what it can tell us about how the site sees *itself*, and the light it sheds on how and why over a hundred million people regularly tune in to view *other* people playing video games, and doing a growing range of other activities, on the internet.

'You're already one of us'

Twitch's marketing likes to push the idea of *belonging*. The site's 2019 advertising campaign, for example, confidently declared to the reader that 'you're already one of us'. The *already* implies that the user doesn't need to do anything special to get started on Twitch: being interested in and knowledgeable about games and gaming are apparently all that one needs. It perhaps also harks back to the assumed childhoods of these imagined users, childhoods in which gaming has played a central role for more and more citizens in industrialized nations in the past fifty years. The *us* speaks to the sense of strong social bonds that are essential to Twitch (a topic I explore throughout this book) and implies a degree of in-group belonging. It suggests a demarcation between *us* and *them* before immediately reassuring the reader that they – that you – are already in the *us*, and need not worry about being left out in the cold with *them*. Both aspects of this slogan are designed to appeal to a young game-playing population. It emphasizes ideas of belonging and the naturalness of that belonging, setting up a divide between the 'gamers' who apparently belong on Twitch, and everyone else, who apparently doesn't. Gaming has long been framed by many of its participants (and its marketers) as an exclusive or elite pastime (Kirkpatrick, 2017; Massanari, 2017; Paul, 2018; Huang & Liu, 2022; cf. Sjöblom et al., 2019: 25; Welch, 2022: 523) requiring deep skills and acquired knowledge, and Twitch is very clear in trying to connect to this sense of distinctiveness that many game players feel.

Understanding why this slogan was chosen for a website

predominantly (although no longer exclusively) associated with *gaming* tells us immediately what Twitch is trying to do, and who Twitch is trying to bring on board. In an earlier era before ubiquitous internet access when games were a less visible pastime, a shared interest in gaming offered a fundamental form of connection. Working out how to run a game on home computers such as the ZX Spectrum or Commodore 64, or navigating different compatibilities or graphics cards or sound cards in early eras of PC gaming, also further bolstered the (not wholly unreasonable) sense that those able simply to get games to run were, indeed, displaying some degree of technological and technical prowess. This sense of gaming being something *apart*, something *different*, or even something suggestive of membership in a technological elite, has unfortunately metamorphosed into one of the main sources of the toxicity and exclusion now found across gaming culture (Paul, 2018; Schott & Horrell, 2000). Yet for those on the *inside*, gaming could nevertheless be a source of deep belonging and a way to identify with others who had the same experiences and pursued the same ludic pleasures (De Grove et al., 2015; Vella et al., 2019). In this sense every player is, indeed, already 'one of us' from Twitch's perspective. Every player brings some degree of gaming literacy and knowledge and the potential to quickly connect to other Twitch users via a shared interest in gaming or in specific games or genres.

Twitch is noteworthy for how rapidly a user can get started on the platform. There is no sign-up requirement and Twitch's homepage immediately offers the interested viewer a range of channels. I might find someone playing a game I like, or a game I know nothing about but want to learn about, perhaps because I'm considering buying it. Maybe the 'streamer' (the broadcaster/player) rather than the game grabs my attention – it might be that they look like I do, or talk like I do, or seem to have had similar life experiences. Instead of the streamer or the game, maybe what grabs my interest is the text-based chat room associated with a channel. Perhaps the conversation between viewers there is highly amusing, or they're talking about games or non-gaming topics that interest me. Speaking personally, even after almost a decade of researching Twitch there is still something compelling about entering a channel and immediately seeing how actively and enthusiastically its viewers are taking part in the broadcast. It suggests that one has stumbled on a whole world of peers one didn't know of, and that surely if there's something here many others are enjoying, I might enjoy it as well?

Finding such a connection on Twitch immediately positions the viewer as being a member of Twitch's *us*: a member of a set of demographically similar players, or people who enjoy similar games, or people who live in similar places, or people who make and laugh at similar jokes (cf. Johnson, 2022). Although gaming is ubiquitous and the games industry is big business, comfortably eclipsing many other creative and media sectors in terms of yearly economic output – with most estimates placing it somewhere around $200bn (Monahan, 2021) – it is for many game players that sense of *connection* that is sought and valued, and Twitch indeed provides this. Yet this connection on Twitch, as elsewhere in gaming, is not equally available to all. The archetypal straight white male 'gamer' (Paaßen et al., 2017; Taylor & Chess, 2018) may well easily identify as 'one of us' – Twitch's semi-real and semi-imagined proposed community of online gamers sharing their experiences and their passion for games – but this cannot be taken for granted outside that demographic.

Research has comprehensively demonstrated the varied and subtle but often explicit means by which women (e.g., Guarriello, 2019; Ruberg et al., 2019; Orme, 2021), queer players (e.g., Taylor, 2018: 20; Welch, 2022: 523; Lawson, 2023: 12) and ethnic minority players (Chan & Gray, 2020; Evans & Llano, 2023: 5; Han et al., 2023) are denied full engagement in gaming communities, including game streaming. Players who do not match the implicit norm of the 'gamer' – white, male, young and heterosexual – can struggle to find acceptance in gaming communities, representation and presence in games (Orme, 2018: 156–7), or form friendships and sociality around gaming, and often suffer bullying and bigotry. Being outside the demographics that games and game companies – including Twitch – implicitly or explicitly frame themselves as appealing to, can easily feel alienating or hostile. Twitch's *us* is presented as an unquestioned and almost axiomatic expression of the apparent deep connection between *gamers* the world over, but in fact hides – as so many gamers are eager to do in their rejection of 'politics' in games (Phillips, 2020; Ruch, 2021) – a far more complex reality.

Who is, therefore, 'one of us'? Who is not, and who gets to decide? What powers do 'us' members possess to shape and define gaming on Twitch and beyond, that those outside do not? I argue in this book that Twitch is a central public forum for the debate and creation of meaning and importance in gaming, which in turn requires us to ask who gets to speak, and who is listened to. This contestation is vital to our understanding of Twitch because there is a deep reciprocal relationship between what is considered important on Twitch and what sorts of streams get the most attention, and *who* is behind those streams and hence what sorts of content and ideas they put out into the site. There are few game players more prominent than those on Twitch and few games more prominent than those with large numbers of Twitch viewers, yet the politics of these phenomena are far from transparent. By examining Twitch we examine the politics of contemporary gaming through an extremely important but generally overlooked pair of questions: what *matters* in gaming, and *who* gets to decide? Figuring out the answers to these questions, as well as presenting an overview of this major gaming-focused – but no longer gaming-only – internet platform in the 2020s and beyond, are the key objectives of this work.

We have always watched games

Arguably the earliest scholarship in the discipline we now call 'game studies' that really addressed the *spectator* experience of gaming was that which explored spectating in arcades. Largely now a reminder of a bygone past in most countries – although Japan maintains an active arcade scene – it is with arcades that the watching potential and the social potential of gaming first became truly apparent (Schofield & LeDone, 2019: 1; Groen, 2020). The colourful cabinets, the large and bright screens, the interesting sounds of arcade machines drew in children, teenagers and young adults (Kocurek, 2015). Arcade spaces were designed to highlight the newest and potentially most interesting games, and to enable others to gather around them (Orme, 2021: 2253). This setting not just allowed spectators to view what was taking place on screen but also offered something of a free tutorial in a game. Those perhaps intimidated by the reflex or knowledge demands of gaming – or just unaware of how to play the latest title – would be able to watch others first before potentially playing themselves (Taylor, 2018: 38).

This was important because people in arcades could not just watch others playing the games, but could also expect to *be watched* when they played. Alongside this inherently spectatorial framing of the space and the possibilities it afforded, arcades also facilitated a kind of asynchronous spectatorship via high-score lists (Stenros et al., 2011). These enabled players to see what scores others were achieving on a given machine without having to be physically present at the time of play. Some arcade cabinets even allowed for viewing replays of other players' achievements, allowing viewers to spectate – at a temporal distance – a session of play that had yielded a compelling high score (cf. Johansson, 2021: 8). Watching play in this earliest era of digital gaming expanded, therefore, beyond both its spatial and temporal borders, and rapidly established an important social dimension of gaming culture and the exchange of knowledge, achievement and prestige. Spectating also had an economic benefit, as the development of skill through observation potentially reduced the impact on one's own stack of coins when seeking to reach a later level or achieve a particular in-game goal.

Yet early digital game spectating was not limited to the arcade. The rise of home gaming consoles and the popularity of gaming among children and teenagers increased opportunities for spectatorship, especially in singleplayer games where siblings or friends would take turns watching and playing (Dixon & Weber, 2007; Taylor, 2018: 37–8). I remember playing real-time strategy games like the *Command and Conquer* (1995–2020) series with my friends as a teenager, taking it in turns to play perhaps twenty or thirty minutes of an online multiplayer contest before handing over to the person sitting by and watching. This sometimes led to frustrations – we always wanted to be taking *our* turn at the end of a battle so that we could deal the final blow to our opponents – but also enabled a higher level of observation and tactical decision making, one that was only possible with a second player *watching* and entirely free to think and strategize, rather than making moment-to-moment inputs into the game itself. Much of the game advertising and marketing material of the era shows children or teenagers gathered around a console or PC with one playing and the others watching. Although presumably a marketing strategy to imply the potential excitement of gaming even for those who might not consider themselves *gamers*, it nevertheless reflected a reality for many families and in many homes.

Another antecedent of the recent eruption in game spectatorship on Twitch can be found in esports, which is to say competitive and often professionalized video gaming (Taylor, 2012; Reitman et al., 2020). For around two decades now gamers have been able to attend events in person to watch highly skilled gamers duke it out in different games. Major live events were a rarity for a long time, however, and it was often instead through the internet that the achievements of the world's leading competitive players were broadcast and shared (Major, 2015: 13). Videos of competitive gaming matches have been uploaded to video- and file-sharing websites for the last few decades, while in South Korea (Jin, 2010; 2020) whole television channels are dedicated to StarCraft and StarCraft II. Here gaming has not taken on the arcade spectatorship experience of looking over the shoulder at someone else's skilled play, nor the home spectating experience with friends or family enjoying a singleplayer game together, but rather a spectating experience that is closest to professional physical sports. Competitions can be watched in person or with friends and family, of course, but broadcasting offers an experience where viewers might be tuning in from anywhere at any time in any context.

People have thus always found watching games (just as with physical sports) to be compelling, through the games of the arcade and the newly-digitized modern home – and now Twitch. In a medium often thought of as being defined by its *interactivity* – in a way that literature or cinema are not – it is perhaps surprising how much pleasure and satisfaction can evidently be gained by forgoing that interactivity and instead allowing someone *else* to be interactive with a game, and simply watching what happens (cf. Orme, 2021). Twitch is the site that exemplifies this like no other, with well over a hundred million spectators regularly tuning in to watch several million other people playing digital games. This is not simply 'instead' of playing games themselves, but rather the relationships between a person's Twitch game viewing and a person's own game playing can be complex and multi-layered. The dynamics can range from viewers watching skilled players of their favourite games in order to learn something and improve their own play skills (Burroughs & Rama, 2015; Olejniczak, 2015; Lin, 2019), to people watching a Twitch streamer as 'passive background entertainment'

(Ask et al., 2019; cf. Taylor, 2018: 39–40) while taking breaks in the working day or even gaming themselves, to people using Twitch as a source of something akin to a game review (Johnson & Woodcock, 2019b; cf. Nieborg & Foxman, 2023) to inform a potential future purchase decision (Speed et al., 2023), to people who don't play digital games at all nevertheless enjoying the spectacle and the community (Orme, 2021; cf. Baldauf-Quilliatre & de Carvajal, 2021).

Twitch therefore takes some of the established dynamics of game spectating, and pushes the acceleration pedal *hard*. Rather than watching one friend, you can now watch as many different people playing games as you can find on the platform. Rather than being watched by a handful of friends, now you too can be watched by hundreds or even thousands of eager spectators. Rather than watching someone playing a game at a high level in person, you can watch them from the comfort of your own home or on your phone on the subway, and rather than skilled singleplayer gamers being known only from their three-letter tags in the local arcade machines, they are now globally visible, and globally seen. We might therefore conclude that something like Twitch was waiting to happen, with the antecedents I've discussed in this section telling us much about how compelling it is to watch the digital gameplay of others. Yet just as the physical space of the arcade or the home shaped earlier spectating practices, what can we say about the actual dynamics and experiences of spectating or broadcasting on Twitch? In the arcade one looks over the shoulder of a fellow player, while on the television channel one watches the celebrity playing. On Twitch a person can do both of these, but the platform also adds new dynamics to the spectatorship experience that were (are) not present in these other forms. It is to this I now turn in order to give a sense of what streams on the platform are really like and what it means to spend time on, and to experience, Twitch.

On experiencing Twitch

Twitch is first and foremost a platform on which an individual can 'live stream' (broadcast) themselves doing something over the internet with accompanying video and sound (Sjöblom et al., 2019). Twitch does not allow content it deems to be sexual or otherwise unacceptable (Ruberg et al., 2019; Brown & Moberly, 2020) – though the barriers are porous and poorly policed (Cullen & Ruberg, 2019; Ruberg, 2021) as I discuss later in this book – but anything not within those categories is generally considered fair game. Live streamed sexual content has been an adult staple on the internet for decades. Some of this originated in the phenomenon of 'cam girls', who were women broadcasting themselves live on the internet with a range of objectives, only one of which was sexual or erotic (Senft, 2008) – although they are now often remembered as being solely about this, which is itself a telling reminder of how the internet often frames the activities of women. Cam girls represent an important precursor to Twitch (Ruberg, 2021; cf. Henry & Farvid, 2017), albeit one the site likes to distance itself from. Most broadcasts on Twitch can be viewed live and re-watched after the initial stream without needing to sign up for an account (Uszkoreit, 2018: 165), although some streamers make their recordings exclusive to committed fans. An account allows you to comment in the text 'chat' window accompanying a live stream to talk to the streamer or other viewers, and allows you to start your own channel with that username. A streamer is free to watch channels any time they are not streaming (or indeed when they are streaming), while a viewer can watch any number of channels simultaneously, in any broadcast language or from any time zone, and can stop and start their viewership of a particular channel at any time.

Although no longer the complete picture, Twitch is still primarily associated with, and predominantly features, digital gaming streams. In a gaming stream the four most common aspects of a broadcast are the streamed video of a game being played, a live webcam image of the streamer's face and sometimes upper body, a voiceover commentary from the streamer, and the 'Twitch chat' window alongside the live video. The first (the main video) most often takes the form of a screen capture on the streamer's computer using software specifically designed for this, such as Open Broadcaster Software (OBS) or StreamLabs (Woodhouse, 2021: 30). These record the image on the user's screen and transmit it to Twitch, which then relays it to the viewers on that channel. This video content is usually broadcast at a high frame rate and these days is generally of a high quality such as 720p or 1080p, although lower-quality options are generally available for viewers on mobile phones or with limited data plans. The second (the webcam) is not universal but certainly the expected standard, and has hence received a high degree of scholarly attention (Sjöblom et al., 2019: 23; Brown & Moberly, 2020; Woodhouse, 2021; cf. Ruberg, 2022). Most streams on Twitch have a webcam focused on the streamer's head, neck and sometimes upper body, allowing the viewer to see their facial and sometimes bodily responses and reactions to what is happening in the game (or other activity) or being posted in the chat window. Channels without a webcam, meanwhile, sometimes have a 'VTuber' (Sutton, 2021; Turner, 2022) avatar instead (Brett, 2022), a digitally generated humanoid (or robot, animal, etc.), which mirrors the real-world actions of the streamer through voice and motion capture, but without showing their actual image.

The third (the commentary) can range from a moment-to-moment stream of consciousness commenting on, and giving immediate responses to, whatever is happening in the game, to occasional comments and observations about the channel, to anything in between (Payne, 2018: 287; Taylor, 2018: 19–20; Ruberg et al., 2019: 473). Twitch channels without voice commentary only find an audience in the most unusual of cases (Johnson & Jackson, 2022), suggesting that this sense of personal interaction and seemingly off-the-cuff conversation is key to a channel's appeal. The fourth (the chat) entails a text-based chat window which sits alongside the streamer's video broadcast. Viewers can type messages to the streamer and to other viewers, and there are icons next to viewers' names. These denote whether they are a financial supporter of the stream and if so to what extent and for how long, whether they are a stream moderator, or any one of several other statuses (Cai & Wohn, 2021: 9–10; Carter & Egliston, 2021: 14; Johansson, 2021: 44; Jackson, 2023a: 151–2). Known as 'Twitch chat' or more casually just 'chat', this window is the main way that viewers talk to the streamer and each other and has itself seen a significant amount of research (e.g., Ford et al., 2017; Recktenwald, 2017; Lo, 2018; Nematzadeh et al., 2019). Twitch chat is one of the most distinctive elements of the platform, with its low-fidelity text (Hamilton et al., 2014) sitting alongside the high-fidelity audiovisual content (Ruberg, 2021: 1683) being key to enabling many of the platform's most distinctive practices and complex interactive possibilities (Harris et al., 2023).

Digital gameplay dominates Twitch in terms of the volume of broadcast content and in terms of how people (gamers and otherwise) think about the site, but it is not the entire story (Payne, 2018: 287; Consalvo & Phelps, 2019). Non-gaming streams exhibit similar traits, except that, rather than capturing gaming video, they might capture a second webcam showing the streamer doing something (e.g., making a costume), or just a single webcam image that shows the streamer and their activities but nothing else besides. One of the most popular non-gaming broadcast types is the so-called 'Just Chatting' category (Kersting et al., 2021: 6; Lamerichs, 2021: 182) in which live streamers are simply having conversations with their viewers, either from home or while travelling. Many of these streams are quite relaxed and try to generate an atmosphere of cosiness and comfort (see Johnson, 2021: 1012; Youngblood, 2022; cf. Wohn et al., 2019: 103) through a sense that one is simply having a nice chat with one's friends (Speed et al., 2023; cf. Leith, 2021: 112). These are all dynamics of Twitch addressed more fully later in the book but here it is enough to note that this sense of easy friendship and mutual interest between a streamer and their viewers – whether incidentally in a gaming (or non-gaming) channel, or as the focus of a chatting channel – is a key dynamic for our understanding of Twitch culture.

These observations lead us to one of the major ongoing debates about Twitch and one of the key themes of this work: what is Twitch *for*? Platform infrastructures and technologies can easily lead to unexpected outcomes which can be capitalized on by a platform's owners, resisted by them, or continue to exist in states of tension and debate. There are examples to be found on many platforms, such as the curious forms of humour and poetry and 'bots' which exist on Twitter* (e.g., Veale & Cook, 2018; Dynel, 2020) or the emergence of cultures of sexual and gender openness, expression and exploration on Tumblr (Tiidenberg et al., 2021). The internet has long been renowned for users' ability to find unintended uses for websites and facilities and infrastructures that go far beyond original design goals and specifications. As I examine in chapter 1, Twitch exploded to wider popularity following the unexpected success of its gaming content – and its subsequent self-framing as being *for* gaming – but that does not mean such a situation is set in stone. I therefore cannot address Twitch solely in its primary state as a platform for gaming, but rather it must also be addressed as a platform whose purpose is *itself* in flux, contested, and intertwined with the politics of the activities it hosts on its millions of channels. This is one of the most important current dynamics of Twitch and must be examined alongside its powerful role

---

* This website was known as 'Twitter' for the duration of my research and I therefore use the name here; I also do so as a (very) minor act of resistance against Elon Musk's vandalism of the site.

within gaming if we are to gain a comprehensive image of what Twitch is, what it is used for, what roles and functions it fulfils, and where it might be going.

On researching Twitch

My own research on Twitch started in 2015 after completing my doctorate and acquiring a small grant from a UK funding agency. With this money my colleague Dr Jamie Woodcock and I travelled to Twitch's annual 'TwitchCon' event in 2015, 2016 and 2017. Amongst the many thousands of attendees we conducted around a hundred streamer interviews, some of quite significant length. These streamers had gathered at the event to meet their fans, promote their channels, network with other streamers and potential sponsors, and in many cases simply to *experience* the extraordinary rise of this gaming platform of which they were a small yet important part. Many gave their time generously to discuss their experiences and reflections on the platform, their labour, their perceptions of Twitch, game streaming and its future. All of this made it particularly valuable to get such a large volume of data, especially at a time when Twitch scholarship was in its infancy.

Since then I've published scholarship on Twitch addressing a range of topics – labour, culture and monetization being three of the most central – yet throughout this entire research process there has been one theme not yet fully examined. Specifically, I have continually observed how *important* things that happen on Twitch seem to be for gaming and for gamers, how much they are talked about and discussed, and how much of a continued life and continued influence they hold beyond the platform itself. This process began with the broadcast of esports events on Twitch, which were key moments in the communities and politics around competitive games (Burroughs & Rama, 2015; Taylor, 2018), but has since expanded massively across games and genres. Now it is not just individual broadcasts of individual moments in games that are of consequence – a new world record speedrun, for example (Scully-Blaker et al., 2017) – but rather Twitch's collective interest in a game (Stuart, 2020), or lack of interest in a game, can shape the financial success of that game and its wider popular reception (Johnson & Woodcock, 2019b; Parker & Perks, 2021). Major accomplishments in gaming streamed on Twitch garner immense amounts of gaming press and responses from players (e.g., Moyse, 2018; Gault, 2019). New games are often released by having famous streamers broadcast their play of the game – sometimes before others have access to it – such that their responses shape initial cultural reactions. Game developers change aspects of games to appeal to streamers and to be compelling on Twitch (Johnson & Woodcock, 2019b; Parker & Perks, 2021), sometimes even including big-name streamers in their advertising and sponsorships (Sjöblom et al., 2019; Woodcock & Johnson, 2019; Kersting et al., 2021). Controversies on Twitch immediately spill over into other social media platforms and gaming – as well as non-gaming – news sites (e.g., Hern, 2022; Park, 2023). Yet we also see increasing contests over, and diversity in, what Twitch is or should be for (e.g., Taylor, 2018: 22; Ask et al., 2019; Cabeza-Ramírez et al., 2021), and these contests inevitably intersect with ideas of what gaming is, who gaming is for, and who 'gamers' are.

All of this makes Twitch an exemplary site for research when trying to understand contemporary gaming (and other streamed activities, as I explore in later chapters). Researching Twitch offers a tremendous availability of content and behaviour for study; streamers eager to talk with you if you're actually able to get in touch with them; and data applicable to a wide range of research agendas and interests – not only gaming and games. Yet streamers can exhibit neoliberal and optimized thought processes about their time that makes securing interviews and the like for academic research very difficult, and the complexity of what the site offers necessitates engaging with numerous disciplines and approaches if one wishes to make serious intellectual progress. Nevertheless, Twitch has manoeuvred itself (and by the immense labours of its streamers and, to a lesser extent viewers, has been manoeuvred) into a position of massive visibility and importance in gaming, and increasingly in other domains as well, making it a key site for contemporary internet and digital cultures research. In this book I hope to present the reader with a comprehensive and novel sense of the site and its significance through the combination of synthesizing contemporary scholarship and presenting new analysis – in the latter case through a new argument that seems clearer to me with each passing year of studying Twitch. That is, specifically, the role that Twitch plays as a kind of *agora*.

The gaming agora

Sociologist T.L. Taylor (2018) published the first monograph on Twitch, building on her esports interests (Taylor, 2012) by giving professionalized and competitive gaming a dominant place in the analysis presented, and examining in detail the central role Twitch has played in the rapid growth of esports. It also examines Twitch's history, the emotional and affective work of game live streaming, and its legal and regulatory complexities. Taylor (2018: 23) identifies 'multiple cultural trajectories' that collide in game live streaming, specifically television, 'broader cultures of gaming and spectatorship', user-generated content and 'telecommunications'. We are told that Twitch in turn emerges from a conflux of 'television transformations, internet culture, and multiplayer experiences' (ibid.: 38). These observations remain as true as they were in 2018, but the emergence of other key factors in the last half-decade – particularly the rise of *celebrity influencers* on the site, and Twitch's intensification as a *monetized and metricized* platform – now demands our attention. Equally, broadening out from a focus on esports is another way this current volume looks to update our understanding of Twitch to the 2020s and beyond. Taylor's framing of gaming channels as being either 'esports' or 'variety' in nature (Taylor, 2018: 3, 6, 35) is no longer able to capture the now immense range of genres of gaming channels, the rise of many non-esports competitive gaming channels which focus on a single game, and the simple fact that esports is now just one part of gaming content broadcast on the site. As Taylor (2018: 6, 19, 22) puts it, her work is fundamentally concerned with the question of what happens when 'private play' becomes 'public entertainment' through a site like Twitch – this volume, by contrast, looks to update our understanding of Twitch to reflect a deeply changed platform, and integrate new analyses that reflect numerous major changes Twitch has undergone in recent years, especially in terms of Twitch's increasingly key role in the wider gaming ecosystem.

In this book I therefore build on Taylor's discussion of Twitch's role in the increasing publicity of private digital game play, by posing the question: what, therefore, *does Twitch mean for gaming*? What does this site mean for how we understand what gaming is, what gaming is not, what gaming entails, and what is important in gaming? In other words, what is Twitch doing to our ideas about gaming, *and* how is Twitch changing and shaping how those very ideas are debated, contested, and settled? While I retain a strong interest in the individual streamers and viewers of Twitch and much of this book will be concerned with their experiences, interests, behaviours and motivations, it is these broader political and ideological (and economic) questions that now come to the fore. Twitch has grown to such a size that the site is no longer just a location for individual experiences, but instead a major actor *in its own right* in gaming and gaming media. The experiences of individuals on the platform are not just their own but *collectively constitute* the nature of the much larger actor that Twitch has become. Twitch's influence as a platform is constructed from the behaviour of all its users, but much like the relationship between a state and its population, the actions of the former cannot be seen as simply an aggregate of the individual actions of its members.

To address these topics I propose in this work that Twitch should be understood as a leading – perhaps, now, *the* leading – gaming *agora*. The *agora*, in ancient Athens, was a city square in which 'administrative, political, judicial, commercial, social, cultural, and religious activities' (Camp, 1986: 6; cf. Sennett, 2016: 2) were all carried out and, importantly, were *seen* to be carried out. This might involve debates over political issues, important trade deals between leading figures, major religious ceremonies or observances, discussions over philosophy or history, and affairs of state or the public settling and proclamation of legal or civil matters. In a pre-digital era this gathering of people in one place, and this gathering of significant matters in one place, did much to define matters of importance and give large numbers of people some degree of say and engagement with them. Just as the most popular speakers in the ancient *agora* dominated through their 'rhetorical skills' (Davenport & Leitch, 2005: 143), so too do Twitch's most popular streamers command massive audiences and hold the ability to shape perspectives on major issues in gaming. This occurs because an *agora* fundamentally allows people to 'speak in a public forum' and exhibits three key characteristics: the equal 'right and opportunities to speak', a sense of 'shared values', and 'informal controls on debate' (ibid.). The totality of Twitch's millions of users, tens of thousands of channels, its infrastructures and affordances, its content, its cultures, together create a dynamic and influential *agora*. It is from an *agora* that 'reasons, purposes and norms emerge' (O'Kelly & Dubnick, 2014: 9) within a given culture or society, and it is the emergence of these articulations of importance and consequence in gaming, and for gamers, that are at the core of this book. I therefore select the *agora* rather than any of the other (more commonly invoked?) scholarly metaphors for the internet or websites, such as 'third places' (Steinkeuhler & Williams, 2006), 'third spaces' (Graham et al., 2015), the 'virtual sphere' (Papacharissi, 2002), and so on. It is the *agora*'s focus on speech and presentation, its explanation of the elevation of some speakers above others, and its emphasis on ideas of norms, debates and ritual, which are all key to developing a new perspective for understanding Twitch.

In exploring this *agora* two of the key questions are who speaks in it and who listens in it, and hence the power dynamics around Twitch's diverse set of users. The platform has become one of gaming's primary places for influencing gaming trends, creating famous gaming moments, forming game communities and even enabling gaming careers, but also one of gaming's primary places for shaping and reinforcing harassment, exclusion and prejudice. At the very same time the 'exclusivity' of that forum for gaming-related content and hence gaming-related concerns is *itself* being challenged, with many other streamers – offering cooking channels, artistic projects, chat shows and more – recognizing the potential of the platform for matters beyond the politics and play of digital games. The Twitch *agora* is an absolutely central hub for the politics and contests and meanings of modern gaming, but a second level of politics also plays out about whether other matters, not just gaming, can or should be accommodated within Twitch's walls. All of Twitch's streamers are standing on the *agora*'s cobblestones when holding their debates with their fellow gamers and more generally their fellow Twitch users, but some are also levering up those stones and trying them out in new orientations at the very same time (cf. Harris et al., 2023). These two layers of debate on Twitch – what matters in gaming, and whether or not 'what matters in gaming' should be the exclusive focus of the site – co-exist, and are the source of much of what makes Twitch so interesting as well as the source of some of its strongest controversies, challenges and issues. Throughout this work the *agora* perspective will, I hope, allow us to focus more thoroughly than before on many of these dynamics key to understanding the site, and (game) live streaming more broadly.

This work consequently has several goals. One of them is to give an outline and overview of Twitch as it stands now in the early to mid-2020s. Some of this foundational work can be found in Taylor (2018) and in the hundreds of journal and book chapter publications that now exist on Twitch, but the site is also a constantly evolving experience. A half-decade has passed since Taylor's book and this is ample time for new dynamics (e.g., the celebrity influencers and metricized monetization mentioned previously) to rise to prominence on any platform, especially one evolving as rapidly as Twitch. We are therefore due an updated look at the platform and what takes place on it, who is involved in it, but also how the platform *as an actor*, and its impact on gaming in particular, can be understood and categorized – another goal of the work is to provide exactly this. Twitch has grown into such a prominent force in gaming across most countries with gaming communities that political and ideological questions about Twitch's role – and the roles of its streamers and viewers – in gaming culture are now of the utmost importance. Twitch often still frames itself as a grassroots social experience and in some ways it is, but like all platforms that grow to such a size Twitch cannot *help* but become a major influence in the field it occupies, like a massive gravitational force pulling at the very fabric of digital gaming (cf. Burroughs & Rama, 2015; Nakandala et al., 2017; Hilvert-Bruce & Neill, 2020: 308; Bowman et al., 2022: 7; Siuda & Johnson, 2022). We need to understand what effects this presence is having and to not just acknowledge the individual experiences of the millions who use the platform, but to start seeing Twitch as an actor in its own right which reinforces and sometimes challenges the norms of gaming, while also developing new aspects of gaming culture that expand far beyond the platform itself. We also just as urgently need to understand all of Twitch's increasingly prominent *non*-gaming aspects, the tensions these sometimes generate with its gaming origins, and what these new dimensions might tell us about the site, about live streaming, and about emerging digital cultures of content creation and consumption.

Outline of the work

To properly examine Twitch and to understand its role in the framing and contesting of what *matters* in gaming and in some cases beyond, four main areas of analysis stand out: Twitch as a platform (infrastructural and technological), the streamers and viewers who spend time on Twitch (personal and psychological), the content created by the first group and consumed by the second (creative and communicative), and the cultures and communities arising out of all of these (social and communal). Each of these should tell around a quarter of the story and will together give a comprehensive image of Twitch as it stands in the 2020s, while also interrogating how Twitch's particular combination of infrastructural and technological, personal, creative and cultural factors simultaneously generate something highly distinctive with an increasingly important role and influence in and on digital gaming, and internet culture beyond gaming as well.

In the next chapter I therefore start my analysis with a focus on Twitch as a platform. This chapter considers the history of the site, what one actually *does* on the site, and then, with these basic elements developed, I consider three main points in the chapter. Firstly I show how the infrastructure and technologies of Twitch allow for an unusually high degree of customization, helping us understand how Twitch's streamers not only make statements on the site but also construct the very platforms (in the more traditional sense of that word) from which those statements are made. Secondly I argue that some of these same foundational elements of Twitch also contribute substantially to its unfortunately ubiquitous harassment and toxicity, framing this for now in platform terms before we explore it in other ways later. Thirdly I highlight the key roles played on Twitch by metrics and money and argue that these are not background or secondary elements of the site – and nor are they present only in the experiences of aspirational or 'successful' streamers – but rather they are essential and irreducible components of Twitch.

The second chapter moves on from examining Twitch as a platform to consider Twitch's users. I examine both the streamers and the viewers of Twitch, what they do on the platform, and how their actions and activities contribute to making Twitch such an effective and compelling *agora* for the gathering of 'gamers' and the mediation of 'gaming'. I then propose three core arguments. Firstly I introduce a concept I call the 'Twitch we' – a register of speech used almost universally by Twitch's streamers to develop an implicit connection between themselves and their viewers – which allows us to understand the sense of belonging, identity and comfort experienced by Twitch's users. Secondly I interrogate how Twitch is unusually capable of presenting individuals as being both celebrities and friends, and how this is integral to our understanding of Twitch as such a compelling gaming *agora*. Thirdly I unpack the complex role of the 'moderator' who sits somewhere between a viewer and a streamer, and how they adjust our understanding of the authorship of a stream, and hence the ability to speak in Twitch's *agora*.

The third chapter then examines what is broadcast on Twitch – which is to say, what Twitch streamers and viewers alike call 'content'. After looking at the founding role played by esports broadcasts, I examine the far greater diversity of gaming content that we now see through both 'variety' streamers – who stream a wide range of content – and what I term 'focused' streamers, who emphasize a particular game or genre. With these foundations I then develop two core understandings of Twitch content in this chapter. Firstly I argue that both focused and variety streamers and their channels work to articulate answers to the question of *what matters?* in the contexts of gaming as a whole, and also in specific gaming communities. This helps us to understand how and why Twitch has acquired such a central role in contemporary gaming. Secondly I use several prominent non-gaming content types – creative streams, real-money gambling streams and so-called 'Hot Tub' streams – to in turn interrogate the contested nature of this *agora* beyond its core gaming content, and the role of *creativity* on the site more broadly.

The fourth chapter then addresses how communities form and are maintained on Twitch through largely Twitch-specific cultural practices such as 'raiding', the extensive use of 'copypasta', and the vital role played by Twitch's 'emotes' – small icons that represent 'objects, symbols, or emotional expressions' (Vandenberg, 2022: 445) and are sent by viewers in Twitch chat. On these foundations the chapter then develops three key ideas. Firstly I examine how many streamers and viewers conceive of a channel as being a kind of digital 'place' as a result of its aesthetics, in-jokes and language, and that understanding this place-ness of the Twitch stream is key to unpacking what viewers and streamers alike find so compelling about it. Secondly I look at how the communities and cultures of Twitch are increasingly growing and expanding beyond the platform through other sites such as YouTube, Twitter and community-focused instant messaging app Discord. This expansion can serve strategic roles for some streamers, but also highlights the ability for a Twitch channel to be a *hub*, not merely a *place*. Thirdly I focus in depth on the use of 'emotes' in Twitch and how they function as 'characters' that viewers slip in and out of in their conversations on Twitch, simultaneously facilitating rapid and easy communication yet also limiting and constraining the full range of discourse expressed.

In the concluding chapter I argue that Twitch has led to an unprecedented degree of game spectating but also an unprecedented *position* and status for spectatorship itself as a practice within gaming culture more broadly. It is no longer something comparatively rare and small scale, but now something massive and large enough to exert an influence on aspects of gaming, ranging from game design and the games industry (Consalvo & Phelps, 2019; Johnson & Woodcock, 2019b; Parker & Perks, 2021), to the emergence of gaming celebrities and the pursuit of gaming careers (Johnson & Woodcock, 2017; Taylor, 2018; Partin, 2020; Yu et al., 2021). I then consider the future of Twitch research and identify potentially fruitful directions – studying the actual games played on Twitch (strangely absent from most analyses), the tensions between gaming and non-gaming content on the site, the potential expansion of Twitch into a platform offering more than just live streams, and the future of Twitch in the context of challenges from other sites. Understanding the emergence of the gaming *agora* that Twitch has facilitated shows us the contemporary state of gaming; the politics of gaming and their complex relationships to gender, bodies, money, leisure, aspiration and more; and how and why spectatorship is now a more central, and essential, part of gaming than it has ever been before.

CHAPTER I

The Platform

A brief history of Twitch

Twitch began life as 'Justin.tv', a website set up by three young American men with the primary goal of broadcasting, twenty-four hours a day and seven days a week, the life of one of their members: a certain Justin Kan. For eight months in 2007 Kan wore a baseball cap with an attached webcam. Viewers saw and heard almost everything that Kan was doing, yielding a strikingly intimate portrayal of his life at the time. While many viewers enjoyed this rather odd and unusual insight into a stranger's life (known by the term 'lifecasting'), others saw it as an opportunity for 'messing with' or harassing the caster. Kan was subject to 'swatting' – reporting someone to the police as a potentially dangerous criminal in order to elicit an armed response team to intervene on a live stream (Taylor, 2018: 222; Uttarapong et al., 2021: 16; Jacob & Tran, 2023) – on numerous occasions (Cook, 2014) and others found equally inventive but less potentially fatal ways to mess with the life of someone broadcasting everything he was doing. Even at this early stage in the history of live streaming there were viewers who were on board with the streamer and the stream's objectives, *and* viewers who sought to disrupt it – attitudes anticipating much of what evolved on Twitch over coming decades. The appeal of these streams thus introduces some of the key themes this book explores: the intimacy of the live stream (Senft, 2008; Dargonaki, 2018; Woodcock & Johnson, 2019; Phelps et al., 2021b), the sense that one is watching the life of a friend instead of the distant life of a celebrity, and the potential for viewers to both engage with – and mess with, potentially seriously – its broadcasters.

Over the following years the site grew in popularity and in the variety of its channels. In 2011 Justin.tv launched a gaming-specific section called Twitch.tv, or just Twitch (Rao, 2011). This reflected how successful gaming content had become at that point, having eclipsed the site's original lifecasting focus. Twitch enabled anyone with the appropriate technology, internet speed, and ability to figure out then-opaque live-streaming software packages, to broadcast their gaming. At this time there was a now little-remembered competitor to Justin/Twitch known as 'Own3d.tv' – 'owned' being a term in gaming denoting resounding victory over one's opponent(s) in a game – which was hosting solely gaming content, but by the end of 2013 Own3d had shut down, leaving Twitch as the only site of any size focused on game live streaming (Peel, 2013). Twitch at this point was far from the size it would later reach, but the fact that the gaming component of live streaming had come to dominate the rest of the site – which allowed for the streaming of essentially any non-adult content – was telling. In early 2014 Justin.tv Inc. changed its name to Twitch Interactive (Popper, 2014) and later in 2014 Justin.tv stopped broadcasting, explaining that resources had to be focused entirely on Twitch. Only weeks after this it was widely reported that Amazon had purchased Twitch for a fraction under US$1 billion (Wingfield, 2014).

Twitch continued to expand and evolve under Amazon's aegis. One of the most important aspects of this was the addition in 2016 of the on-site currency 'Bits', through which one can 'Cheer' for streamers and give them the money that the Bits represent. Twitch donations had previously gone through PayPal and moving to Bits enabled Twitch to keep a greater portion of revenue circulating within the site rather than going to a third party (Partin, 2020). Around the same time Twitch also introduced the 'Twitch Prime' membership for those with an Amazon account (Ask et al., 2019; Cai et al., 2021a); this essentially allowed for a free subscription to a streamer of the viewer's choice using their Amazon account. Between 2019 and 2022 Twitch also introduced exclusivity agreements. This meant that someone who signed up to stream on Twitch was – if contractually 'partnered' (Twitch enabling the streamer to earn income through the site) – only allowed to broadcast on Twitch (Parrish, 2022). One of the last major developments in this period saw Twitch reduce the revenue share given to some of the most successful streamers. There is no doubt that running a live-streaming platform is much more financially demanding in server time and capacity than a non-video-based website with an equivalent userbase, but this shift also shows Twitch focusing increasingly on maximizing income. The site's profitability – which remains surprisingly opaque, although the consensus seems to be that Twitch does not generally turn a profit (Bussey, 2020; Grayson, 2023; Tassi, 2023) – drive much of its public decision making, and are often used to justify firing staff to reduce costs. Nevertheless the resentment that many smaller streamers and even viewers felt – to the fact that the largest streamers earning over $100,000 a year would now earn *slightly less* – is revealing. This solidarity towards high earners tells us something about the sense of personal connection that viewers can feel towards streamers, which we return to throughout this book.

A decade and a half has seen Twitch utterly transformed. Beginning as a niche (though later quite well-known) site for the lifecasting of a single person and later a small group of people, it has now become one of the fifty or so most-visited websites on the planet, valued in the billions of dollars, and a central force in digital gaming culture. Unsurprisingly the interface and possibilities of the platform have also expanded since then, with a constant stream of new features reshaping the site. What, therefore, is Twitch now like to use in the mid-2020s, after its transformation from a platform for a handful of lifecasters to, instead, a thriving hub for over a hundred million gamers?

The Twitch interface

Most people moving onto Twitch for the first time will be presented with the Twitch homepage. A selected channel will start playing. Underneath this lead stream the site offers numerous sets of possible streams in different categories, and the further one scrolls the greater the range of possibilities. If not enticed by the largest streams at the top of the homepage, the user perhaps scrolls down and sees a category that interests them – or something unknown which intrigues them – and gains some initial sense of the size of the platform and variety of content. Twitch's initial 'pitch' to the new viewer is therefore focused on streamers and their audiovisual content, rather than on joining communities or having viewer-to-streamer interactions.

Clicking on any of these channels takes the user to that streamer's channel, taking the form Twitch.tv/[username]. The selected channel now expands to take up most of the screen. This is the main video of the live stream in which one watches the streamer doing whatever they might be doing. Joining a channel for the first time, one inevitably jumps in part way through a broadcast. Sometimes stream content can be easy to pick up but in other cases – especially if a streamer is taking a break, or doing something slightly out of the ordinary, or responding to their viewers – one joins a channel in a lull, with seconds or even minutes passing before 'normal' content on the stream resumes. Viewers sometimes make jokes about these interstitial moments as a way to pass the time and interact with each other while waiting for a streamer's return. When joining a stream, the Twitch chat window also loads. If the channel is highly active messages will begin appearing immediately; if the channel is less active the chat window sometimes appears empty for some time until a first (from your perspective) message appears; and if the channel has few if any viewers the chat window might remain empty. The chat window turns the channel from something one might just watch without any social engagement into a 'digitised spac[e] for sociality and communication' (Chesher, 2024: 36). Without a username the new user cannot comment in Twitch chat but is allowed to read it; signing up to the site allows the new user to begin chatting immediately.

Once a viewer has found a channel they want to watch, they have options. The simplest is to watch and listen to the broadcast. Streams might last only a few seconds or minutes – though streams of this sort often indicate a technical issue or some kind of humorous or light-hearted statement on the part of the streamer – but usually last much longer. It is hard to state an average length of broadcast as the variation is immense across people and communities and types of channels, but the hundreds of streams I have observed in the last almost-decade of researching Twitch have generally come in around three to five hours. Streamers seem to tend towards a stream length that is long enough for viewers to really settle into the channel and for the broadcaster to play a substantial amount of the game they're focusing on (or do a significant amount of the activity they're doing), but also not so long that the streamer gets burnt out or needs to take a break. Regardless of the length of broadcast, however, the viewer can dip in and out – there is no obligation to stay.

An account-free viewer can access every stream that a viewer with an account can access, but an account holder can also interact in the Twitch chat window, give money to streamers, and engage with a number of other site features connected to one's account (and in some cases to one's wallet). Chat is the most used function. For the new viewer – to the platform or to a given channel – Twitch chat messages might simply be greetings or enquiries about what's going on in the stream, while for the long-term viewer conversations and discussions easily and often arise between viewers about the broadcast itself, or related topics of interest (Barbieri et al., 2017; Nakandala et al., 2017). Other messages might be responses to comments that another viewer posted, jokes or humorous comments about the stream, questions for other viewers to respond to about gaming or other topics, 'copypasta' messages – a series of repeated sentences with a humorous motif (Ford et al., 2017; Seering et al., 2017a) – or strings of Twitch's small graphical emotes (Jackson, 2020; Wolff & Shen, 2022) that, as I argue later in this book, are vital to understanding both the specific interactions taking place in a channel as well as the framing of, and limits to, these interactions (cf. Jackson, 2023a). Any of these might be picked up and responded to by other viewers or the streamer in real time, or might simply vanish into the aether with little or no effect on the broadcast. Regular 'chatters' – viewers who speak up often in chat – become known over time in a channel and are often acknowledged by the streamer who might respond with interest, amusement or pleasantries when that viewer has something to say.

Having a Twitch account also gives the user the option to support streamers financially (Siutila, 2018: 133; Johnson & Woodcock, 2019a; Törhönen et al., 2020: 168). This can be via a donation (e.g., Sjöblom et al., 2019; Partin, 2020), which is a one-time payment of anything from a few pennies or cents up to an essentially unlimited ceiling, or by subscribing (e.g., Uszkoreit, 2018; Küper & Krämer, 2021), in which case the viewer commits to give a certain amount of money to the broadcaster every month to express their appreciation – although around half of that goes to Twitch. The social, hierarchic, status and prestige dimensions of these financial contributions are both complex and essential and will be covered in more detail later, but for now suffice it to say that in a Twitch channel a viewer can watch and listen, chat and interact, follow the streamer to elsewhere on the internet, and sometimes support the streamer with financial donations. All these interactions are important, and will appear multiple times in this book, highlighting the centrality of monetization and metricization (see later in this chapter) to contemporary Twitch, and to how users are able to, and encouraged to, interact on the platform.

Channel customization

The above section should give the reader a clear image of what Twitch is like and some of its key infrastructural elements – stream channels, audiovisual content, text chatting and so on. Another important part, however, is the fact that compared with other social media platforms Twitch gives its streamers the freedom and tools to achieve an unusually high degree of channel *customization*. A YouTube account or TikTok account – to use obvious video-focused points of comparison – can only have the barest amount of customization. YouTube users can select the banner on their profile, their username, their on-site name and the display picture alongside their name, but none of these features is especially unusual or unique to the site. The user has significant control over what videos they upload, but the only place where profile information can be written requires several clicks to access, and is comparatively rarely seen. On TikTok the user has arguably even less control as there is no way to customize banners, and it is only really in an individual's 'bio' and profile picture where any degree of specificity can be achieved using text and emoticons. Both are sites with immense popularity and impact and huge userbases, yet neither offers any significant degree of customization to the profile from which a user sends out their content – the focus is far more, all but exclusively, on the content rather than the page from which it originates.

Twitch is different. Rather than a person's profile being simply the source of the content being broadcast and looking very similar to anyone else's profile, what we see on Twitch is the ability for streamers to construct a profile that is entirely unique. Sjöblom et al. (2019: 25) describe the importance of the 'personalized profile visible underneath the video stream' which is 'freely customizable'. This can contain information about 'what games [the streamer] play[s], their streaming schedule, and other social media profiles' (Uszkoreit, 2018: 164), and sometimes data on 'the tools and technology they use to stream' (Sjöblom et al., 2019: 25), as well as information showing viewers 'the structure of the stream through elements such as the rules and schedule of the stream' (ibid.). These are key observations for understanding Twitch. As with many other platforms based on user-generated content, the ability to produce that content and distribute it widely is integral and taken as read. However, where Twitch stands out is in the *additional* capability to construct a distinct and highly customized profile from which that content is launched out into the world. Through working on their profile streamers can 'generate the structure of the stream and their community' (ibid.) and establish an overall framing for what they're doing, who they are, and what people should expect on their channel. A streamer's Twitch page is far more distinctive to *them* than anyone's YouTube or TikTok page, for example, could ever be in the mid-2020s.

This degree of customization applies not only to a streamer's channel page, but also to the form of video being broadcast. One channel might have a video broadcast filled with aesthetically complex and handmade border graphics with pictures of the streamer, information about their other social media sites, and just relatively small parts of the video for a game and their webcam image. Another channel might be entirely a game without any webcam (or just a small webcam) to be seen, while another might be a rebroadcast of someone else's channel while this streamer talks over what's currently going on in someone else's stream. Ten channels in a row one visits might have a recognizable human speaking, but the eleventh channel one visits might instead have a Vtuber cat 'speaking', with its virtual avatar mouth attempting to copy and echo what its human controller is saying to a reasonable degree of accuracy (Sutton, 2021; Turner, 2022). Another channel might simply involve the streamer talking from their bedroom to their viewers about a range of topics, while other stream videos might be filled to the point of information overload with graphics and animations that play regularly whenever a viewer subscribes, donates or follows. Another might have a webcam image of the highest quality that shows the live streamer in a clear light, while another might be filmed by a low-quality webcam or broadcast across a low-quality webcam, offering only a pixelated smudge where a human live streamer is presumably sitting.

All of this leads to a striking divergence between streams. No two Twitch channels are 'exactly the same' (Cai et al., 2021b: 63), with the high degree of personalization possible in a Twitch channel compared to a YouTube or TikTok account. There is a strong sense among users that someone's Twitch channel is a digital *place*, in a particular and interesting way that cannot really be said to be true on other social media sites. In this regard Twitch is in some ways more akin to something like MySpace or Bebo (or blogging) – those earlier social networking sites before Facebook came to dominate. They too were known for the striking degree of customization offered to users. Customization, and the sense that as a user you were carving out *your* space on the internet, were essential to the appeal of these early sites. Users could even insert – within limits – their own HTML into their homepages, enabling different kinds of music to play or graphics to appear or animations to run (Miltner & Gerrard, 2022). Other pages on some sites could even have little games embedded, or trackers which monitored how many people had visited, or the now-ancient practice of the digital 'guestbook' where site visitors could leave a short message. What all of this meant was that each page on these sites was wildly different from all others, and was specific to what that one person was trying to present or articulate. Modern social networking sites like Facebook emphasize updates from friends, sponsored content and following celebrities, but we easily forget that earlier social networking sites were much more about establishing one's own *place* on the web, rather than learning what one's friends were *doing* moment by moment.

These more personalized approaches developed out of an early-internet aesthetic that was far less slick and homogeneous than the corporate platforms we see today. They instead focused on a kind of information overload where features and images and sounds and videos were poured into the viewer's awareness at speed. There is an almost incalculably greater number of websites and online possibilities than there were three decades ago, yet the modern internet is in many ways far more *uniform* and much less constantly *unexpected* than the early internet. Long gone are the days of shock images popping up around every corner, music or sounds loudly playing against the user's control as soon as one visits a website, and dozens of animated 'gif' graphics playing in every corner of a person's homepage. This is in many ways for the best, yet in an era of increasing corporate control over the internet via the largest platforms (Poell, 2020) we should note that this older, looser approach was very antithetical to modern corporate thinking. Rather than consistent branding across every page that unifies them as belonging to a single site, MySpace and Bebo (and now Twitch) allow(ed) users latitude and functionality to separate themselves from the pack and to create something genuinely distinctive, even at the cost sometimes of pages that were confusing to navigate for the uninitiated.

The space and capacity for individuality are not just aspects of Twitch that are deeply appealing to streamers but are also integral to understanding how Twitch functions as an *agora*. The key point here is that each Twitch streamer is not just making their statements into the gaming *agora*, but they are also constructing the *rostrum* (the place where a speaker speaks) – each one being unique – from which they *make* these same statements. Other sites certainly allow people to post a broad range of content much as Twitch does, but the digital location from which that content emanates generally looks the same from one user to another. Twitch goes further by not just providing the means to stream, but also the *framing* of what sort of profile and channel that broadcast is coming from. On Twitch one develops something akin to a television channel (Dargonaki, 2018: 105; Lin et al., 2019; Sjöblom et al., 2019; Spilker et al., 2020; Sixto-García & Losada-Fernández, 2023) with a particular brand and audience demographic, not just the programming that goes live on that channel. Certain properties in a rostrum (a channel) in turn make it more or less likely for a streamer to be listened to, with high-quality webcam images and engaging humour, for example, making a stream more likely to be successful than one with no webcam and little or no entertaining commentary.

All of this adds a second layer of information to the messages being broadcast – a context and a setting and a presentation of those messages through a highly personalized and customized digital presence, in a way that most other contemporary social media platforms lack. By giving its users a tremendous degree of control over how they present their channel, the site enables streamers to construct a position from which they speak. This gives a Twitch channel a kind of weight – almost quasi-institutional in nature – that is lacking on many other social media sites. A Twitch channel looks, sounds and functions at least somewhat differently from every other Twitch channel, giving users a website, an *agora*, of essentially five million television channels each with its own branding and its own group of dedicated viewers. Each channel is essentially one of the millions of conversations going on within the *agora*. The freedoms and styles and attitudes that characterize Twitch are what most fundamentally underpin its *agora*-like qualities. The Twitch platform is not just a service or a technology, but rather presents a relatively open-ended, freewheeling agglomeration of communities and individuals and channels, each of whom is able to speak and to construct how, where and when they speak. This is a powerful combination of characteristics, and one that is key to Twitch's success.

Safety and moderation on Twitch

Streamers on Twitch have significant power over the crafting and construction of their profile and their stream. These elements are built into Twitch's infrastructure as a platform. Another way this power manifests is in terms of control over moderation policies for their channels, such as what sorts of words and behaviours are acceptable or unacceptable to be posted in Twitch chat. Yet whereas the control over their profiles and streams enables streamers to heavily customize and personalize their channels, the control given to them by Twitch over their channel's moderation serves a very different purpose. This book's discussion of harassment and toxicity on Twitch and their place in the *agora* is spread across several chapters, but usefully begins here by establishing some of the key causes of harassment on the site, and Twitch's lacklustre and politically troubling responses to them. These are aspects fundamental to Twitch as a platform and which must be understood to get a sense of the true everyday of using the site.

Toxicity and harassment in gaming communities are frequently part of the gaming experience for many people. Online games and gaming are known for toxic conversations between participants and 'misogynistic behaviors' (Lin et al., 2019: 4) that generate 'toxic and misogynistic environments' (Uszkoreit, 2018: 163). Both 'gaming masculinity' and broader 'toxic geek masculinity' (Welch, 2022: 522) manifest and reinforce one another within 'hypermasculin[e]' (Salter & Blodgett, 2012: 401) gaming spaces. This as an example of what Massanari (2017: 333) more broadly calls a 'toxic technoculture', one in which 'retrograde ideas of gender, sexual identity, sexuality, and race [push] against issues of diversity, multiculturalism, and progressivism'. All of this makes 'gaming spaces unsafe for women, queer folks, and people of colo[u]r who are not seen as authentic members of the gaming community' (Welch, 2022: 523), and in much of gaming there is often a more generally 'hostile response to the expression of a female identity or femininity' (Salter & Blodgett, 2012: 401). As Ruberg et al. (2019: 470) write, distinguishing between apparently 'real' and 'fake' gamers – which is to say, men and women respectively (Scott, 2019; Tran, 2022) – is part of a cultural project of apparently deep importance to many male gamers seeking to 'protect' gaming culture as a masculine space (Ruberg et al., 2019: 478) supposedly incompatible with feminism and other social justice ideals (Cullen, 2022b). The toxic meritocracy of much of gaming (Paul, 2018) in turn further strengthens these issues. There is no level playing field for women and racial and gender minorities in gaming; any lack of 'achievement' then becomes evidence of their lack of gamer credentials; and thus objections to their presence are reinforced and repeated. It is in this context that Twitch's game streamers themselves have been noted as often performing a similar 'reification of geek masculinity' (Welch, 2022: 521), with harassment and toxicity being frequently noted as a major issue on the site (Gray, 2017; Cai & Wohn, 2019; Catá; 2019; Jackson, 2023a).

The first issue in Twitch's infrastructure which helps us understand the platform's struggles with harassment and toxicity is that of *anonymity*. Twitch has a high degree of anonymity (Ruvalcaba et al., 2018: 308) for its viewers compared to some contemporary internet platforms. Only an account holder's username is shown to others (Freeman & Wohn, 2020; Groen, 2020) with no additional information about real-life location, or interests, or other associations, unless they are deliberately added to the profile. A banned account can easily be remade with relatively little effort, and Twitch has no method for checking who is signing up nor what their intentions might be. A site like Reddit is even more anonymous than Twitch – needing no email address to sign up and allowing a user to have an unlimited number of different and unconnected accounts – but many major corporate platforms have moved increasingly in the other direction, with increasingly rigorous regimes of confirmation and spam detection leaving Twitch as something of an outlier. It has been well demonstrated that 'anonymous and pseudonymous' online spaces bring clear regulatory challenges because of users being able to 'behave in virtually any way they like without fear of reprisal or loss of reputation' (Seering et al., 2017a: 111). Users' regulation of their actions appears to be reduced in these contexts, as is the sense that others care what they say or do (Hilvert-Bruce & Neill, 2020: 304; Fox & Tang, 2017: 1292; Uttarapong et al., 2021: 8); harassment and toxicity in online gaming are thus 'increased by the anonymity of other players' (Cote, 2017: 139). The high degree of anonymity of *viewers* is therefore a key aspect of understanding Twitch's moderation problems, and in turn contributes much to the rise of harassment practices such as 'hate raids' that I discuss in chapter 4.

The second challenge posed by Twitch's infrastructure comes from the nature of Twitch chat messages, as the site in effect provides potential harassers with an unusually large number of ways to harass someone *without* being caught by algorithmic moderation. One of the most obvious examples is the use of 'emotes' – the small images that one can post in Twitch chat – in ways that are subtly offensive (Alexander, 2018a; Taylor, 2018; Evans & Llano, 2023). One well-known example is how emotes of black streamers are often used in chat when black people are mentioned, when racial issues might come up, or even when watermelons or fried chickens are mentioned in chat, by a streamer, or appear in a game. The issue here is that an automated moderation system cannot capture the *context* in which the emotes are being deployed – since these contexts are complex amalgams of the streaming video, the streamer's commentary, any discussion going on in Twitch chat, and the wider norms of a channel – and thus harmless use and offensive use are difficult to differentiate algorithmically. In turn the fact that comments in text chat (something easy for an algorithm to monitor) almost always riff off what's going on in the streaming video (a hugely complex source that is difficult for an algorithm to monitor) significantly increases the challenges of catching the comments of hostile actors and distinguishing those from commonplace comments. This is even *further* complicated by the fact that much of the commentary and humour on Twitch used by both streamers and viewers alike can be sharp, caustic and antagonistic (Johnson, 2022, cf. Lybrand, 2019) and hence even more challenging to separate from potentially almost identical statements that might be meant as part of a shared source of cutting humour.

The third element of Twitch's infrastructure that is important to understand in this context is the degree to which a streamer is – psychologically speaking – 'open to attack'. Twitch's very nature as a platform – a site for live streaming, for people to show their real faces and their real bodies and use their real voices from their real bedrooms – represents a place where someone is showing or offering far more of themselves than is the case in almost any other online or gaming context (with the obvious exception of adult internet content). Scholars have noted that live streaming is, by its nature, highly *non*-anonymous: one's 'control of presentation' is reduced when voice chat is present (Charles, 2016: 20), and it is only the 'on-camera content creator' who *lacks* the anonymity that everyone else enjoys on Twitch (Evans & Llano, 2023: 4). Twitch therefore by its very nature offers the streamer – almost exclusively the target of harassment, which is only very rarely targeted at viewers – very little in the way of psychological or personal protection against an aggressor. The aggressor is immediately given access to a far greater amount of information about the streamer than is the case in purely text-based online abuse or even via voice chat (cf. Wadley et al., 2015), even though these are both also sites of significant toxicity. On Twitch the potential attacker (the viewer) is unusually well defended and safe, while the potential attacked party (the streamer) is 'giving' an unusually large amount of themselves on the site. On most sites users who might be under attack, and users doing the attacking, are often much closer in their degree of exposure or power. On Twitch, however, the roles of attacker and attacked are almost always clearly delineated between viewer and streamer, respectively, with markedly different degrees of control and security.

Understanding this combination of factors in the infrastructure of Twitch – high anonymity for *viewers*, the challenges of automatically catching hostile interactions, and extremely low anonymity for *streamers* – is important for assessing how the technological choices made on Twitch, and the infrastructure it has yielded, are not conducive to preventing or managing harassment. What, therefore, is Twitch's response to the challenges of moderation on their platform? Its answer is to put the labour and the expectation of moderation onto its streamers, rather than taking that burden on itself. Although Twitch's built-in moderation removes a small number of unambiguously hostile words in chat, most of the control over this is given to streamers in two ways. The first is how streamers can use AI-driven moderation through the 'Automod' function, which they can customize and set (Cai et al., 2021a; Uttarapong et al., 2021; 2022). A given streamer can set different levels of moderation for different kinds of potentially objectionable chat comments. Twitch defines these categories as 'Discrimination' (including 'hate speech'), 'Sexual Content' (words about 'acts and/or anatomy'), 'Hostility' ('provocation and bullying') and 'Profanity' (expletives and so on). The second involves streamers recruiting moderators for their channel to offer human-standard moderation alongside Automod. Moderators are usually drawn from the streamer's pool of viewers, and are generally fans who are particularly committed to that streamer's channel, show up often, and with whom the streamer has begun to build a closer relationship. This is almost always unpaid labour from the viewer but is seen as a positive reward by many, as it demonstrates a streamer's trust in a viewer and the viewer gets to play a more active role in the creation and maintenance of the channel.

Twitch presents these offerings of moderation control to streamers in a very positive light. Twitch's own guidelines state that with Automod 'broadcasters can establish *their own* reliable baseline for acceptable language and around-the-clock chat moderation' and hence this tool is 'a way to create a more positive experience' for the streamer and their viewers (Twitch, 2023a, emphasis mine). Selecting good human moderators, which is to say the streamer's viewers who decide to take on this job, is meanwhile described as 'one of the best things *you* can do for *your* channel' (Twitch, 2023b, emphases mine). In all these framings Twitch presents this degree of customization as something highly desirable and empowering and emancipating for streamers – which is to say, very much like the rest of the customization that Twitch enables. *Rather than relying on us to moderate for you in ways you might not want,* the implicit suggestion goes, *we are giving this power to you, the streamers, just like we give you tremendous power over most other aspects of your channels.* We have already seen the diverse ways that streamers – and as we'll see later, viewers as well – can shape the construction of a channel, and on the surface this appears to be another element of this same trend. It can of course be argued that self-managed moderation fits with the ethos of Twitch's *agora* – it is up to the community to debate, set and police the standards – but this is in fact an area where the platform's style masks a deliberate dereliction of corporate responsibility. Twitch is relatively uninterested in delivering the relevant labour and resources to protect its marginalized streamers; it is perhaps concerned about alienating hypermasculine gamers from the site; and it understands that just as unpaid labour shapes so much of the site in line with the platform owners' desire to profit, the same model can easily be applied to moderation as well. Twitch's struggles with moderation are therefore not incidental, but actually key to our understanding of it as a platform and how it can be used safely, or potentially not used safely, by streamers as a *platform* for streaming games (and other activities) and articulating their ideas into the wider gaming *agora*.

Metrics on Twitch

The detailed crafting of a channel through its visual, aural, cultural – and content moderation – elements is not the only way that Twitch channels mirror television (Dargonaki, 2018; Ask et al., 2019; Sixto-García & Losada-Fernández, 2023). Another is in the use and functions of *metrics*. Television channels compete for viewer numbers, with ratings figures being essential to securing advertiser income and bringing in the most talented television workers to create broadcast content. This is not only the case on television, of course, with many scholars in the past two decades noting the growing 'metricization' of our political, social, cultural and personal lives (Beer, 2016; Mau, 2019; Poell et al., 2021). Economic matters have long been simplified into quantitative terms, but metrics now represent one of the fundamental intellectual and institutional currents of contemporary industrialized societies. Metrics are also a central element of Twitch, and like money they exert a shaping effect on the content of Twitch broadcasts. They offer an idealized streamer personality with particular perspectives and orientations to be mirrored and replicated. Twitch streamers 'play with metrics' but are in truth, as David Beer (2016: 3) would put it, 'more often played *by* them', and as I will show in this section, the platform is constructed in such a way as to maximize this effort. As with questions of content moderation, metrics are not simply a side note to understanding the infrastructural foundations of Twitch, but an integral element of them.

Although metrics have long been a part of physical sports (Burroughs, 2020) – such as 'batting average' and 'strike rate' in cricket or 'possession' and 'corners' in football – and arcade machines via the high score mechanism (Stenros et al., 2011), it was the growth of esports and speedrunning which really brought metrics into regular gaming parlance. As Tom Brock (2021: 132) has argued, the 'gameplay metrics used to measure player performances in video games enable the competitive logic of capitalism, and a neoliberal subjectivity'. They do this by allowing for the ranking and measuring of things beyond the most obvious – winning and losing a game – and breaking down the possibility of winning and losing into a greater range of information such as how many clicks one makes a second, how rapidly one upgrades one's character, or how many shots or attacks land correctly on target, and so forth. By allowing for the measurement of 'ranking, comparing, and evaluating player behavior' (ibid.: 133), players are given seemingly tangible ways to improve themselves, precisely and variedly, in comparison with others. Brock describes how metrics cultivate feelings of anxiety, uncertainty and inadequacy, which are then (ironically) tackled by boosting those same metrics, a process that allows the gamer's or streamer's psyche to be 'stabilized'. Competitive gamers are encouraged towards 'methods and techniques of self-training and risk management' (ibid.: 141), and just as worn devices like the Apple Watch encourage us to 'continuously measure and evaluate our bodily routines against a set of performative goals' (ibid.: 136), so too do metrics in competitive games. Although such trends find their origins in competitive gaming, they have come to exert a massive effect upon game live streaming.

Twitch is the latest gaming context in which metrics have risen to prominence (Pellicone & Ahn, 2017; Phelps et al., 2021a). Twitch's 'stats' pages tell a streamer their average numbers of concurrent viewers, how many new followers (or subscriptions) they have acquired within a given period (and whether this number was more or smaller than previous periods), how many clips have been made of their content, how many times in total their stream has been viewed within a given period, and so on. These are easily accessible for streamers on their Twitch 'dashboard' and are updated constantly. Twitch's metrics are also connected to the possibility of making income from one's channel – they tell the streamer where their revenue has been coming from day by day, analysed by categories such as donations, subscriptions, adverts and so on. As for what all these metrics are *for*, Twitch's own guidelines state that the use of their analytics 'empowers you' as a streamer so that 'you can make informed decisions' for your channel. First and foremost of these, Twitch's guidelines suggest, is 'how to improve your content, grow your audience', and indeed 'hit your streaming goals' (Twitch, 2023c). Such language is immediately familiar to scholars who have studied metrics, as well as related practices like gamification, with their deployment of language designed to meet ideas of (self)-improvement and the pursuit of one's goals (Whitson, 2014; Woodcock & Johnson, 2018). We also see an obvious commonality with how the abrogation of corporate responsibility for moderation is framed – this is a positive, empowering part of our platform, Twitch says, that will let you get what *you* want out of our site.

Metrics and the means to navigate them and process information about them are all given to a new streamer *immediately*. There is no obvious grace period in which a new streamer gets to grips with other aspects of the platform before being shown these metrics and the tools associated with them; rather they are presented as an integral and unquestioned aspect of what being a Twitch streamer *is*. Introducing the metrics and tools so rapidly is intended to immediately shape how new streamers think about the platform and what they do on it; the implicit objective to begin boosting and growing those numbers is there from the very first moment. In turn, the implicit 'doing better' or 'doing worse' nature of quantification cannot help but begin nudging what a streamer is doing on Twitch. This is not only the case for the aspirational streamer but also for the hobbyist streamer who is presented with these same statistics, unavoidably suggesting to them the existence of a more instrumental orientation they might not naturally have thought about. Only by making an active effort to ignore the metrics pages and the tools designed to – apparently – *enhance* your channel and make you a *better* streamer can a streamer seek to escape these neoliberal logics. Twitch indeed often shows the highest-viewed categories and the highest-viewed streamers in each category, making metrics key to the visibility of one's channel. Metrics of this sort can both 'fulfil neoliberal dreams' but also be 'presented in the pursuit of neoliberal rationalities' (Beer, 2016: 16) as a promissory framing encouraging the streamer down an apparently desirable path. Through these practices Twitch is relatively transparent in terms of the metrics one needs to be 'partnered' or otherwise eligible for monetization, whereas other sites are often rather more cryptic.

Metrics have significant effects on games and streamers alike. Brock (2021: 136) describes how esports players' monitoring of 'personal bests' and 'goals' serves to 'reward self-interest and normalize the idea' that players' lives should be oriented towards competition. On Twitch the apparent embracing of its metrics can be seen in how aspirational streamers commonly articulate clear metric goals for themselves, and in turn note with interesting mixes of pride and humility when they have accomplished a goal. Most streamers whose channels are above a certain size display clear neoliberal and entrepreneurial rationalities when describing their goals, their actions, and their broader orientation to Twitch as a platform (Johnson & Woodcock, 2017; Guarriello, 2019; Johnson et al., 2019). It is common for them to set targets for a broadcast in terms of how much money they'd like to make or how many new followers or subscribers they're hoping to acquire (although there is no research yet on whether being public about these goals makes a streamer more or less likely to achieve them). This appears to serve a primarily instrumental goal in trying to encourage viewers to help the streamer reach that goal, but for some streamers this appears to take on a more psychological dimension. By making clear what their objectives are, the streamer seems to be trying to hold themselves accountable – many online sites and support groups emphasize the importance of 'accountability' and monitoring oneself in trying to reach goals, a discourse that has clear echoes in 'self-motivated' domains such as live streaming (Walker, 2014). These targets therefore appear to be ways for streamers to hold themselves 'accountable', to focus and commit to their stream, and to remind themselves of the objectives they are working towards. In this regard metrics are certainly doing their intended job.

Streamers also often show these metricized targets in their channels (although, of course, not showing targets does not mean that streamers haven't set them). The public *achievement* of set goals encouraged or shaped by the platform's metrics is important for many Twitch streamers, and this can take several forms. When a streamer becomes a monetized 'partner', for example, they often throw celebration broadcasts to discuss with their viewers what custom emotes they should now add to their channel for subscribers. This involvement gives viewers a feeling of being active participants in the stream and its subsequent construction, and demonstrates that this streamer was able to reach this target (and hence others might also now be in reach – as long as viewers keep giving their support). Posts are also often made on sites like Twitter, Facebook or Reddit, announcing with satisfaction that a major milestone has been achieved. These milestones might be in terms of the streamer's income or ability to do streaming as part or all of their income, or for smaller streamers might represent reaching a certain number of followers or a certain average viewer count. Such posts are interesting for how they sometimes adopt a very proud register, expressing the streamer's joy at having grown their channel to a certain level, or reached a point where they can become a partner, or expressing how 'hard work' or 'dedication' or 'focusing on your goals' (or similar constructions) can apparently make anything possible (cf. Marwick, 2013; Mendick et al., 2015). Yet they are also often accompanied by a demonstration of modesty, expressing thanks to all their viewers who 'supported me' or 'made this possible', an appreciation of the fact that so many people are interested in their channel, and the use of what I will later call the 'Twitch we' – phrases like 'we did it' or 'we made it here' or 'we built this stream', and so on. Metrics are therefore not only something that Twitch streamers use to understand their broadcasting and something that Twitch the platform actively pushes, but have also become part of the expected *performance* of a live streamer, especially one with active intentions to grow their channel.

The ubiquity of metrics defines what streamers are 'meant' to be doing on Twitch. They are also key to how many streamers, especially the more aspirational ones, define themselves and their actions on the site. Metrics on Twitch of course take much from the growth of metrics in (competitive) gaming, but also take much from the metrics of 'older' media – circulation numbers for newspapers, ratings for radio and television, and so forth. In this regard Twitch's metrics are understandable not just through a gaming lens but also through the television-like aspects of the site, and the emphasis TV metrics place on viewer numbers and viewer retention. These are all essential metrics (or so we are told) for the aspirational live streamer looking to pursue streaming perhaps a little more seriously than others. Yet the metrics are key to hobbyist streamers as well – streamers' celebrations for reaching a hundred followers or an average viewer count of ten are, if anything, even more common than the more 'impressive' equivalents. This ubiquity demonstrates that this is an *agora* which is fundamentally focused on the reach of one's message far more than the content of one's message. Financial rewards such as higher income and psychological rewards such as higher metrics and more 'influence' flow to those who climb the metric ladder in making their statements into the *agora*, rather than necessarily those whose statements might be the most interesting or compelling. The comparison here with populist politics rewarding the loudest speaker rather than the most coherent is clear, especially when we note that controversies tend to surround the most visible streamers far more than those lower down the ladder.

Yet just as 'better' on the metrics does not inherently equate to 'better' content (whatever that might mean), 'better' on the metrics also does not inherently mean 'better' for the streamer. Many are simply looking to engage with a community, broadcast something for their friends, have a downtime hobby, practise public speaking, or any number of other motives which explicitly or implicitly reject the teleological impetus of the metricized platform (Baym, 2013; Van Dijck & Poell, 2013; Poell et al., 2021). Equally, in trying to make a 'better' stream for themselves, a streamer is also making a 'better' stream for Twitch – which is to say a stream that brings in more viewers, and might later become a monetized stream, generating income for the company. Metrics are therefore not the harmless and beneficial statistics and figures which Twitch so generously offers to its streamers to 'help' them along their streaming journey, but in fact their presence, their usage and their ubiquity all have specific strategic intentions behind them. Their pervasiveness shapes the dynamics of every channel and every streamer in Twitch's *agora* and the platform must thus be understood by appreciating both what the metrics are used for, and also what their mere presence implies, suggests and pressures a streamer towards. Like moderation-related decisions, metric-related decisions taken by Twitch as a company and built into Twitch as a platform are essential baselines for everything that takes place on the site, and a key aspect of how the activities of streamers and viewers alike are seen, understood, portrayed and *captured* for a range of different instrumental purposes.

Money on Twitch

Money, like metrics, is a fundamental part of Twitch, and has seen far more study (e.g., Ask et al., 2019; Johnson & Woodcock, 2019a; Ruberg et al., 2019: 475–8; Wolff & Shen, 2022). It is again not just something which flows beneath the surface for a few financially successful streamers, but something whose manifestations on the platform are consistent, highly *visible* and analytically essential. Almost all major internet platforms are tremendously effective profit-making machines, and internet advertisers and sponsors generally flood the largest of the internet's sites. Yet this aspect is rarely all that visible to the average user on Facebook, for example, who pays nothing to Facebook and would be surprised to learn any of their friends were paying money to the site. On Twitch, by contrast, the ability to give money to streamers – and hence to Twitch, which takes a significant cut of all money transferred – is a core functionality of a viewer's account, and the receipt and appreciation of income is central to the actual broadcast content of so many streamers (Partin, 2019; De Wit et al., 2020; Jodén, 2020: 31; Yoganathan et al., 2021). Many of the most financially successful streamers make five-, six- or even seven-figure incomes and, after Twitch's recent streamer income leaks (Purtill, 2021), it is widely known how much money the most successful can make. What is important here is that the constant flow of capital is not taking place behind the scenes on Twitch but is explicitly foregrounded and *normalized*, to the point that the flow of money has become central to the broadcasts of all the largest streamers, represents a point of pride and aspiration for many smaller streamers, and is entirely unsurprising to the regular Twitch viewer. An outsider with no experience of the site might be surprised to discover how much money flows from viewers to streamers, especially when Twitch streams themselves are free to watch.

Donations and subscriptions are the two main methods by which streamers make money on Twitch, and two key paths through which the site itself makes its income. The former involves a one-off payment given to the streamer – originally via a third-party site like PayPal, but these days generally self-contained on Twitch itself (Johnson & Woodcock, 2019a; Partin, 2020) – while the latter is an ongoing but easily cancelled commitment to provide the streamer a fixed amount of money each month, generally US$5, US$10 or US$25. Donations are usually single or at most double-digit amounts of money, but can sometimes climb to extraordinary levels (Uszkoreit, 2018: 165; Partin, 2019: 156). These are normally done via an in-platform currency called *Bits*, which Twitch sells at a small markup. In popular streams donations are regular occurrences often accompanied by a message sometimes read out by the streamer (Guarriello, 2019: 1751) and sometimes by an automatic text-to-speech system (Consalvo, 2018: 97; Jackson, 2023a: 120) – such messages generally express appreciation for the streamer, offer a joke or a reference, or ask a question. Subscriptions can include a message to the streamer they might or might not read out, but almost always yield a verbal statement of appreciation from the broadcaster – 'thank you [username] for the [x] months subscription!' (Partin, 2019: 156; Carter & Egliston, 2021: 14; Wolff & Shen, 2022: 9). Subscriptions also allow the viewer to have a little icon next to their name, generally uniquely designed either by the streamer or a third party (Johnson & Baguley, forthcoming) and chosen for a given channel, which highlights the number of months for which they have been a consistent subscriber. In this case Twitch generally takes around half of the subscription fee. The amount of a donation and the regularity of a subscription are both platform-facilitated methods for viewers to demonstrate their appreciation for a streamer but also their commitment to, and hence perhaps status in, a given channel.

Many Twitch streamers – usually the more 'successful' – also make money from sponsorships (Payne, 2018: 290; Uszkoreit, 2018: 165; Törhönen et al., 2021). Smaller channels are sometimes able to secure them too, and often leverage them to progress to larger audiences and greater visibility. Most sponsorships on Twitch are from games companies or more broadly from companies and organizations that have, or aspire to have, a clear link to gaming, or geek or nerd culture more generally (Johnson & Woodcock, 2019b). A few lucky streamers get sponsored directly by games companies to play their new games – this can be blockbuster games companies but also applies to indie game developers and mobile games developers too. Such a sponsorship generally requires the streamer to play the game in question for some minimum period and might sometimes specify things like the time of day in which broadcasts should take place, or the exact in-game content which can, cannot, or must, be shown to the viewers. Clearly such sponsorships do rather imperil any possible idea of the game streamer as a neutral arbiter of taste who is just hanging out with their friends and discussing a game or games which they all enjoy. If a game streamer were to accept a sponsorship from a company in exchange for broadcasting their game, only to proceed to insult the game and disregard it, it seems unlikely that company would recruit that streamer again (Johnson & Woodcock, 2019a). This inevitably encourages a streamer to be at least reasonably positive towards the game being played, yet it is not difficult to tell when a streamer is underwhelmed by a sponsored game. Responses like 'this is certainly interesting' or 'this definitely has potential' can seem strained and don't really indicate genuine praise. The contrast with the various markers of more genuine streamer enthusiasm is hard to miss (see, e.g., Taylor, 2018: 86; Ruberg & Cullen, 2019: 94; Jodén, 2020: 31).

What we see here is therefore a clash between two roles for the streamer in the *agora*, as complicated by the financial value of sponsorships: the neutral arbiter or the everyday gaming friend wants to speak truthfully, but the businessperson inevitably has their statements about a new game reshaped by the money. Game streamers have, however, found ways to address this money-generated clash of roles, and how it might 'corrupt' the honesty of the *agora*. One of the earliest methods here was simply to acknowledge that a game was sponsored, rather than a game that the streamer was playing entirely of their own volition. This might seem like an obvious thing to say in the interests of transparency, but this was not originally a norm on Twitch. Acknowledging a sponsorship is one way that a streamer can demonstrate honesty and openness, and present a sponsored stream as *the channel* collectively looking at a game, rather than *the streamer* being paid to broadcast a game. Many streamers who do sponsored streams will also regularly stress to their viewers that their opinions on the game will not be shaped by the fact it is sponsored. Statements such as 'I will always give you guys my honest opinions', 'I'm always going to say it straight' or 'I only accept sponsorships from products I like' are common, although it is difficult to gauge how convincing (or truthful) they are. Twitch streamers – hobbyists as well as professionals or aspiring broadcasters – consistently prove themselves highly resourceful and able to innovate, and here we see streamers finding ways to navigate the tensions of what Lark (2022: 468) calls the 'artifice and authenticity' of live streaming (cf. Wu et al., 2022: 11).

There are many other ways to make money on Twitch, each of which has some influence on Twitch's role as an *agora*. Advertising is one such, although some streamers actively resist putting adverts on their channel as much as possible and make a very vocal point of saying so. This seems to be designed to endear viewers to the streamer, reinforcing authenticity (Lamerichs, 2021; Welch, 2022) – I'm just a gamer like you, money isn't my priority – over aspiration and ambition. Yet advertising and marketing finding their way into such spaces is not a new trend. Some scholars of the ancient *agora* emphasize its transactional and indeed economic quality, with Camp (1986: 6) describing 'the use of the area as a marketplace' and Eble and Breault (2002) framing it as a 'market square' for both the selling and consumption of goods. Davenport and Leitch (2005: 138) similarly note that where a 'large gathering of citizens occurs' market activities 'naturally' emerge at such locations, and this led to a 'blending of the civic with the commercial' (Gottesman, 2014: 28). It is interesting to note that in earliest sources the 'primary function of an agora was as a political meeting place' (Camp, 2016: 310), but in later sources 'the commercial aspects' of the space become more prominent, leading to a point where the *agora*'s function being 'primarily' that of a marketplace becomes the norm. The same appears to have taken place on Twitch, with advertising becoming both ubiquitous and a point of contention. This shouldn't be a site, many streamers suggest, for companies to hawk their wares, but should instead be focused purely on gaming without this corporatized aspect – both sides thus agree on the nature of Twitch's *agora*, but disagree about what parts are more or less important.

Streamers also deploy competitions between their viewers over who gives them the most money as a method for encouraging and gamifying financial support from their fans (Siutila, 2018; Johnson & Woodcock, 2019a; Abarbanel & Johnson, 2020). As mentioned previously, an *agora* can be easily understood as a site of competition, where the most compelling voices and speakers come to dominate over others (Davenport & Leitch, 2005). Twitch has integrated this very competition into its platform infrastructure such as by noting donation 'leaders' at the top of Twitch chat windows, enabling streamers to also rank their own viewers in this way. Markets are readily seen as ways to 'legitimise and authorise' (Beer, 2016: 28) behaviours and practices and we can perceive this here on Twitch as well. Once again the question of whether the site is for gaming or for money, or for making money through gaming, raises its head with these sorts of competitions, blurring our understanding of the precise nature of this space and how different actors understand it. Some streamers also set public challenges for *themselves* for their channels, such as daily or weekly targets for the number of followers they want to hit or hours they want to stream, and this target as well as their progress towards it will often be visible on a broadcast. As with celebrations of metric success, some streams will highlight this, often by giving a sense that they (the streamer) are *working hard* to grow the channel and anything that viewers can give is appreciated; others, however, will simply have the metrics up on their broadcast without it being anything they directly talk about. Just as in the ancient *agora* speakers were 'giving accounts of themselves to their peers' (O'Kelly & Dubnick, 2014: 13), here on Twitch we see streamers using the pursuit of higher metrics and more money as ways to legitimize themselves as speakers who are putting in appropriate degrees of effort, and who are taking Twitch sufficiently *seriously*. All of this is facilitated by Twitch either explicitly, through the site's dashboard (Pellicone & Ahn, 2017: 4864; cf. Beer, 2016: 92), or tacitly, through the dominant cultural position metrics occupy on the platform.

It should be clear from this discussion of metricization and monetization how incredibly *visible* money and economic exchange is on Twitch. All major digital platforms have numerous ways for the platforms and the users creating content on those platforms to make money, otherwise they would not be the multi-billion-dollar enterprises that so many are, but it is rarely as *obvious* as on Twitch. Facebook's users are not constantly presented with information about how much money is being spent or earned by 'Pages' nor the precise systems by which sponsored content appears on their feed. Advertising on Twitter has generally been comparatively rare and unobtrusive, and almost never seen if one simply tweets without following the tweets of others. On the internet more broadly, most users are now very good at automatically ignoring adverts on many websites, with adverts running in banners down the side or at the top or bottom of a webpage often being simply unnoticed by the experienced user. On Twitch, however, the presence of money and the presence of potential money to be given or received cannot be escaped. This constant flow of money between users – viewers to streamers – and to the platform from *everyday users* – viewers and streamers alike – is highly unusual, as is the extent to which Twitch's streamers are often discussing money, framing their ambitions in terms of becoming sponsored or partnered, and thanking viewers (Partin, 2019; Wolff & Shen, 2022) for their generous donations.

When discussing money, one of my very first interviewees in 2015 said that Twitch was 'like the gold rush' (Johnson & Woodcock, 2017). We see here that not only does this statement acknowledge the money potentially to be made on the site, but it also – looking back over the past decade and the increasingly ubiquitous monetization of Twitch – speaks to the *role* that money plays on the platform as well as its availability. The gold rushes of the American West and late-1800s Australia were not just opportunities for the lucky, resourceful and sometimes unscrupulous to become wealthy, but were also cultural and social contexts in which gold as a concept and a point of discussion became a fundamental part of everyday life. On Twitch the exchange of money is not something that only happens to a few streamers, but happens to many. It is also not something which is hidden or in the background, but is in fact highly visible on those Twitch channels where money changes hands. In these channels it is not some distraction from a stream's primary content, but actually *is* a core part of that stream's primary content. It is unlikely that any streamer would admit this – streamers define their streams according to the gaming or other content it focuses on, rather than an endless sequence of people giving them money (cf. Taylor, 2018: 96; Sjöblom et al., 2019: 25) – but this does not change the fact that the exchange of money is integral and takes up a significant amount of broadcast time. Some streamers actively downplay the possibility of donation to avoid appearing 'money hungry' (Sjöblom et al., 2019: 25; cf. Jackson, 2023a: 252–3) – though of course it is only the most successful streamers who are in a position to demonstrate their disdain. Beer (2016) tells us how metrics do not merely measure but actively shape behaviour, and the same can be said of money on Twitch. A full understanding of the platform is not possible without appreciating its monetization possibilities, their regular presence on the site, their visibility to streamers and viewers alike, and how they shape and contest what is meant to be taking place in Twitch's gaming-focused *agora*.

Designing and building the agora

In this chapter I have sought to describe and interrogate Twitch as a platform – its history, its interface and navigation, and the roles played by customization, moderation, money and metrics. All these factors, together, give us the techno-logical and infrastructural foundations of a platform that is far from neutral and in no way free from the creation and reinforcement of certain kinds of power relationships, while nevertheless still evidently being highly appealing to streamers and viewers alike. The openness of the platform and the ability to construct a channel that is distinctive enough to begin to take on its own identity – something we return to in chapter 4 – offers something unlike most other contemporary social media platforms, where the platform's own branding remains overwhelmingly dominant. Twitch streamers not only produce content just as we see on other social media sites like Instagram and YouTube, but also construct a background identity of a channel, almost a place or an institution, with its own set of aesthetic and cultural brandings that mark it out from other streams. In currently ongoing research I've been exploring how streamers build timetables, schedules and regular streaming routines in order to give viewers a sense of consistency and reliability to their channel (see, e.g., De Wit et al., 2020; Sixto-García & Losada-Fernández, 2023) – again, like television broadcasts – and the channel customization aspects are also a part of this building of the platform from which a streamer speaks, alongside the building of whatever is actually broadcast. Through money and metrics, meanwhile, we see that Twitch is also an *agora* which tracks both one's construction of a rostrum and what one has to say from that rostrum, both implicitly and explicitly suggesting that live streaming *should* become more than merely a hobby and that all of one's decisions can be carefully planned and rationalized. This is thus no neutral *agora*, but one that actively supports people who commit to certain kinds of labour and who fully embrace the opportunities for customization the site offers in construction of a personal or channel brand.

This heavy degree of customization is a double-edged sword, however. Twitch gives only light-touch tools for the streamer looking to control and manage what viewers say back to them, meaning that hostile actors have a surprising amount of power here to speak back to streamers and potentially disrupt their broadcasts. Twitch frames the options it gives to streamers as a positive, which allows its broadcasters significant control over the chat content in their channel, but this masks a transposition of moderation labour – and the *moral duty* to moderate – from the platform onto the user. Where other platforms do relatively little to excuse their lax attention to hostile and toxic actors, Twitch instead leans into the (genuine) degree of control streamers have over many things as a way to frame user-centric moderation regimes as a similar kind of control, when in fact it represents the opposite. Streamers have minimal control over who talks back to them in their channels precisely because the site's responsibility to handle this has been largely overlooked, and this relative absence of moderation leads inexorably to the sustained harassment of women and minority streamers. These positions that are hard-coded into interactions by Twitch the platform, having previously been chosen by Twitch the company, essentially serve to have their *agora* further amplify the already dominant voices in gaming, and further quieten and subdue the already marginalized voices. Like other platforms, Twitch is not eager to commit the labour and money required to actually police a platform as large as the one they find themselves owning and controlling, and so instead this job is farmed out to the streamers, and in turn to the almost always unpaid moderators they recruit.

Making sure to think of Twitch as a *platform* is therefore particularly useful. It is of course a platform in the sense meant by critical media and internet scholars, which is to say an online service or website that does not 'just facilitate socio-economic, cultural, and political interaction', but actively looks to 'organize and steer this interaction' (Nieborg & Poell, 2018: 4276) through connecting 'users, advertisers, and third-party developers' in marketplaces where 'value increases for all parties as more people use it' (Helmond, 2015: 2; Flew, 2021). Yet Twitch also exemplifies the idea of the platform in the more traditional sense, as a structure or stance or position that allows one to articulate ideas to an audience. Twitch 'gives a platform' to its streamers in a way that few other platforms can manage for their users. We therefore now have a sense of Twitch's foundations as the gaming *agora* able to give astonishing visibility to gamers and their play, and – as I explore in the following chapters – able to transmit to and define for millions of gamers the nature of consequential and noteworthy moments in the wider gaming culture. Yet it is also a platform that beguiles with its apparent realness and verisimilitude, that shapes what its speakers might be doing – and what its listeners might be hearing – according to neoliberal logics of monetary profit and metricized visibility, and that reinforces existing power relationships through doing little to protect, let alone promote, marginalized voices. While Twitch's rise to prominence as a gaming *agora* was presumably not planned for most of the site's existence (although Amazon's purchase tells us much about the potential that the company saw in Twitch's unexpectedly successful game-focused iteration), it has now arrived as one of the most important places where gaming is discussed, shaped and formed. We now know the possibilities, restrictions and infrastructures through which this shaping takes place, but we have said little of the individual people doing the shaping. In the next chapter we will therefore explore: who are the speakers using this platform, and who are the listeners who tune in to receive what they have to say?

Chapter 2

Twitch Users

Introduction

In the previous chapter I looked at what we might think of as the infrastructural or material foundations of Twitch, and hence both the opportunities and limitations of Twitch as an *agora* – a place for speech and debate, the determination of interests and importance, and economic exchange, where speakers have variable degrees of visibility and voice, and rituals and norms form key parts of the interactions there. In this chapter I want to build on these foundations to ask: who are the voices taking advantage of this public forum, and who listens to and engages with whatever those voices have to say?

The chapter is split in two halves. In the first I will summarize research on Twitch streamers and Twitch viewers, giving the reader a sense of what we know about who these people are, what they do on Twitch, how they contribute to Twitch's gaming *agora*, and why. In both cases I will highlight the large number of different scholarly conceptions of streamers and viewers, emphasizing how the complexity of what users are actually doing and experiencing on Twitch confounds the potential for simple development of a single comprehensive framework. In the second half of the chapter, I'll offer three core arguments regarding Twitch's users. In the first I will develop the concept of the 'Twitch we', a mode of speaking on Twitch that brings viewers into a streamer's activities and connects them closely with the successes of a channel – thus building the sense of belonging, of being 'one of us', that I discussed in the introductory chapter. In the second case I look at the tension between streamer–viewer friendships and the celebrification of streamers as a way to begin moving beyond the dominant paradigm of 'parasocial relationships' for understanding streamer–viewer interactions, and to instead dig more deeply into what makes Twitch so very compelling for all of its users, especially when compared to other platforms on which celebrities or friends might be present. In the third case I examine the roles of 'moderators' – non-streamers empowered to have some control and influence over a streamer's channel – and demonstrate that, far from being simply dedicated viewers, they in fact play a vital constitutive role in a streamer's channel by ensuring that broadcast content matches as closely as possible the desired 'vision' of a streamer. In the conclusion I will bring these facets together to demonstrate how Twitch's *agora* has many voices, not just those of the streamers, and that assessing the power dynamics across this plurality is essential for understanding the experiences of Twitch's more than a hundred million users – streamers, viewers and moderators alike.

Twitch streamers

Twitch's users (both streamers and viewers) are by far the most researched part of the site. Beginning with streamers, we note that gaming has long been seen as a male pastime (Cote, 2017: 136; Uszkoreit, 2018: 163; Ruberg et al., 2019: 471). Dynamics of exclusion and expulsion manifested early in gaming communities looking to define themselves not just by gaming, but also through blocking entry for anyone – especially women – who did not fit the imagined gaming archetype (Fox & Tang, 2014; Charles, 2016). Yet in the past decades gaming has become a hobby with almost exactly equal numbers of men and women (Ogletree & Drake, 2007; Sullivan & Smith, 2016; Paaßen et al., 2017), although women, transgender and nonbinary gamers remain relatively unseen and marginalized compared to cisgender male gamers. On Twitch well over half of all streamers do identify as men (Ruberg, 2021), with various sources suggesting that between a fifth and a third identify as women (Woodcock & Johnson, 2019; De Wit et al., 2020). Pervasive misogyny on the site means, however, that we cannot assume all these streamers have the same experiences on Twitch, or the same statistical likelihood of climbing Twitch's ladder of 'success' if equal effort and talent are committed to that objective (Ruberg et al., 2019: 471; Brown & Moberly, 2020: 62; cf. Poeller et al., 2023). Most but not all streamers on Twitch identify as being white (Yosilewitz, 2018). The great majority of Twitch streamers and viewers are in their teens, twenties and thirties (Twitch, 2023d), with streamers forty or older rare and viewers forty or older even rarer (cf. Ruotsalainen, 2022). 'Young white men from North America' (Ruberg, 2021: 1684) are thus the primary, but far from the only, demographic of the site. In terms of educational and career background, meanwhile, Twitch streamers I have interviewed have included current or former students, car mechanics, soldiers, casino dealers and fast-food employees (Johnson & Woodcock, 2017). This highlights how gaming's earlier strong associations with computer science and programming (Kirkpatrick, 2016) have faded away as the medium has transitioned towards the mainstream.

The key point here is the diversity of streamers on Twitch, and this diversity is apparent in scholarly attempts to capture, define and propose typologies for streamers and their activities. There have been numerous different framings proposed in the past decade from scholars working in a variety of fields – primarily and unsurprisingly media studies and communication studies, but also psychology, human–computer interaction, sociology, and marketing and business. While none captures the entire dynamics of streamer orientations to their streaming practices – 'the motivations to stream are complex' (Young & Wiedenfeld, 2022: 382) and so are streamers' behaviours on Twitch – each captures an important part of the picture. I want to look first at the demographic of Twitch streamers most often studied. This is the 'professional', 'aspirational', 'successful' or 'full-time' streamer. This growing body of research began with a paper (Johnson & Woodcock, 2017) in which my co-author and I interviewed around a hundred professional and semi-professional Twitch streamers – which we defined as making the majority, or a substantial part, of their income from the practice – to understand their labour practices, professional orientations, and economic opportunities and challenges. Since then, the position of these broadcasters as an object of study within Twitch scholarship has expanded significantly. Although such streamers are only a tiny percentage of the overall demographic of Twitch, they are by far the most visible and influential streamers, and the ones who serve as inspirational or aspirational role models for others interested in taking their Twitch practice more 'seriously'. They mark an unusually compelling case study at the intersections of celebrity, gaming, digital labour and digital economy, and are also of course the dominant speakers in Twitch's *agora*.

To begin with, the motivation behind a person deciding to approach their streaming activity on Twitch in a 'professional' manner appears to come from the idea that streaming as a career can produce a significant sense of purpose and fulfilment. In a previous publication I argued that when 'the future looks bleak for many' young people, the pursuit of a career as a game streamer is emerging as a 'novel for[m] of life project' (Johnson et al., 2019). This echoed Taylor's (2018: 70) observation that many are attracted to live streaming by the combination of their 'love for gaming' and 'otherwise dire job prospects', suggesting that 'meaningful and fulfilling work' might only be found in this space. To 'carve out a career' (Chan & Gray, 2020: 360) that is 'self-made and flexible' (Meisner & Ledbetter, 2020: 1180), and to do so from a 'passion or hobby' (Yu et al., 2021: 55), is immensely appealing. Gaming is a passion that many take very seriously and commit huge amounts of time and energy to, while also often becoming central to the identity and sense of self that many players have. It is equally often framed culturally as a purely leisure activity – hence not *work*. When we bring these together we see how the lure of a career playing games appeals both because it speaks to a deep passion and enjoyment on the part of the player, *and* presents itself as being very far away from the world of work so daunting in teenage years and young adulthood. In this vein Törhönen et al. (2020: 166) situate it within a growing trend of 'turning leisure activities, such as gaming, into productive endeavours' which might indeed yield feelings of 'self-actualization and personal well-being'. For many of Twitch's predominantly young ambitious streamers, these hopes of realizing a dream do seem to 'merit the time and effort investments they require' (Johnson & Woodcock, 2017: 345), even while the demands of the job can be intense (Johnson & Woodcock, 2017; Johnson, 2021). While there are many ways to stream, it is this framing for streaming that appears to yield by far the largest audiences, the most monetary success, and hence the most influence over Twitch's gaming *agora*.

Part of the appeal of this orientation appears to lie in the lure of becoming a digital gaming *celebrity*. We live in times of an unusually high fascination with celebrities, and research in this area regularly conceptualizes successful broadcasters on Twitch as being 'microcelebrity streamers' (De Wit et al., 2020: 1) and 'digital celebrities' (Johnson, 2019: 516). It appears that the allure of celebrity status in gaming can be a 'powerful motivator' as many top streamers are, indeed, famous on the site and to a certain extent beyond it (Taylor, 2018: 91). Others discuss the 'micro-celebrities and influencers' on sites like Twitch (Törhönen et al., 2021: 1) as a key framing to understand their behaviours. Streamers in fact rarely call themselves influencers, perhaps preferring the site's ludic and meritocratic framings instead, but there is much overlap between what the most 'successful' do on Twitch and what takes place on sites more commonly associated with this phenomenon, such as Instagram. These are some of the allures of Twitch – to enjoy a life pursuing one's passion, a life (seemingly) of play rather than work, a life that will transform you into one of the select few making a living from such competitive and strategically demanding career paths, and a life of attention and celebrity within a culture you care about a great deal. The idea of *aspiration* is particularly important, with Taylor (2018: 70) discussing the 'professional aspirations' of streamers, and others mentioning the importance of understanding streamers' aspirations to turn a 'passion project into a paycheck' (Meisner & Ledbetter, 2020: 1180), as well as the fact that those who make it become, in their turn, 'aspirational figures' (Kowert & Daniel, 2021: 3) for others. The role of identity is key, with streamers 'aspiring to create a new professional identity' (Taylor, 2018: 68) as 'a professional broadcaster' (ibid.: 82) through the apparent possibilities for 'achievement and self-development' (Törhönen et al., 2019: 2560) offered by Twitch.

Scholars have written extensively on what being a professional Twitch streamer actually entails. Despite the profound appeal of live streaming as a career, the reality can be extremely taxing (Johnson & Woodcock, 2017; Johnson, 2021). There is now widespread agreement amongst researchers that being a 'successful' live streamer is a 'laborious lifestyle' (Yu et al., 2021: 55) and that 'being financially successful' on Twitch 'demands a lot of work' (Groen, 2020: 98). The various demands of managing one's stream, community, viewers, income, sponsorships and so forth can be 'strenuous and difficult' (Johnson & Woodcock, 2017: 338) and certainly every bit as demanding as more traditional jobs, if not sometimes even more so. As most full-time Twitch streamers are self-employed, there is a constant risk of burnout (Yu et al., 2021: 56). Succeeding in the job also requires management of a 'complex assemblage of microphones, video cameras, green screens, second or even third monitors, fast, stable internet, and high-end computer hardware' (Partin, 2019: 155), all of which require varying degrees of technical expertise and on-the-job learning. Another significant part of the labour demands of the job comes from questions of *time*, as Törhönen et al. (2020: 177) note that more time invested in streaming tends to lead to potentially rapid 'career development'. This time is primarily time spent streaming (Brown & Moberly, 2020: 60), but a lot of unseen and often unappreciated work takes place off-stream as well (Johnson, 2021). Streamers also need to generally broadcast regularly and on 'fixed schedules' to get 'consistent viewership' (De Wit et al., 2020: 2; cf. Johnson et al., 2019), and these streamers often have a 'personal schedule of streaming times' which enables users to 'rely on' being once more able to tune in (Wulf et al., 2020: 332). Live streaming with a professional or aspirational orientation may well be hugely compelling, but extensive research shows that the reality is extremely demanding and challenging.

Scholars have also shown that successful streamers also put in a lot of work whilst streaming to create and manage a community that can, and that wants to, financially support them. Successful Twitch broadcasters are not silent (Taylor, 2018: 75) but are generally talking constantly to build rapport and connection with their viewers (Woodcock & Johnson, 2019). Ruberg and Cullen (2019: 93) cite a streamer who explains that successful streamers must be able to 'talk without pause', use 'expressive body movements' and often try to make 'eye contact with viewers'. In turn streamers stress the importance of demonstrating 'that they are excited to stream' (ibid.: 94) and should appear 'motivated, confident and proud', but also 'appreciative and humble' (ibid.: 97) that they have this unusual and highly sought-after career opportunity. One of the key challenges for a stream is to keep 'the uncut stream entertaining between eventful action-packed moments' (Jodén & Strandell, 2022: 1970), a challenge not faced by YouTube gamers who can edit and polish their videos before release (cf. Postigo, 2016). Taylor (2018: 75) calls streamers who manage all of this 'accomplished', and this sense of achievement is echoed by Li et al. (2019: 14) who frame a successful streamer as a 'masterful director', who manages performance and engagement. With these sorts of activities these streamers 'entertain the audience through narration and emotional expressiveness' (Seering et al., 2017b: 437) with the goal of 'craft[ing] a strong sense of identification, connection, and community with their audience' (Kersting et al., 2021: 10). Jodén and Strandell (2022: 1983), meanwhile, describe this as creating 'emotional energy' in a channel, and note that this and other kinds of social interaction are essential for 'successful streams on Twitch' (ibid.: 1971).

The importance of money and income are also regularly highlighted in studies of these 'top' streamers, unsurprising given their key role on the platform. Some of the most successful streamers earn millions of dollars a year (Chan & Gray, 2020: 355), and those with the most clearly work-focused orientations to their live streaming are generally the ones who bring in these 'highest levels' of income (Törhönen et al., 2019: 2558). Part of this striking flow of money is connected to the sorts of affect and labour discussed in the previous paragraphs – Groen (2020: 98), for example, argues that having even 'modest financial success' as a live streamer requires 'creative energy'. This is a finding that connects to Walker's (2014: 439) comments about how these streamers, whom he defines as having an 'active posture' regarding their streaming practice, need to 'develop a public identity connected to play style, on-air personality, comedic reper-toire, their relationship with teammates or co-streamers, or even a style of critique'. This is only part of becoming a 'top' streamer, however, as one must also learn to master the metricized 'tools and monetization mechanics' Twitch gives to streamers (Sjöblom et al., 2019: 21) and find ways to constantly encourage donations, subscriptions and so on (cf. Johnson & Woodcock, 2019a). Gender is also implicated here in these top streamers and their monetization, as Ruberg et al. (2019: 475) note that male streamers are often 'celebrated for their enviable financial success' while female streamers are 'criticized when they earn money through streaming' because it implies 'a focus on money rather than on video games'. Such a double standard shows that the idea of the professional gamer – or more exactly a professional game streamer, in this case – is constructed as a normative identity in contrast to femininity (Dargonaki, 2018: 107). Within a 'patriarchal gaming culture' (Tran, 2022: 509) some gamers are legitimized to pursue money and income in ways that others are not (Cullen, 2022b), and this shapes the potential to reach these highest levels of Twitch 'success', which are neither equally distributed nor equally available.

There is therefore extensive work on professional or aspirational streamers, and this is a demographic we now have a strong understanding of. There is far less literature, however, that directly addresses what we might think of as hobbyist streamers, which is to say those understood as performing actions opposite to the professional or aspirational streamers, or whose orientation is very specifically not focused on the dynamics described above. These streamers have nevertheless been mentioned by a few authors, possibly first by Walker who describes 'passive' streamers (in contrast to 'active' streamers) who 'do not go out of their way to set up additional equipment or software' and are more generally 'limited in their ability to build any sort of personal reputation and cannot attract communities around their play' (2014: 439). Others use the term 'amateur' in contrast to the above framing, such as Kersting et al. (2021: 6) who describe these streamers as hosting channels in which 'the relationship between streamer and audience' is more 'closely-knit' than in other – larger – alternatives, and Guarriello (2021: 143) who also discussed 'amateur livestreamers' who are 'not monetizing or aiming for corporate sponsorship for their content'. However, streamers have also been examined according to *size* rather than according to the status or orientation – professional or hobbyist – of the streamer. When it comes to stream size, large channels have seen less study than small channels, which is mostly because these are generally seen as synonymous with the much-studied aspirational or professionally orientated streamers. Yet there is a body of literature that covers large channels and this sits alongside, but distinct from, research that instead counts 'successful' streamers as being those of the professional or aspirational orientation. For example, Catá (2019: 137) describes the importance of a 'large consistent following' for streamers looking to achieve 'success' with their channels; Carter and Egliston (2021: 9) mention 'the largest streams' on Twitch; Diwanji et al. (2020: 9) also talk about 'large streams'; Glickman et al. (2018: 193) describe some of the social dynamics in 'larger streams'; and Phelps et al. (2021a: 2863) define a 'large stream' as one with 'hundreds or thousands of viewers'. Placing specific numbers on these is also common, with Guarriello (2019: 1757) noting that 'the game live streamers who earn the most money on Twitch [are] those with thousands of live viewers'. These numbers are also important for a streamer who wants to 'prove they have an audience' in order to become an 'affiliate or partner' (Brown & Moberly, 2020: 60) and hence be able to earn money through Twitch's platform affordances; this is 'highly competitive' (Pellicone & Ahn, 2017: 4871) with only a minuscule fraction of users – estimated at '0.075% of streamers [gaining] affiliate status and 0.0135% gain[ing] partnerships' (Brown & Moberly, 2020: 61) – having channels large enough. Having already discussed the importance of metrics on Twitch, we therefore see that the metrics of viewer, follower or subscriber counts give an easy means of categorizing channels in a way that partly, but not entirely, overlaps with the more aspirational and work-focused streamers, and allows researchers to capture a sense of the appeal of different speakers (and different communities) within the *agora*.

Small channels and small streamers, however, have seen quite a bit more attention than their larger cousins. In the case of smaller channels and streamers, a dominant perspective and terminology – 'microstreamers' – has emerged in recent years. These are similar to what Brandis and Bozkurt (2021: 170) call 'clique streamers', who 'targe[t] the smallest audiences', but the framing of the 'microstreamer' has become the main perspective on these broadcasters. This has brought with it a growing body of incisive research examining these individuals on Twitch (who do of course make up the overwhelming numerical majority of the site's broadcasters). In terms of the numbers being used to define this demographic, definitions differ – Phelps et al. (2021a: 2863), for example, note the 'long tail' of streams on Twitch with 'average audience sizes approaching zero', and consequently define microstreamers as those with 'small audiences' of 'fewer than 100 concurrent viewers'. Young and Wiedenfeld (2022: 381) similarly use the 'small audiences' terminology, Carter and Egliston (2021: 9) mention streamers with a 'handful of viewers', while Lin et al. (2019: 3) note that most streamers 'have few (if any) spectators' watching their streams, a finding echoed by Scully-Blaker et al. (2017: 2035) who state it is 'not uncommon to find channels with viewer counts of 1 or even zero'. While the precise size of a micro-streamer varies across researchers, therefore, there is a clear distinction being made here with larger broadcasters. The fact that these streamers are the overwhelming majority on Twitch, yet have little representation or visibility in the site's gaming *agora*, further emphasizes the importance of monetization and metrics previously discussed.

As well as the size of their channels, motives for streaming also differ for microstreamers. Many authors suggest a primacy here for intrinsic rather than extrinsic motivations, such as 'innate interest' in whatever they're streaming, a 'motivation to share that activity' with others (Phelps et al., 2021a: 2863–4), the pursuit of personal 'autonomy', and the role of a 'community leader' through 'skill competence displayed to an audience' (Young & Wiedenfeld, 2022: 381). Scholars have proposed that microstreaming meets needs for these streamers, such as 'the need to relate' to others (ibid.: 393), 'uplift others' and 'create connections' to 'make new friends' (ibid.: 390), build confidence, and simultaneously 'find their people' and do so through 'an ongoing process of personal development' (ibid.: 394). Hence for most of these broadcasters 'streaming activity is a mediated extension of their personal leisure activities' (Phelps et al., 2021a: 2863), although this does not mean that microstreamers 'have no ambitions' towards larger streams, nor that some of the labour issues described above are not applicable. Our understandings of streamers exist on a sliding scale rather than in absolutes. The arguments proposed here are not that larger or more professional streamers always lack the intrinsic motivations above, nor that smaller streamers always lack drive or don't have to face labour issues – rather that streamers in many regards can be seen as a *spectrum*, rather than a binary, but that we can nevertheless identify *general* and common distinctions between these different categories of streamers.

Microstreamer behaviour, as well as demographics and motivations, has also been examined. Their channels offer what are often 'more intimate spaces' (Phelps et al., 2021b: 1) than those of larger channels, with viewers normally all being acknowledged by name when they enter (Carter & Egliston, 2021: 9) and the channels offering 'an amateur warmth and charm that can feel absent in larger streams' (Phelps et al., 2021b: 3). For viewers this is why many choose to participate in these channels rather than other parts of the wider Twitch *agora*, as here 'they experience[e] more meaningful interaction' (Hamilton et al., 2014: 1316). Microstreamers, although small in size, are often highly 'passionate' about and 'deeply driven' to support their 'microcommunities' (Phelps et al., 2021a: 2870). This is closely related to Scully-Blaker et al.'s (2017) distinction between 'playing along' and 'playing for' in Twitch game streaming, with microstreamers generally playing more actively *along* with their viewers and engaging in more direct communication than their larger counterparts. Money, or its absence, is also an important part of microstreamer experiences. Young and Wiedenfeld 2022: 391) note that their interviewees classified themselves as 'small streamers' precisely because they earn 'little to no income' from their streaming, and Consalvo et al. (2023: 2326) similarly stress that most microstreamers never make money from streaming, and indeed never attempt to. This is one of the most obvious and key distinctions between larger and smaller streamers – and the more hobbyist or the more aspirational streamer – and with money so deeply integrated into the platform and the aesthetics of bigger streams, the inclusion or exclusion of financial elements marks out a major difference across channels.

Twitch's streamers are thus diverse in their backgrounds, their orientations to streaming, and the size of communities they craft, manage and in some cases rely on for income. The *agora* offers a tremendously varied range of speakers not just in terms of what they have to say, but also how they present and say it, their attitudes towards metrics and money, and the ways their listeners might or might not be directly or indirectly involved. It is streamers who create the primary content and it is streamers whom viewers tune in to watch. It is the streamer who plays the game (or carries out some other activity), who laughs and shouts and interacts with whatever they are streaming, and the streamer who takes the credit for successes – overcoming a challenging boss, for example – and also the responsibility for defeat, or for disagreeable or problematic behaviours. There are clear distinctions and categories but these exist on sliding scales, not as absolutes; plenty of microstreamers can be aspirational while 'successful' streamers can seek to generate a sense of relaxedness in their broadcasts, to name just two examples. Yet as following parts of this chapter show, the popular idea of the streamer as the creator and the viewer as the consumer is far too simple. This is partly because viewers both as individuals and as a collective mass *do* shape a channel's content and the experience of being in that channel (sometimes to a quite profound degree), and partly because of the existence of 'moderators', empowered viewers who have a major impact on a Twitch channel and its content. This, in turn, will lead to new insights I explore through what I call the 'Twitch we' in terms of how streamers perceive their roles on Twitch, how viewers and moderators see their roles, and the power dynamics and discourses that underlie what is actually a deeply interwoven mutual co-creation of Twitch content. Streamers, however small their viewer numbers, are broadcasting to *viewers*, or at least understand themselves implicitly as doing so (Scully-Blaker et al., 2017: 2030) even if there's nobody actually there – what can therefore be said of these viewers, Twitch's other key category of user?

Twitch viewers

We now come to Twitch's viewers rather than its streamers. Given that plenty of streamers are also themselves viewers, and viewing streams can indeed be part of the networked labour of streaming (Johnson, 2019), here we are primarily talking about viewers who do not themselves stream – which appears to tacitly be the framing of most viewer-focused research projects – while also acknowledging that where there *is* overlap, we are discussing these individuals when they are in the viewer 'frame', rather than when they are in the streamer frame. There have been numerous scholarly attempts to define various categories of viewers in a way that offers us more clarity about their behaviours, interests and motivations. While no typology is ever perfect, there are clear recurring themes from these research projects which tell us much about viewers and, like streamers, we can identify both important lines of distinction between viewers as well as an understanding of how scholarship to date has defined and understood this demographic. Much like understanding streamers tells us key insights about who is doing what on Twitch, and why, understanding viewers will offer us the second half of this picture. A comprehensive sense of how viewers have been understood also highlights the sheer range of what is taking place on Twitch, and the diversity of approaches being taken to attempt to capture this astonishing variety.

More scholars have developed typologies for understanding the interests and motivations of Twitch viewers than has been the case with streamers. The reasons people watch Twitch 'vary significantly among individuals' (Partin, 2019: 156) and to begin this section I want to look at some of these highest-level typologies for Twitch viewers, before then going into more depth about some of the most important viewer dynamics we see on the platform. The first comprehensive typology, chronologically, appears to be that of Sjöblom and Hamari (2017: 985) who propose that viewers watch Twitch streamers because of five motivations they define as 'cognitive, affective, personal integrative, social integrative and tension release'. Hilvert-Bruce et al. (2018: 58) then proposed six key motivations: 'social interaction, sense of community, meeting new people, entertainment, information seeking, and a lack of external support in real life'. In the same year Taylor's (2018: 39–40) monograph on Twitch also proposed six, but a different six, in this case arguing for the importance of 'aspirational' (wanting to emulate a streamer), 'educational' (wanting to improve at a game), 'inspirational' (fandom surrounding a game), 'entertainment' (the pleasure of watching something), 'community' (being part of a wider social experience) and 'ambience' (the channel as background noise) drivers in viewer attention to Twitch streams. Wohn et al. (2019: 105) then split viewers into those who are 'casual fans' and have little investment in what channel they watch, 'celebrity fans' particularly focused on a streamer, and those with a deeper 'emotional attachment' to a broadcaster. Later Wu et al. (2022: 5) listed what they presented as an integrated summary of existing research on live streaming and identified key motivations as wanting to 'relax, kill time, keep up with "fashion", make more friends, communicate with others, improve skills, find a community, gain new knowledge', and 'seek the feeling of company'. Most recently, Speed et al. (2023: 1) argue for four groupings in the 'general Twitch audience' – those who watch to inform their gaming decisions, those who watch but reject social interaction, those who follow particular streamers but do not interact, and those who focus on the social and interpersonal aspects of the site.

The key takeaway here, of course, is that Twitch's viewers are every bit as complex as streamers, and that research is still grappling with fully understanding them. Moving beyond these high-level categorizations, however, perhaps the best place to start is in a separation between active viewers and lurkers. The term 'lurker' has pre-Twitch internet usage and refers to users who 'regularly login to online communities but seldom post' (Sun et al., 2014). As previously noted, there is no obligation to engage in Twitch chat, and many users – including, in fact, myself – are lurkers (Jackson, 2023a: 41). Several scholars have therefore examined those who 'only' engage with the audiovisual part of Twitch and do not talk in chat nor interact with channel communities, and this has generally been from two angles: those who watch Twitch in the background, and those who are 'just watchers' (Orme, 2021) for other reasons. In the first case Taylor (2018: 40), discussing her 'ambience' motivation for Twitch viewing, notes that for many viewers a Twitch stream can be 'a kind of comforting background noise and movement'. This is echoed by Jodén and Strandell (2022: 1971) who talk about 'passive viewers' of the platform who don't engage in the social dimensions of Twitch, Spilker et al. (2020) who discuss a 'passive' orientation to consuming Twitch as being akin to channel-hopping on the television, and Orme (2021: 2259) who notes 'multi-tasking' is very common with Twitch viewers. For many the site allows for people to enjoy aspects of gaming without it being a *foreground* activity. Much like many half-watch television programmes in the background of their living rooms, many also appear to use Twitch streams for the same purpose.

In turn, however, Orme's recent work goes into particular detail about these viewers by studying what she calls 'Just Watchers', a demographic who don't engage with social and communal aspects. Going beyond the background-noise motivation described above, Orme explains how these users watch Twitch because games can come with a 'mental, emotional and social toll' when playing oneself (2021: 2260); because being skilled at games can yield 'exhaustion, stress and anxiety'; and, for Just Watchers with marginalized identities, Twitch channels are a way to engage with games while largely evading other, potentially toxic, gamers (ibid.: 2261). Others want to experience game stories, Orme explains, or watch games they don't have the expensive hardware to play, while another part of this group 'experience a thrill from watching skilled players pull off feats that they themselves cannot' (ibid.: 2262) – an obvious comparison here with esports viewing (Taylor, 2018) and indeed physical sports viewing, and one that demonstrates how displays of skill can be relative, as well as absolute. Ultimately many Twitch viewers have some combination of 'limited skill, time and money' (Speed et al., 2023: 2), and the existence of these lurking viewers shows us how the motivations to watch games, and to play games, can therefore easily differ (Hilvert-Bruce et al., 2018: 64). Given their obscurity, gathering data on these viewers is somewhat more challenging than others, but it is clear they represent a significant part of Twitch's viewer demographics.

Beyond these lurkers, however, Twitch viewer research focuses on those with more active interactions with streamers and with each other. One of the defining elements of Twitch is that 'viewers can interact with streamers in real time' (Wulf et al., 2021: 649) by watching the game being played, hearing a streamer's commentary, and responding or commenting in the text chat (Young & Wiedenfeld, 2022: 381). Viewers 'value the quality of liveness' (Glickman et al., 2018: 188; cf. Auslander, 2022; Persaud & Perks, 2022) that allows streamers to 'view and respond to the chat' (De Wit et al., 2020: 11) – viewers like it when streamers 'individually address their audience and answer chat messages' (Wulf et al., 2021: 652), while viewers can 'respond synchronously' to the streamer with messages, donations and so forth (Goh et al., 2021: 508). In the chat window 'viewers express support, opinions, suggestions, requests, even criticism' (Speed et al., 2023: 6) and this can also reach a point where viewers and streamers discuss 'intimate' (Dargonaki, 2018: 105) issues such as mental or physical health (Johnson, 2019; cf. Dunlap et al., 2023), careers and so forth. Research suggests that viewers feel more comfortable interacting with a streamer when they appear authentic and genuine (Wohn et al., 2019: 103) and this can indeed lead to some strikingly private and personal conversations. As a final point here, the size of channels has been implicated in streamer–viewer interactions – smaller audiences enable a streamer to 'offer a more personalized experience for the viewer' (Johansson, 2021: 8) through which to 'build rapport' (Nematzadeh et al., 2019: 10) – but as with streamers this is a spectrum, not a binary. The interactivity of this *agora* therefore appears essential for viewers, most of whom are interested in something 'more' than being passive viewers.

We therefore see that many viewers are keen to interact with the streamers they watch, especially in smaller channels where such interaction is more feasible. However, a strong line of research in the last half-decade has questioned the nature of these interactions, often by framing them as 'parasocial relationships' between viewer and streamer. As Kowert and Daniel (2021: 1) put it, in parasocial relationships 'a person extends emotional energy, interest, and time in the relationship while the other person, the media figure, is unaware of the other's existence'. In the case of Twitch this would entail a viewer feeling that friendship or affection exists between them and the broadcaster, but this would not be felt the same way by the broadcaster. It is a 'one-sided intimate connection with a media performer such as a streamer' (De Wit et al., 2020: 3) that bears a lot of surface commonality with other more reciprocated interactions – which helps make it compelling to the party making the effort to forge the parasocial interaction – but ultimately remains 'asymmetrical' (McLaughlin & Wohn, 2021: 1715). In this understanding viewers thus find themselves in relationships which are not in fact as strong or as mutually meaningful as they first appear to be. According to this model a streamer 'intentionally or unintentionally creates an illusion of intimacy' that serves to make 'viewers feel special' (Wohn et al., 2019: 108), and much of viewer behaviour and motivation on Twitch can be thus explained. One article to date (Kowert & Daniel, 2021: 1) begins to move this discussion towards acknowledging that asymmetry does not inherently mean parasociality – streamers *are* aware of viewers, even if the back and forth is uneven – but overall the parasocial framework remains highly dominant.

It has been argued that live streaming might actually be more prone to the creation of parasocial interactions 'than any other form of media studied previously' (McLaughlin & Wohn, 2021: 1729). Sherrick et al. (2022: 50) suggest that this is from a combination of 'platform affordances' such as Twitch chat, 'livestreamer characteristics' such as the accessibility and openness discussed in the previous chapter, and 'cultural norms' such as viewers and streamers sharing private details. I agree entirely with the importance of these aspects, and yet they are rarely examined in much depth in assessments of parasociality on Twitch. The parasocial framework is right to identify the potential imbalance in streamer–viewer relationships but runs the risk of failing to take into account what aspects of Twitch specifically – such as metrics, monetization, platform infrastructure, platform cultures – deeply influence viewer interest in, and practices of, chatting with streamers in the Twitch chat window. We have seen that Twitch's gaming *agora* is far from a neutral space and is one with a tremendous number of specific idiosyncrasies shaping what can take place there. The idea of parasocial relationships on the platform does tell us something about why and how viewers develop 'emotional attachment to the streamers' (Wohn et al., 2018: 7), but either overlooks Twitch's distinctive aspects or reduces them to variables rather than foregrounding them as key analytic factors in their own right. We should therefore look beyond parasociality for a full sense of what viewers are doing on Twitch, and why, even while it does lay some important foundations that are worth keeping in mind.

Another way to understand viewer behaviours and motivations on Twitch is therefore through the lens of money. Motivations for giving money often appear 'targeted' towards the streamer. Monetary donations are a form of 'tangible support' through which the viewer expresses '*intangible* support', which is to say emotional and interpersonal approval, to a streamer (Wohn et al., 2018: 7, emphasis mine). Doing so enables viewers to 'pay for the entertaining experiences they enjoyed' (ibid.: 5) and to subsequently 'feel good about supporting that particular streamer' and hence facilitating them in continuing to make content (Sjöblom & Hamari, 2017: 992; cf. Wohn et al., 2018: 6). A streamer seen as 'genuine in their personality or actions' throughout their broadcasts motivates financial support (Wohn et al., 2019: 103), but so do live streamers who simply show overt interest in donations (Hou et al., 2020: 149). In turn a channel's viewers often subscribe to 'build deeper involvement' with a wider channel community rather than the streamer specifically, and to 'feel like a larger part of shared experiences' (Hilvert-Bruce et al., 2018: 64). The ability to socialize 'with other viewers and the streamers' on Twitch and beyond

– keeping in mind that those who financially support a stream are often the most visible in that channel – has been identified as 'an important motivation' for paying money to a streamer (Uszkoreit, 2018: 166), especially as subscribers are seen as exemplars of 'ingroup norms' that new viewers might want to emulate (Seering et al., 2017a: 113). Thinking about these sorts of *transactions* is therefore a fruitful complementary way to think about viewer behaviour on the platform, and one that takes seriously the specificities of Twitch as a unique platform.

In a similar vein, perhaps the dominant explanation for why viewers are so willing to give money to streamers – keeping in mind that almost every Twitch channel can be viewed without even having a Twitch account, let alone without having to donate real-world money – comes from an understanding of *rank* and *status* in Twitch channels. Subscribing, for example, puts one in a 'more exclusive "social club"' (Sjöblom & Hamari, 2017: 992) within that channel, demonstrating one's 'importance' to the channel as a financial supporter (Hou et al., 2020: 148) showing 'explicit loyalty' to the streamer (Seering et al., 2017a: 113). Thinking back to the discussion of gaming celebrity earlier in this chapter, it is not hard to see the potential appeal of creating and showing one's social proximity to such a figure. This also takes place when streamers thank viewers who give money (De Wit et al., 2020: 11), while the usernames of donors (and often the 'top' donor for a given day) are also often shown on a channel (Johnson & Woodcock, 2019a: 7; Partin, 2020: 5; Meisner & Ledbetter 2020: 1186; Jodén & Strandell, 2022: 1974). Being highly ranked and visible through such systems are seen as having significant cultural value (Abarbanel & Johnson, 2020: 406). These viewers who send in financial gifts are thus able in live streams to 'display their social status' (Gong et al., 2023: 4) as 'outstanding citizen[s]' (Wohn et al., 2019: 11) in a highly monetized and highly metricized environment. Another kind of visibility viewers pursue by donating can also be found in the unlocking of channel-specific emotes and subscriber icons (Speed et al., 2023: 2); such 'visual indicator[s]' (Sjöblom & Hamari, 2017: 991) of one's rank are highly sought-after in some channels and motivate a lot of donations (Brown & Moberly, 2020: 61), as these are seen as 'special privileges' in a channel (Cullen, 2022a: 32). Money – one of the key elements of Twitch – affords us additional insights into how this aspect is used by viewers to achieve various goals, and how a viewer's interest in a channel or in a streamer can be more fully understood.

These findings tell us much about viewer–streamer inter-actions, but only touch on viewer–viewer interactions. What is clear, however, is that a sense of *community* (cf. Jackson, 2023a: 119–24) is central to many non-lurking Twitch viewers. The interest in social interaction and a 'sense of belonging to an online community' have been called the 'most consistent and strongest motivators of live-stream engagement' (Hilvert-Bruce et al., 2018: 64). The social dimension here is already 'baked' into the Twitch experience, not requiring the fan to seek out other locations to develop and maintain social ties around particular media. The site offers opportunities for interaction and the formation of 'social ties' (Küper & Krämer, 2021: 1) for those who 'follow streamers and become part of their community' (De Wit et al., 2020: 8). As I show in chapter 4, Twitch communities readily spill outside of Twitch onto other websites as well, but even just on the platform itself there is a strong sense of community involvement with a streamer one watches avidly and for long periods. Over time viewers can gain a 'deeper involvement' in a particular channel community and feel like a part of that community's 'shared experiences' (Sjöblom & Hamari, 2017: 992), with watching a channel alongside others becoming 'a collective social experience' (Taylor, 2018: 89). In turn viewers don't just share private or intimate information with the streamer as discussed earlier, but also do so with each other, often 'in hopes of helping out someone else in a similar fashion'

(Uttarapong et al., 2022: 8). Many of these possibilities, of course, are to some extent 'coded' into the platform. Twitch's design 'facilitates the development of communities' in streaming channels (De Wit et al., 2020: 5), and the site's features – such as the subscription icons and so on discussed above – 'encourage viewers to come back to the same stream' and 'identify themselves with the community' within that channel (Houssard et al., 2023).

What position do viewers thus occupy in Twitch's gaming *agora*? On the most obvious immediate level it is the viewers who are the crowds jostling and bustling in this public square, moving from speaker to speaker – or sometimes remaining hooked on a certain speaker for a long period of time – and whose collective actions and the force of their collective attentions and interest determine, in sum, which speakers are the most listened to and have the largest reach, and which speakers are striving to make their voices heard above the wider din. Most are tuning into channels from a culture and community they themselves have a deep involvement with, while others interestingly are not – they are exploring a space which interests and intrigues them, perhaps getting some of the benefits of gaming (experiencing interesting creative media products, albeit secondhand) without some of the drawbacks (physical requirements, toxicity and harassment, intimidating cultural knowledge, and so on). Ultimately Twitch's viewers, much like Twitch's streamers, are complex and multi-faceted, and we see a wide range of motivations, interests and behaviours manifesting in both groups. They interact in a diverse range of ways shaped by their personalities and their desires, but also by the nature of the platform, its foregrounding of metrics and money, and its distinct specificities that mark Twitch and its users out, like so many other dominant internet platforms, as being a novel object of study in their own right.

The 'Twitch we'

There are far more viewers than streamers, and naturally some overlap between the two, but scholarship on each has led to distinctive categorizations and ways to understand the two groups. To interrogate their *connection*, however, I want to begin by studying one of the registers of speech used almost universally by streamers. Outside of passing mention in two papers (Karhulahti, 2016: 7; Jodén & Strandell, 2022: 1977–80) it appears that the practice in question has not been addressed in research – perhaps because it is so ubiquitous that it has managed to fly under the radar – but I think it is in fact highly significant. If, for example, a particularly challenging level of a game is completed or a fearsome foe overcome, the streamer will almost never say 'I did it!' or 'I won!' or some equivalent. Instead the streamer is far more likely to say something like 'We did it!' or 'We won!' – even though none of the viewers materially contributed to overcoming a gaming challenge. Almost always such moments of victory, long-awaited by the viewers as well as the streamer, will elicit a flood of positive and congratulatory comments in Twitch chat which will sometimes directly congratulate the streamer. Yet they will also sometimes echo this *we* formulation (e.g., 'we did it, chat!'), suggesting that perhaps viewers *did* contribute to this victory in some way, or that the victory is a victory for the channel and not just the streamer.

I call this phenomenon the 'Twitch we'. It is modelled after the so-called 'royal we' (*pluralis majestatis*) famously deployed by the British royal family. In its regal context the royal *we* involves the individual human speaker also representing the state, the government or broader population. Queen Victoria's likely apocryphal 'we are not amused' is perhaps the most famous example, suggesting that not merely is she not experiencing jollity but that the same, at least to some extent, can be said of the state, government and nation as well. Perhaps one of the most curious but overlooked things about Twitch is the similar deployment of this pronoun by its streamers. This phrase shows up in almost every gaming channel and has become so normalized and standard that in my almost-decade of researching Twitch I have never seen a single viewer, across hundreds of channels and thousands of hours, even post a chat message of the sort 'We? But we didn't do anything!'. As such, the 'Twitch we' – the *pluralis ludio*, if you will – emerges as a subtle but surprisingly universal piece of performance on the part of Twitch streamers. When they make this statement they might be speaking out to a handful of viewers, or hundreds of thousands (not to mention other people who view their channel sometimes, but might not be viewing it at that exact moment). In a conventional understanding of gaming as an interactive activity that one person is controlling (or several people if it's a multiplayer game) such a statement would be ludicrous. None of the viewers offered even a single input into any of the games being played, and as I discuss below, many streamers are actively hostile to their viewers attempting to contribute ideas, insights or suggestions to their play.

Yet why does the Twitch *we* exist, and why is it so ubiquitous? It serves a number of different functions, and examining them is important if we are really to pin down this streamer–viewer relationship. The streamer seems first to be implying some degree of joint achievement in a game, a tying of the viewer's emotional support to the streamer's ability to make progress. It is far from uncommon for game streamers on Twitch of all skill levels to become stuck at a difficult part of a game, to find their existing strategies proving insufficient for some new hurdle, to repeatedly try some sequence of a game without quite achieving success, or to lose certainty over where to go next or what to do next within a game. The Twitch *we* suggests that the viewers' presence perhaps gave the streamer the resilience or the determination to make progress against a difficult challenge. It can also be used to give a subtle nod to financial support. The streamer might be saying with this use of the Twitch *we* that the stream has only continued to this point, or perhaps has only reached this point of commitment to and success in a game, because of its viewers' financial support. Twitch is often used by viewers as a means to watch games that might interest them but they feel disinclined to buy, and this sense of the Twitch *we* implies a collective playing of the game and a collective progression that the viewer gets to enjoy, without having to commit the physical and mental effort themselves (cf. Johnson & Woodcock, 2019b; Parker & Perks, 2021).

The Twitch *we* can also be used to imply that the viewers had to be there – had to be watching – to encourage the streamer to *keep going* with the challenge. This is not quite the same as the first point, although it is closely related. This sense of the Twitch *we* evokes the idea in some of these more intense challenges that the challenge would only have been performed and attempted for such a long period of time – and hence would only have been accomplished in the end – if it was, indeed, a *public* act (cf. Jackson, 2023a). As substantial as any internal motivation would be, it is not hard to understand both a positive pressure – I want to impress my viewers and reward them for their dedication – and a negative pressure – I don't want them to feel like their time has been wasted – for playing on-stream rather than off. In this regard the viewers are presented as being, in fact, integral to the challenge. Attempts to complete said challenge only went on for so long and only resulted in success because there were enough people present that the streamer committed to securing the achievement. Viewers might not have contributed button inputs, strategy, or any direct attempts at the challenge, but they contributed their presence – their *time* – to the streamer's reserves of enthusiasm, interest and perseverance. All of these interpretations have something in common, which is to say a sense of unity and togetherness between the streamer and their viewers, united – emotionally, psychologically, financially, temporally – in the pursuit of gaming.

It is this final sense – that the *channel* is functioning in a collective sense – that is perhaps the most important. The use of the Twitch *we* reduces the perception of distance between the streamer and the viewer. The channel as a whole accomplished something and hence the viewers are entitled to – and indeed, should – feel some degree of ownership and accomplishment in their *own* right as a result of whatever just happened on stream. It is not hard to see how this might be a positive emotion to generate in one's viewers, especially given that a viewer needs to expend little energy – merely tuning in – to be discursively positioned as possessing at least some agency in a streamer's victory.

The Twitch *we* shows that streamers are therefore keen to tie viewers into the sense of accomplishment and achievement, and hence belonging, in their channels (Sjöblom & Hamari, 2017: 992; Hilvert-Bruce et al., 2018: 64, Evans & Llano, 2023: 4). Yet this picture is complicated by the times that streamers actively *reject* their viewers' support or interest, in this case because of a practice known as 'backseat gaming'. Backseat gaming or simply 'backseating' involves a viewer instructing the streamer on what they ought to be doing in a game (Cai et al., 2021a: 292; Uttarapong et al., 2021: 14; Mihailova, 2022: 1845). This can take several forms. In a singleplayer game that the player (streamer) is playing for the first time, a viewer might backseat by telling them that there's a hidden item in the room they're currently in, or offering a solution to the puzzle the player is currently pondering. In a multiplayer game backseating might involve a viewer telling the streamer some kind of superior strategy or superior build that might do better than the one currently used, or reminding them about something important in the current match that maybe the player overlooked. Backseating is different from 'spoiling', however, with 'spoilers' being pieces of information about a game that the streamer hasn't yet uncovered, but are generally not to do with strategy, tactics or decision making (Johnson & Woodcock, 2019b). A viewer might 'spoil' a twist in a game's plot, or spoil the general direction that a story might be going, or that maybe something exciting or something challenging might be coming up.

These are interesting dynamics to consider because they mark contexts in which a streamer *rejects* support or backup from their viewers, and in many cases becomes actively hostile towards viewers who attempt to offer advice (whether well intentioned or not). This reinforces the Twitch *agora* as being, in some sense, only for streamers and not for viewers, and this marks out a clear tension with much of the rest of the platform's infrastructure and culture that so strongly promote viewer engagement. For example, during the play of a new game – especially one long-awaited by a streamer – some broadcasters will deliberately stop interacting with their viewers for the duration of that broadcast, ignoring their chat window and even turning off donation or subscription messages so that viewers cannot sneak them information by that path instead. These broadcasters will often explicitly say that they're looking to play the game completely unspoiled, while also finding ways to emphasize to their viewers that they still value them and are glad they're on board. Others will suggest that the viewer gets the best viewing experience from an unspoiled streamer, and hence the wise viewer will accept no back-and-forth interaction for that game. Many streamers, however, go further in their avoidance of spoilers and backseating and actively punish viewers perceived to be doing this, such as immediately banning from their chats anyone who spoils an aspect of a game. Banning viewers for spoiling is far more common than banning viewers for backseating but both can regularly be seen on Twitch. A small number of streamers go even further, railing against 'backseating' even in games where there is nothing left to be spoiled.

There is thus a tension here between the ubiquity of the Twitch *we*, and the hatred most streamers espouse towards viewers who spoil or backseat. These two discourses run seemingly counter to each other but in fact define what relationship between streamer and viewer during gameplay is *valid*, and what relationship is *invalid*. It defines the rules and limits of what contributions to a streamer's part of the Twitch *agora* are acceptable, and what contributions are not. To put it another way, when is the streamer speaking, and when is everyone speaking, within the same space? Valid assistance is thus framed as passive and not active, and might involve the viewer answering a question the streamer poses – 'can someone remember whether I picked up Item X?' – or simply offering moral support and just *being there* to observe and appreciate the streamer's play. Invalid assistance, however, involves telling the streamer what to do, trying to 'speed up' the streamer's progress, offering suggestions out of exasperation or boredom, accidentally or deliberately revealing something secret or presently unknown, or in rare cases backseating or spoiling specifically *because* they know it will bother the streamer. Jackson (2023a) has proposed a novel use of Mia Consalvo's theorizations of *cheating* (Consalvo, 2007) as a valuable and incisive way to address backseating. Jackson suggests that most Twitch streamers understand backseating as a specific kind of cheating: that, in being backseated, the streamer is *being cheated* out of the experience that they were meant to have. Backseating changes the streamer's experience from being one where they get to explore and hopefully enjoy a game from scratch, and instead into one where at least some portion of that experience has been taken from them by a viewer.

I therefore propose that this strong hostility to backseating, when coupled with the use of the Twitch *we* – two elements that seem at first glance to be counter to one another – tells us much about the psychological orientation of the streamer to their own position and role in Twitch's *agora*, and the behaviour of their viewers. Streamers seek support from their channel and recognize that this inclusive discourse ties viewers more closely to their streams, but also want to ensure that *they* remain the primary speaker. The viewers might have supported me, this pairing says, but it was nevertheless *me* who completed this game or triumphed over this challenge. In this regard a Twitch streamer has their cake (support from their channel) and gets to eat it (claim all the success for themselves) too. The Twitch *we* and the responses of streamers to backseating are hence ways to control and navigate these tensions of individuality and collectivism. Davenport and Leitch (2005: 138) state that the term *agora* is related to two ancient Greek words that describe congregation and gathering on the one hand, and delivering a speech on the other, and we see both aspects coming through here. Viewers gather and support the streamer, and the streamer delivers a performance. Yet because the 'participatory nature' of sites like Twitch can 'alter audiences' perception of proximity, accessibility, responsiveness, similarity, and other relevant celebrity features' (Kreissl et al., 2021: 1022), there is a deep tension here that has to be resolved in each individual Twitch gaming stream. Agency itself is something contested on Twitch among streamers and viewers, with streamers simultaneously understanding the importance, for the success of their channel, of seeming to share that agency, and the importance of keeping that agency to themselves as a means of psychological gratification.

Are streamers celebrities, friends, or both?

In streamer–viewer relationships streamers thus seem to occupy many different roles and positions in relation to the viewer. On the one hand the streamer can be somewhat inaccessible, especially in large channels, with relatively few viewers getting to engage with them directly. The more aspirational streamer in particular will be someone who has developed and continues to develop their online brand, and who broadcasts potentially quite a slick final product to their viewers. Yet the streamer is also someone with whom viewers communicate, and in some cases build up something of a relationship. Some streamers and viewers – and commentators and scholars – dismiss the relationship as being merely 'parasocial' in nature, but others form what certainly appear to be genuine bonds and friendships through the platform (cf. Johnson, 2019; De Wit et al., 2020; Persaud & Perks, 2022; Uttarapong et al., 2022). This is one of the fundamental tensions – *and* one of the fundamental appeals – of Twitch: a streamer can occupy simultaneously the dual roles of *celebrity* and *friend*. In balancing these roles, the streamer can become massively attractive to viewers in ways that celebrities, and arguably even friends, on most other social media platforms cannot. This is a key component of how Twitch functions as such a compelling gaming *agora* for viewers, how its speakers are presented through both the technical and cultural elements of the platform, and how its primary speakers are seen by their fans.

We can understand these dual roles as being constructed through different aspects of activity on Twitch (and elsewhere), as well as through the platform's infrastructure and the communities generated around the site's users. The *celebrity* (Brandis & Bozkurt, 2021: 170; Leith, 2021: 113; Speed et al., 2023) brings in between hundreds and tens of thousands of viewers on *Twitch*; probably boasts a Twitter account with tens of thousands of followers; maybe has a private subreddit or Discord server accessed by subscribers only; has deals and sponsorships with major companies; gets on stage at TwitchCon; and, ultimately, makes their living *playing video games on the internet*, which for many game players seems an astonishing and hugely compelling career path (Johnson & Woodcock, 2017; Guarriello, 2019: 1751; Johnson et al., 2019; Chan & Gray, 2020: 360). They are somewhat inaccessible but also impressive and admirable precisely because of that same inaccessibility. The *friend*, meanwhile, chats with you when you decide to chat to them; uses your username (or maybe even your real-life name) in the way that other everyday friends might; seemingly wants your opinion on the games you're playing or the game they are playing, or on other relevant topics of geek or nerd interest; uses everyday language and a friendly body posture when they're interacting with you; and might be someone with whom one can share problems and struggles, and they share theirs back. They fill many of the same sorts of roles that friends outside of Twitch do, and act in many of the same ways.

Look now at the picture on other platforms. Celebrities on Instagram or YouTube, for instance, can be compelling to follow (and compare oneself to) but are invariably very *distant* individuals, whose posts or videos might accrue thousands of comments lacking even a single response from the creator. Making a 'real' connection with them almost never happens, and many fans know that much of what appears on such websites is performative and heavily edited and curated (e.g., Garcia et al., 2021; Savolainen et al., 2022). The liveness (Auslander, 2012; 2022) of live streaming, meanwhile, although curated by the most skilled streamers to some extent, nevertheless retains a vitality and immediacy (Johnson & Woodcock, 2017; Cabeza-Ramírez et al., 2021: 6; McLaughlin & Wohn, 2021: 1715; Yoganathan et al., 2021: 1007; Persaud & Perks, 2022) and a *closing of distance* (Taylor, 2018: 200; Küper & Krämer, 2021: 6; Welch, 2022: 522) that these other sites lack. Friends meanwhile – perhaps on Facebook or WhatsApp, let's say – are people with whom one interacts regularly, people whose private lives one sees at least to a certain extent, and whose interactions with us and ours with them have a relaxed, familiar pacing to them. Outside of live streaming it is very rare for someone to appear to be a celebrity and a friend at the same time; to be famous and noteworthy but also someone *you* personally interact with; to have all the excitement and the glitz and glamour of apparently being someone enjoying global renown and admiration, while also having (seemingly) forged a friendship and a relationship with *you*. Interacting with this celebrity is made all the more compelling because they also appear to be one's friend, marking out that friendship as somehow special, something to be treasured. Interacting with the friend is made all the more compelling because they are also a celebrity, and one has a sense of access to the private life, the personality and activities of a famous figure.

This celebrity–friend dynamic has massive implications for understanding why Twitch is such an effective *agora* for gaming (and any other activity with a sufficiently large amount of on-site interest). By combining the affective dimensions of *both* of these framings of an individual and one's online interactions with them, Twitch becomes transformed into a space where one can achieve both the sense of pride, consequence and involvement one gets when interacting with someone who is 'famous', but *also* the sense of comfort, familiarity and intimacy one gets when interacting with a friend who chooses to spend their time with you. Studies of parasocial interactions on Twitch have covered the latter to a significant extent, but have overlooked how closely the former is interwoven with, and constitutive of, these dynamics. Viewers are therefore not just choosing to spend time with a streamer, but there is a further sense for viewers that the streamer is choosing to spend time with *them* (cf. Kowert & Daniel, 2021). The streamer could be off gaming privately but instead they made the choice and the effort to do it on their channel, with all those who might be watching. Twitch gives viewers access to people who transcend being celebrities *and* who transcend being friends, and instead become something more: someone of importance and consequence and note, *and* someone who is friendly, approachable, and seems genuinely interested in *you*. This combination flows through the liveness of the live stream, the functionality of the chat window, and the immediacy of the webcam and the streamer's voice, and is fundamental to what makes these affective bonds between streamers and viewers so deeply compelling.

Moderators

The Twitch *we* and the celebrity–friend dynamic both highlight the complexities of interactions between the different users on Twitch. Both involve relationships between streamers and viewers but go beyond what Twitch's oft-cited parasocial relationships or parasocial interactions (Catá, 2019; De Wit et al., 2020; Leith, 2021; McLaughlin & Wohn, 2021; Wulf et al., 2021; Kneisel & Sternadori, 2023; cf. Kreissl et al., 2021) would seem to suggest. Rather than one-sided interactions in which a viewer mistakenly perceives a relationship with a streamer, we instead see how platform and norms and behaviours are constructing shared and overlapping identities, and making for a far greater degree of authorship and the blurring of in-channel roles than is immediately obvious.

Another example of these trends can be found in studying Twitch's human moderators. The general understanding of moderators is that they are essentially highly dedicated viewers (Taylor, 2018: 72; Johansson, 2021: 8, Seering & Kairam, 2023: 2) who help to manage a channel's chat window. They are not themselves broadcasting (Wohn, 2019: 2) on a streamer's channel (as only the streamer is doing that) and they do not have access to any of the behind-the-scenes tools or functionality that the streamer has (unless the streamer specifically grants them access). They are not directly earning income from the viewers who contribute to the channel unless the streamer elects to share income with them; they are certainly not the person nor the content that viewers came to watch and engage with; and they are presumably not physically located wherever the streamer is broadcasting from. They cannot control when a streamer is live and not live, and cannot exert direct control over a channel's broadcast content. All of this seems to tell us that moderators are simply viewers with a little bit more power – within the confines and strictures of what the streamer allows them – yet the real picture appears to be rather more complicated. By examining this more complete alternative we will be able to take the observations in the previous sections and deepen them again, showing how these most visible and powerful 'viewers' are in fact essential to a streamer's construction of the channel, demonstrating that the gaming *agora* on Twitch is even less dependent solely on the streamers than it first appears.

The Twitch moderator's main job is – especially in larger channels – to assist the streamer in *managing* the crowd of people watching the stream (Lo, 2018: 31; London et al., 2019). This can take different forms. A moderator might need to time out or ban an individual who posts something unpleasant or inappropriate (London et al., 2019; Wohn, 2019: 6–7; Seering & Kairam, 2023), or simply just something which is against the rules of that particular channel (e.g., 'no spoilers'). This is one of the main roles given to moderators. Having a moderator or moderation team reduces the number of things a streamer needs to keep track of. A moderator will also often be the first responder to a question posted in chat, especially in large channels with active chats (Cai et al., 2021b: 70; Wolff & Shen, 2022: 6). Sometimes a moderator uses copy-and-paste responses to routine enquiries such as 'What game is [streamer] playing?' or 'Are we allowed to do [whatever] in this stream?', but other times the questions of viewers require tailored responses. This is again ordinarily a task for a streamer. In these examples – saying hello to people joining the channel, answering regular questions, and the like – the streamer transfers responsibility to a moderator. This changes what is being broadcast by the streamer (they might no longer have to say the same thing every five minutes) but also changes the constitution of the stream, with the moderator having a role in *creating* a broadcast that aligns with what a streamer wants. The imagined stream desired by the streamer is brought into being in part by the moderators (Johnson, 2021) who are able to shape the channel's success and are consequently much valued by streamers.

Moderators enjoy other privileges and some of these begin to further blur the relationship between streamer and viewers. One of the most obvious is how some moderators (and other dedicated viewers) play games directly with the streamer. This would normally involve a moderator joining a voice chat application with the streamer and potentially other moderators (or other streamers, or friends of the streamer, etc.) to make up the numbers for a multiplayer game. This appeals to the streamer because bringing in a 'random' member of their chat is far riskier than bringing a moderator into their channel: a viewer who decided to spout racist invective after having been granted voice access to the streamer's broadcast could have massive repercussions for the streamer (but few for the viewer). The sensible wariness about doing this makes it a significant reward for the moderator who *is* allowed to be a part of the streamer's gameplay (Groen, 2020: 100) due to the implied demonstration of trust. This reward again blurs our understanding of who is *doing* the streaming, and who can be trusted to stand alongside the streamer in their corner of the wider Twitch *agora*. We noted above that a moderator actively moderating a channel ensures a closer alignment of the broadcast to the streamer's wishes – they therefore have a constitutive role in creating the stream, even if they are not directly influencing anything that appears on camera. The same can readily be said in this context, with the sum total of all players invited by a streamer into a game having at least some role in the creation of that streamed audiovisual broadcast. A streamer who wishes to stream a cooperative game, for example, cannot do so without people who can be trusted – and this gap can be filled by moderators. The current configurations and expectations of Twitch make much of this moderator impact invisible, thus masking what are actually valuable contributions to the Twitch *agora*.

What would a Twitch channel look like without moderators? In a small channel there would often not be much difference. A streamer could likely see and respond to every comment in the chat, and although an unpleasant or inappropriate comment might remain for seconds or minutes until the streamer notices it, the comment would normally still eventually get deleted and the perpetrator dealt with appropriately. In mid-sized and large channels, however, differences become readily apparent. Without a moderator to handle messages in the volumes we see in larger channels, a streamer would be faced with two options – to leave their chat completely unmoderated, which would come with its own problems and potentially exacerbate some of Twitch's exclusion, harassment or discrimination issues; or to spend a disproportionate amount of their own time moderating their channel, which is time-consuming (Li et al., 2023: 5), labour-intensive (Kim et al., 2022; cf. Cai et al., 2023: 16), and hardly makes for compelling viewing. Thus, moderators do not just perform key roles for the streamer, but their absence would be highly noticeable and would introduce a lot of what we might think of as *static* for a streamer trying to broadcast the stream they want to broadcast. A streamer with moderators speaks to a crowd who are kept well in check according to the streamer's desires; a streamer without moderators might speak to anything ranging from that same kind of crowd to an unruly mob, or anything in between. To extend the ancient Greek analogy we might think of moderators as the burly guards standing around a speaker in the *agora* who is getting enough attention, or who is sufficiently controversial, to merit potentially hostile responses from those around them. Moderators thus end up with 'complex interpersonal relationships with the streamers and viewers' in which 'emotional labor, physical labor, and fun are intertwined' (Wohn, 2019: 1).

Despite the work that being a moderator involves, it is easy to see what the appeal of the role is. Moderators are understandably attracted to what amounts to a deeper closeness and connection with the streamer (Wolff & Shen, 2022: 6; Seering & Kairam, 2023: 2; cf. Küper & Krämer, 2021). They would not have stuck around long enough to become moderators if they did not enjoy a streamer's content or feel a personal connection with them, and so becoming a moderator only happens to those who, by definition, are attracted to the role. Moderation is also – in the microcosm of a single stream within the entire Twitch *agora* – a role with a great deal of status. Becoming a moderator gives you a green sword-shaped badge by one's name in that channel's chat, which 'mark[s] out mods' (Lo, 2018: 70) and is 'considered a literal and figurative status symbol' (Wohn, 2019: 4). Moderators stand out from the wider crowd of the *agora* and gain a position above and beyond that of most of their fellow viewers. They are co-creators of any Twitch channel in which they feature, both enforcing and actively creating rules and hence the possibilities of what can and cannot, and what does and does not, get broadcast and experienced on that stream (cf. Cai et al., 2021b: 70). I have previously discussed how both metrics and money shape social status and prestige on Twitch, and a moderator icon is a further step 'up' beyond the rest of the crowd. It demonstrates that one has the streamer's trust, one plays an important role in the stream – and one is perhaps even a streamer's (celebrity's) friend. It is also a way to give back to a stream by supporting the channel. It is not uncommon for streamers to become important touchstones in a viewer's personal and emotional life (e.g., De Wit et al., 2020; Goh et al., 2021; Chae & Lee, 2022), and moderation is a way to give something back. Just as the streamer is not a straightforward 'sole creator', so their viewers and moderators are not a passive audience. Moderators serve a key role in the construction of a Twitch broadcast, and, much like viewers, their relationships with streamers, viewers and other moderators can all be complex and multi-layered.

Speaking and listening in the agora

In the previous chapter I explored Twitch's technological and infrastructural aspects, and how they influence some of the social dynamics on the site. In this chapter I have focused in on the streamers and viewers who serve as the speakers and the listeners in Twitch's *agora* – although the distribution of roles is complex. What we see is that any broadcast–receiver model of the streamer and viewer is inadequate to fully conceptualize Twitch. This is certainly how the site goes about presenting the roles of its streamers and viewers, but it is too simplistic a framing for the purposes of critical analysis. Instead we should see each streamer's channel as being comprised of many different speakers, each with a role to play in the construction of a broadcast. The streamer is of course the most obvious speaker and the individual who is framed by the platform as being *the* speaker. This is also a framing that streamers are keen to reinforce, as noted here in our discussion of the Twitch *we* and the discomfort with which streamers address any sense of mutual construction of their channel, even while promoting those very same ideas in order to build a sense of shared engagement and interest. Yet the streamer's speaking is entangled with what viewers do on their channels. How viewers respond to the streamer and their content, how viewers understand their own contributions to the platform, and how viewers have the ability to interact both with each other and with the streamer, all shape viewers as not inherently passive actors – although they *can* choose to 'lurk' if they wish – but rather speakers in their own right who contribute to the conduct and style of debate in a channel, including the interactions between the actors. Moderators exemplify this by straddling the two categories and making a far more obvious contribution to the construction of a channel than the 'average' viewer, although still in most streamers' and most viewers' minds making only an instrumental and functional contribution.

Yet these multifaceted understandings do run counter to how Twitch presents itself, and how both streamers and viewers tend to frame their behaviours on the platform. In its advertising to streamers and its encouragement for users to become or continue as streamers (rather than viewers), the clear sense is given that Twitch is essentially a platform for streamers to come and do *their* thing (gaming or whatever it might be), and for viewers to come and watch if the thing is sufficiently compelling. The high degree of customization, the deep integration and ubiquity of metrics and monetary exchange, and the power that streamers have to frame their channels and produce video content while viewers communicate solely by text (Freeman & Wohn, 2020; Sheng & Kairam, 2020; Uttarapong et al., 2021: 8), all contribute to this sense. This is reinforced by how streamers appear to see themselves and their communities – whatever they might say to the contrary on social media – and indeed the widespread framings of the streamer as essentially the sole arbiter of what takes place on a channel. This also suits Twitch who are always looking to recruit more streamers onto the site, much like other platforms – Uber being a well-researched one – in which users are facilitated to essentially do their own thing and the platform takes a cut of their efforts. The 'emergent cascade of negotiations, exchanges and favours' (O'Kelly & Dubnick, 2014: 9) one finds in an *agora*-like space is nevertheless far more complex than those who own the space like to suggest, and Twitch is no exception.

To conclude: streamers, viewers and moderators on Twitch are the second key component for understanding Twitch, after the investigation of the historical, technological and infrastructural dimensions of the platform itself in the previous chapter. By examining the users I have sought to review relevant existing literature and offer novel understandings of site characteristics such as the Twitch *we*, the celebrity–friend dynamic, and the collaborative construction of a stream via regimes of moderation. At the same time, the discussion of this chapter points towards those in the following two chapters. In the next, I will look at what streamers actually *broadcast* – what is the content that gets streamed and watched on the site? The discussions here also have important implications and foundations for the discussions in chapter 4 of Twitch's 'characters'. These are shared imagined identities that Twitch viewers slip into through the use of on-site emotes in order to achieve easy communication, and to shape the norms and practices of the site. This will move us from understanding the creation of Twitch content as the preserve of the streamer – and viewers and moderators – to an understanding of how Twitch content is also shaped even by the *characters* who speak through the site's users. Twitch's gaming *agora* is ultimately one constructed out of complex interactions between streamers and viewers and moderators, all of whom have the ability to speak and to be heard; between infrastructural and social incentives to monetize and metricize, but also incentives to interact, relax, and foster community; and between different ideas of agency, control, creation, ownership and influence.

CHAPTER 3

Twitch Content

Introduction

In the first chapter I explored the infrastructural and technical foundations of Twitch – what are the possibilities for the production and distribution of content on the site, and how do its materiality and specificities shape these? In the second I considered Twitch's users – the streamers, the viewers and the moderators – who create and consume live streams on the site, focusing on their motivations and behaviours, and how their actions co-create the complicated relationships and dynamics we see on the platform. In this chapter I want to move on to now explore the *content* of live streams – which is to say, what is actually being broadcast on Twitch.

I will look at Twitch's content by first examining how the site came to prominence via the live streaming of competitive gaming events. Through these, Twitch began as a gaming *agora* focused on impressive gaming accomplishments – an aspect still very important, though less central now – and a place where the live video broadcasts of gaming celebrities could, and still can, be watched. I then argue that a decade on from those beginnings, we can now identify two different primary regimes of content production by game streamers on Twitch – the content created and broadcast in 'focused' channels, and that created and broadcast in 'variety' channels. The content of focused channels has emerged as a way to shape and define what matters within a particular gaming community, while variety channels offer instead a touchstone for, and influence upon, what is currently interesting and fashionable within gaming. In the process the reader will note a transition from discussing streamers to discussing *channels*, a framing that reflects more accurately the mutual construction of Twitch content discussed in the previous chapter and (in the next chapter) the nature of Twitch communities and Twitch's culture. Towards the end of the chapter I then look at non-gaming content on Twitch, and examine the pressure such content is now exerting on the idea that Twitch's *agora* is one solely for and about gaming. This challenge is, however, relatively new, and I therefore start by examining what first developed the site's association with gaming – the rapid expansion and success of esports broadcasts.

Esports and competitive gaming on Twitch

'Esports' – as competitive and often professionalized digital gaming came to be known – was fundamental to the early growth of Twitch. Broadcasting live events allowed competitive gaming to reach an audience vastly larger than ever before (Hamilton et al., 2014; Taylor, 2018). It transformed esports from something some game players knew about but had likely never seen, into something that could be easily watched at home; and from something that many gamers had *not* heard about at all into something which would now begin to establish a presence within the community more broadly. Twitch soon also began to exert an influence on the careers and the politics of esports players, who realized that just as Twitch had boosted the visibility and viewership of their competitive matches (cf. Ruvalcaba et al., 2018: 296), the site could also be used to boost their *own* visibility and viewership as individual players (Leith, 2021: 114). The perception of distance between esports players and their fans quickly became much reduced – think back to the previous chapter's discussion of the *celebrity–friend* relationship on Twitch – and began to generate a noticeable cultural shift. Not just did the players become more accessible but so did their strategies, with viewers now able to watch far more of a famous player's play than might otherwise be the case if they were only being observed during major competitions. For competitive gaming fans esports content was hugely compelling, and integral to Twitch's early growth.

Yet esports is no longer the only context where the most skilled and competitive play can be seen on Twitch. Speedrunning – which involves trying to complete a game as fast as possible (Scully-Blaker, 2014) – is also now well established (Hope, 2023). The practice had existed long before Twitch and even had a substantial supporter community, but it has expanded hugely through visibility on Twitch in the number of games now with active speedrunning communities, the number of people making a full-time living from doing this on Twitch, and the tens of millions of dollars raised in speedrunning charity events (Cook & Duncan, 2016). The rise of 'challenge runs' is in turn another interesting facet of the expansion of competitive gaming on Twitch beyond esports. These involve adding new rules, requirements or limitations that make a game as *difficult* as possible. Challenge run rules might require never dying in a game (a 'permadeath' rule), never sustaining damage in a game, or playing the game with an unusual controller, or playing a game blindfolded, or playing a game without being able to press a certain button or use a certain in-game item or in-game ability. These can bring tens of thousands of concurrent viewers on Twitch – and potentially millions over time, after they are accomplished and later uploaded on YouTube – and are a good illustration of how Twitch continues to serve as a platform for highlighting and facilitating *noteworthy* things in gaming. Not merely the completion of a game many others have completed or an everyday match of a multiplayer game, Twitch instead gives tremendous visibility to – and encourages viewers to value and give priority to – the unique, the unusual and the one-off.

Across esports, speedrunning and challenge runs, the broadcast of competitive and highly skilled gaming content was and remains a key part of understanding Twitch's role as a gaming *agora*. Its ability to give unparalleled visibility to innovative approaches and noteworthy achievements, *and* to do so in front of such large crowds that these events later become points of discussion elsewhere on the internet, is an essential part of what makes its content so compelling. The meritocracy that many gamers perceive as being an integral part of their pastime can have highly problematic aspects (Paul, 2018) but has undoubtedly been instrumental in the growth of Twitch. Competitive broadcasts were a key opening part of Twitch's live stream content and even now esports channels remain almost exclusively available on Twitch in most countries outside of China, and the same is largely true for speedrunning and challenge runs. Twitch has long promoted the highest level of gaming competition just as the ancient *agora*, among many other purposes, served to highlight athletic excellence (Camp, 2016: 312–13) – such spaces offer opportunities for small numbers of elites to show off their skills, in whatever domain or area, to large numbers of people who might never before have been able to tune in. Given many of the more problematic dynamics of gaming cultures discussed earlier in this book, it may be telling that Twitch's gaming *agora* began with competitive world-class skilled gameplay rather than the far more personal, intimate, person-to-person and co-operative modes of interaction that now predominantly characterize the platform.

Taylor's (2018) work examines in detail the esports component of Twitch, but it is in the growth of non-esports competitive play, and especially the ascendance of non-competitive gaming – which now completely eclipses competitive gaming in terms of streamed hours and streamer–viewer participation – that we see the key changes in the last half-decade on Twitch. Almost any game can now be found on the site – there is an overall trend towards more recent games rather than older games, but channels hosting games from older consoles, and even home computers, are not unknown. Major online multiplayer games are one of the mainstays of Twitch, such as 'multiplayer online battle arena' games *League of Legends* (2009) and *DoTA 2* (2013), first-person shooter games such as real-world conflict-inspired *Counter-Strike: Global Offensive* (2012) and cartoonish superhero-focused *Overwatch* (2016), and 'battle royale' games such as the surreal and infamously popular amongst children and teenagers *Fortnite* (2017) and the grungier and more 'realistic' *PlayerUnknown's Battlegrounds* (2017). Singleplayer games, by contrast, tend to enjoy a little less visibility on Twitch, often surging in interest during release and then quickly fading away, although those seen as possessing more 'replay value', which is to say continued interest in repeat play, do stick around. More narrative-focused games often get just one play by a given streamer, and then little afterwards. Yet across all these sorts of games two very distinct sorts of streamers and channels on which gameplay is broadcast stand out, and it is to these broadcasters, and the gaming content they stream on Twitch, I now turn.

'Focused' channels

The great majority of contemporary Twitch gaming channels are not focused on top-level competitive play, and instead tend to frame themselves in one of two ways – as 'focused' channels or as 'variety' channels. The former is characterized by an emphasis on one game or a closely related small number of games, while the latter roams more freely across the full range of games and gaming. I will frame this discussion around *channels* rather than *streamers* because the focus of this chapter is on Twitch's content rather than its users, and because the last chapter showed that streamers are not the sole determinants of their stream (despite the linguistic overlap in those words). A focus on channels rather than streamers allows us to capture the complexities of authorship and relationships that exist within these spaces. Analytically foregrounding the channel also allows us to move beyond many studies (including some of my own) of the streamer as the key actor on Twitch and instead to develop a stronger focus on the activities which are *actually being broadcast*, which remains rarely researched. Examining the spectrum of game channel orientations will demonstrate how different sorts of gaming broadcasts are able to use Twitch as the *agora* to make different statements in, and exert different effects on, the wider world of gaming and gaming culture. Each channel can thus be thought of as one of the thousands of conversations going on simultaneously that together, in aggregate, and in all their diversity, constitute the *agora*.

There are too many different articulations of how focused channels concentrate on certain games to recount here, but three examples will be illustrative. In the first case a focused channel might concentrate on a single game, or primarily on a single game with brief digressions elsewhere. This is the form of focused streaming that we see most obviously in esports and speedrunning, and often with the popular multiplayer games listed above such as *League of Legends* or *Counter-Strike*, but also exists elsewhere. Streamers might run channels focused on relatively unusual or rarely played games; might really push a game which hasn't seen much attention on Twitch; or focus on a game with a clear and immediate fanbase which is large enough to meet whatever their streaming goals might be. In a one-game channel the streamer becomes particularly associated with a specific game and may be able – through the regularity and consistency of this focus, their development of knowledge and enhanced skills, and their formation of a speaking position around that one game – sometimes to exercise significant influence on how that game is seen on Twitch, and within gaming culture more widely. There are comparisons here with specialist television channels, such as MTV's emphasis on 'youth culture' (Jones, 2005), or the deliberate framing of HBO as a brand for unusually high-quality television dramas (Jaramillo, 2002). In chapter 1, I discussed one aspect of what we might think of as channel *branding* through the ability to customize one's profile and one's stream to an unusual degree, and focusing one's channel on specific things is another aspect of branding.

In the second, 'focused', channel scenario, a streamer might focus on a specific genre of game. Digital game genres have been studied for several decades now (e.g., Apperley, 2006; Clarke et al., 2017), with scholarship acknowledging the complexity and difficulty in pinning down these concepts (more than with other media). One concept of game genre – the one I personally find the most useful for its ease of use and its comprehensive sweep – suggests that whereas cinema and literature have solely thematic genres (horror, drama, science fiction, etc.) games have both thematic genres *and* mechanical genres, the latter being definitions such as first-person shooter, strategy, puzzle, exploration, and so forth (Järvinen, 2007; Karhulahti, 2011). What we see on Twitch is that both kinds of genre can be defining rubrics for a channel, framing the contexts in which the streamer is producing content and contributing to a particular discussion. Many Twitch channels define themselves as primarily playing horror games or emotional games, for example, while others will emphasize their play of strategy games or puzzle games. The streamers on these channels will shift between games in their given genre, often playing new games but often also returning to old classics, and will often write the selected genre in their channel information. A streamer focused on modern roguelike or 'roguelite' games, for example, might be likely to play popular indie titles like *The Binding of Isaac* (2011), *FTL* (2012) and *Spelunky* (2012), while titles some would consider part of this genre, and others would not, might also show up – such as *Slay the Spire* (2019). The precise boundaries of a genre are often fuzzy and up to the streamer to define, but all definitions will aim to set out a clear sense of what viewers should expect to find there.

In the third scenario are streamers who frame their channel around games made by a specific *company*. One noteworthy example of this found in many channels is the Japanese developer From Software, and their notoriously difficult and cryptic set of action-focused roleplaying games *Dark Souls* (2011–2016), *Bloodborne* (2015), *Sekiro: Shadows Die Twice* (2019) and, most recently, *Elden Ring* (2022). The unifying channel aspect here is the studio and the associated fact that the games reflect and iterate on a specific and distinctive set of design, aesthetic, narrative and gameplay choices. The streamer is not necessarily expressing any particular connection to the company or interest in the company or its staff beyond their games, but is instead using the company – and the associations viewers will have surrounding their games – to define the nature of their channel. Another example would be the games of Swedish grand strategy game developer Paradox Interactive, known for intricate and exhaustive historical simulation games such as *Europa Universalis* (2000–Present), *Victoria* (2003–Present) and *Crusader Kings* (2004–Present). Streamers playing these games often express a strong sense of association with or praise for the company who produce these games – being, essentially, the only company in the world that produces *exactly* this sort of game – and the dedicated fanbase of the company finds an easy and comfortable community in focused Twitch channels (cf. Gandolfi, 2018; Mihailova, 2022). In focused channels we therefore again see the creation of expectations, and the normalization of what one expects to see in each stream coming from that same channel.

One striking aspect of focused channels is the involvement of the streamers in the companies whose games they focus on playing. In the case of From Software, highly visible game live streamers have in recent years been involved in various company endeavours. Many of the company's games come with strategy guides and 'design works' books, and game live streamers (and YouTubers) who focus on the company's work have increasingly taken on a central role in these publications. This might mean writing introductions or concluding sections in a book, helping to curate parts of the publication, bringing together strategy hints and guides for new players, finding other ways to represent the community, or being used as a source of advice and expertise on the company's fanbase. They might also be allowed to broadcast streams of themselves playing a new product, offering enough to potentially lure in the viewers to make a purchase (Woodcock & Johnson, 2019). These roles previously belonged – and still to some extent belong, of course – to games journalists (Nieborg & Sihvonen, 2009; Perreault & Vos, 2020), whose positions as community figures and taste-makers are used by games companies to advertise products or give special access. Yet times are changing, and through sites like Twitch and YouTube it is now gaming content creators who are being granted such exclusivity and involvement (Johnson & Woodcock, 2019b). In turn, this filters down to the viewers of these channels who feel (to a lesser extent of course) that *they*, as part of that channel and that community, are also a little bit closer to these games companies than they might otherwise be. We therefore see here how game makers can draw on Twitch to improve the presentation of (and in effect, promote) their games, through an understanding that Twitch offers what are essentially advertising opportunities that are distinct from television spots, online banner adverts, word of mouth or press coverage.

Given the ability to attract and retain people interested in those games, and the strength of existing community bonds between players of certain games or genres as a basis for forming a channel community, it is easy to see why the focused channel might seem like an appealing option for streamers. It allows time to explore a game or genre, and especially if streaming becomes a source of income, that favourite game or genre can come to be something that one can 'justify' spending more and more of one's time on. From the perspective of the streamer's ambitions – if they are looking to grow their channel, perhaps to the point of making some income from it – one of the main ways that Twitch's viewers find a new channel is through the *game* being played. Moreover, focused channels also serve to reassure the viewer that they can be confident in consistently being able to see the content they want to see whenever they tune in, and that their expectations will be met. Viewers, it seems, are not only looking for interesting speakers in this *agora*, but also those whose content and performance can to a large degree be predicted. As with elsewhere on the internet there are dynamics here of self-reinforcing preference (e.g., Nguyen et al., 2014; Beer, 2016: 78), with viewers entering the Twitch *agora* (the entire site) with preformed notions of which channels they might spend time in, who they want to listen to, and perhaps even what those people 'should' have to say.

Yet there can be downsides, such as a focused streamer coming to feel that they have been 'locked in' to a specific subset of game live streaming. When this happens the game or genre that boosted their channel's visibility becomes a requirement and an expectation – even if they first selected this game or genre precisely because it is one that they greatly enjoy – and the desire to play something else runs up against the desire (or even the financial need) to maintain the status quo to keep the existing viewer base interested and engaged. One well-noted example comes from a famous streamer of the From Software games who achieved significant success on the back of impressive challenge runs of the game, with one of the most famous having accrued several million hits on the YouTube version of the final successful Twitch stream. After achieving success in both the challenge they had set themselves *and* the construction of a channel focused heavily around this challenge and the associated games – and having made clear the emotional toll that the process had taken – they moved into a very different genre of game in order to decompress. Despite their best efforts this led to significant loss of viewer numbers, in turn generating considerable tension between the streamer's desire to take a break, the viewers' expectations about a return to the 'core' nature of the channel, and the instrumental needs of the streamer to continue making a living from their broadcasts. The fact that self-branding also requires self-governance (Whitmer, 2019: 2) is often overlooked, but we see it here in the focused channels and their delimitation of what is acceptable and unacceptable for a streamer to broadcast.

Focused streamers can therefore find themselves in a situation where what made them can also break them. The game (or series) that might have brought in large numbers of viewers (cf. Hamilton et al., 2014; Guarriello, 2019: 1757; Phelps et al., 2021a: 2863), potentially significant income, maybe even enough to make a living (Johnson & Woodcock, 2017; Johnson et al., 2019; Ruberg et al., 2019: 475; cf. Fung et al., 2022: 384), and which gave them sufficient visibility to maybe secure sponsorships and promotional deals (Dargonaki, 2018: 105; Uszkoreit, 2018: 165; Woodcock & Johnson, 2019), can come to be a *requirement* rather than a pleasure. The self-actualizing choice (that we examined in chapter 2) a focused streamer might have made – to pursue their passion for gaming via games streaming rather than choosing a more traditional career path – now leads to a shrinking and withering of other possibilities if this successful career path is to be maintained. This has sometimes led to heated moments. In one observed stream I saw a viewer make a passing comment about the fact that they were 'only' in the channel for when the streamer was broadcasting their core game, and this sent the streamer in question – already known for being relatively loud and boisterous – into what can only be called a rant. The streamer snapped at the viewer and made it clear that the viewer was the 'kind of' viewer that the streamer had no interest in developing a relationship with, and that the statement of preference for the core game was deeply inappropriate. I cannot imagine the viewer in question did not take genuine offence, despite the generally light-hearted antagonism that defines much of Twitch humour and culture (Johnson, 2022; cf. Pellicone & Ahn, 2017: 4864; Taylor, 2018; London et al., 2019: 59; Welch, 2022: 525). Such intensity speaks to how much pressure focused streamers can be under to maintain their channel as a place for a certain and predictable kind of output they themselves might have lost interest in. Viewer expectation of a certain kind of content thus emerges as a major factor on focused channels and for the streamers who host these channels. Again, the comparison with specialist television channels can be made – one assumes MTV's fans would be displeased if the channel suddenly started broadcasting shows discussing low-cost kitchen appliances.

To summarize, the contribution of focused streamers to Twitch's role as an *agora* for what matters in gaming can be understood in a specific way. Focused streamers are framing and shaping in their channels the answer to the question: *what matters in my community?* Although on one level 'gaming' can be understood as a single community of over a billion gamers ranged across platforms and games and demographics (many of whom never intersect or interact with other aspects of the gaming world), the idea of a single homogeneous gamer (or 'Gamer') block is conceptually untenable (cf. Shaw, 2012; Condis, 2015). Instead, more nuanced appraisals of different gaming communities help us to frame the position of these live streamers as being arbiters of taste in their specific gaming communities. The overall Twitch *agora* has many positions for many speakers, and there is no obligation for mutual intersection between different channels – one might spend years listening to one speaker without hearing a word of the next speaker over. In turn, if we consider two streamers of equal reach who on a given day stream a new strategy game – one of them being a focused strategy game streamer, and the other streaming a strategy game for the first time – they will not have a remotely comparable impact on the discussion and debate surrounding that game. Part of this comes from all the factors already discussed, but also of course from the viewers. Viewers of a focused strategy game streamer will be, on average, far better informed about the genre and the consequence of what they're watching than viewers of a variety streamer. Focused broadcasts also serve to define and shape genres and the connections between games – focused streamers can define or even create connections between games and genres through articulating what the focus of their channel is. This focus then gives a channel an ever-stronger platform to make inroads into that game, that genre, or even that game company, with its speakers (both streamers and viewers) becoming ever more influential as time goes by.

'Variety' channels

We can now look at the other sort of Twitch gaming channel – the variety channel. All game broadcasters on Twitch exist somewhere on a spectrum between 'focused' and 'variety', yet there are relatively few who do not define or tacitly present themselves according to one of these norms. Whereas the focused streamer emphasizes a particular game or sort of game and often deploys this as one of the key appeals of their channel – although as I have shown, that can poten-tially backfire to some degree – the variety streamer plays a far wider range of games (Taylor, 2018: 3; Leith, 2021: 115). Although a variety streamer who might play *every* genre of game or who would be willing to try *any* game probably doesn't exist, most variety streamers will pick and choose from large numbers of games and game genres. For some variety streamers a game might be played to completion – or at least until the end of interest for the streamer – before moving onto the next one, while in others there might be several games which are cycled between for a period before some games drop out of the rotation and others come in. In most variety channels the streamer will make clear at the start of a broadcast what the game of the day is, or what games might be played that day, while other streamers with several games 'on the go' might schedule them specifically – Game X on Mondays, Game Y on Wednesdays, and so on. While no statistics exist on this, eight years of observational work on Twitch tell me that most game streamers host channels closer to the variety end of the spectrum than the focused end, although channels that emphasize the latter are by no means rare. If focused channels carve out a space on Twitch for specific sorts of games and those who play them, what is it that variety channels are doing?

At first glance it might seem as if the variety channel is one with less potential to speak loudly in Twitch's *agora* and impact and shape gaming culture and matters of consequence in the gaming community. Viewers are likely to be more varied in their gaming interests, and the streamer less closely associated with a specific game or game genre and its fanbase. Yet there is a major way in which a variety channel, and especially the entire set of variety channels on Twitch, can have a significant impact on discussions in and around gaming – this is by playing new games, or games which have only recently been 'discovered'. Variety game streamers can therefore be seen as the arbiters of the question: *what's the latest hot thing?* What newest game or newest downloadable content or newest multiplayer or newest live service is currently of interest, is currently noteworthy enough to be considered worth playing? For variety streamers the tone of their channels when playing a brand-new game is often one of consideration and study, almost akin to that of a games reviewer (Johnson & Woodcock, 2019b; cf. Nieborg & Foxman, 2023). The variety streamer playing a new game often deploys the Twitch *we* in describing how 'we' are exploring the game, we are learning it, we are figuring out what goes on, we are seeing what it has to offer. There is a reciprocal relationship here of sorts, of course, where the novelty of some new release is bolstered by variety streamers playing it, while the sense that a variety streamer is truly in tune with the digital gaming zeitgeist is reinforced by their ability to regularly change programming onto the latest fad. We might say that each individual focused streamer has far more influence over what matters in a particular part of gaming than an individual variety streamer, but all variety streamers are collectively a key bellwether of what is currently going on in gaming.

The game *Among Us* (2018) is the ideal recent example of how variety streamers can shape gaming, in this case during the Covid-19 pandemic years. Although released two years before the pandemic appeared, this game only rose to popularity during the early 2020s. It involves players – either who know each other, or strangers recruited for that match – controlling cartoon astronauts attempting to fix a spacecraft. Each player is given a number of objectives but a small number of players are instead tasked with eliminating the other players while pretending to be completing the normal tasks. Every so often a player can be voted out of the game by the others, leading to a social deduction game (Rodriguez, 2020; Montelli, 2021) in which players must balance completing their objectives with trying to deceive, or uncover, the other players. *Among Us* emerged over the space of several months as perhaps the 'perfect game' for 'pandemic quarantines' (Rodriguez, 2020) with the required numbers of friends needed to play the game having little to do except stay at home, and the game's mechanics lending itself incredibly well to the streaming experience. As Grayson (2020) explains, in *Among Us* players 'plot, scheme and scream' live on air, and there's a 'grim thrill to watching a skilled impostor'. For some of the stream 'they're giving you, the viewer, a peek behind the curtain of their diabolical plan', and then as soon as their character is socializing with the other players, 'they're playing a perfect babyface' and 'the imposter player cracks the world's most malicious grin'. The fact that the game's release had actually come years *before* its sudden fame demonstrates strongly the ability for Twitch to catapult an 'unknown game into the limelight at remarkable speed' (Johnson & Woodcock, 2019b: 671) when the right set of factors align.

Through their ability to quickly adapt to a suddenly well-played game – and in the process further establish and cement that game *as* a well-played game – variety streamers thus collectively offer a reflection of something currently happening within gaming as a whole, and individually offer channels which explore a full range of gaming possibilities. A game which suddenly becomes popular on Twitch can capture the gaming public's imagination and attention with remarkable speed, bringing niche or obscure titles aston-ishing and rapid fame – while a blockbuster title that only gets a few days of play on Twitch before fading from view tells us a lot about how successful that game might (not) be in the wider gaming sphere. Seeing 'some of the most popular streamers come together to play, bicker, and deceive one another over and over again is exciting' (Matthews, 2020), and it was the mass move of Twitch streamers into *Among Us* – especially in a period when more and more people were streaming on Twitch *per se* (Kastrenakes, 2020) as a result of the inability to do much else – that demonstrated the flexibility of the site's appeal. As Leith (2021: 115) notes, variety streamers are well positioned to make these adjustments to unexpected games precisely because 'their audience is already prepared for the streamer to change the game that they are playing', and this flexibility is essential to understanding the success of a title like *Among Us*. A niche game thus leaped into a global level of visibility within a tiny amount of time, propelled by the possibilities of Twitch.

Articulations of a streamer's objectives – to develop a focused channel or a variety channel in their little corner of the Twitch *agora* – are hence discursive statements that identify what questions are being answered through the content on a streamer's channel. A variety streamer can show what is contemporary and cutting-edge in gaming, what the conversation about newest games is focused on, and can introduce interesting new games to their viewers and address themselves more easily to the full range of *their* own gaming tastes. The focused streamer, meanwhile, can develop a striking degree of influence within a particular gaming community and is likely to gather viewers with whom a greater depth of conversation is possible, but can find themselves unable to fully exercise the breadth of their own gaming interest once their channel becomes associated with certain kinds of digital play only, and not others. Whereas the focused streamer must consider what game they are playing as a matter of the first consequence (in terms of viewer numbers and viewer interest), a variety streamer has a far larger degree of freedom. The focused streamer offers a deeper engagement and the variety streamer a broader one; the focused streamer gives a sense of persistence and drive to their broadcasts, while the variety streamer gives a sense of wider appreciation and more diverse tastes. A variety streamer's viewing numbers *will* naturally fluctuate to some extent depending on what is being played, as will the degree of a viewer's interest in any specific game, but the viewers come in with the expectation that a range of games will be played.

These two sorts of channels form most of the gaming content on Twitch. All sorts of games are played, but different streamers and their different channels present this content in different ways, prioritize different kinds of play, encourage and engage with different viewers in different ways, and each brings different forms of information to the gaming *agora*. Twitch's gaming origins lie in esports broadcasts that showcased the largest and most important of competitive gaming contests, and which later expanded to esports streamers hosting their own channels, and speedrunners and challenge runners pushing the boundaries of what is possible in singleplayer as well as multiplayer digital games. This created a gaming *agora* for the highly visible accomplishment of challenging gaming feats, bringing those feats to a far greater audience than ever before while at the same time engaging that audience – through the ability to chat, the *liveness* of the site and so forth – with the players broadcasting. Twitch's broader diversification into digital gaming writ large then led to the emergence of two clear and distinct streamer and channel categories – the focused streamer and the variety streamer – who generally rely less on the spectacle of high skill and more on their ability to offer reliable and distinctive experiences of deep commitment or wide interest to their viewers, and in doing so contribute to taste-making and sense-making in games. These two sorts of channels form the foundations of the contemporary state of Twitch, allowing viewers to engage with a particular community or to engage with the contemporary in gaming as a whole, and for streamers to express their perspectives and contributions through experience and expertise on specific topics, or through broader perspectives on the wider game streaming ecosystem.

This gives a comprehensive sense of gaming content on the site – but what else is being broadcast?

Art and creation

We have now looked at some of the core dimensions of the *gaming* experience on Twitch; yet digital gaming is not the only sort of content being broadcast on the site. There are other well-developed and emerging trends in broadcast content, and these are interesting for two reasons. They firstly demonstrate some of the contestation over what Twitch is really for – just gaming, or other things as well? These contests have become increasingly central to Twitch in recent years, eliciting debate, controversy, hostility and online abuse, and show both the complex politics of 'gaming' and the tension between the seemingly solely economic interests of the platform's stakeholders when contrasted with the diverse interests of its users. The second point of interest is how they also shed further light on some of the key dynamics of Twitch regarding celebrity, influence, money, visibility, cultural engagement, and the tensions the site faces. Examining non-gaming content shows us the kind of power that some of the most successful streamers have, as well as how particularly innovative or *creative* streamers can push the boundaries of the site by developing entirely new forms of content. Having explored how gaming content on Twitch shapes the *agora* by exploring what matters in particular gaming contexts, in the second half of this chapter I will now look at three interesting examples of non-gaming content on Twitch. These are not exhaustive of non-gaming content on the site, but each is quite distinct and indicative of some of these emerging contests and uncertainties over the platform's 'purpose', its governance and its culture.

The first major branch of live streaming on Twitch that doesn't involve the broadcasting of gaming content is the growing number of 'art' or 'creative' streams (Uszkoreit, 2018: 164). These channels involve the streamer working on a creative project and allowing the viewers to observe the project taking shape. Some of these are tightly connected to gaming while others are entirely separate. A common kind of creative stream involves the making of 'cosplay' – costume play – outfits, in which the viewer sees every step of the process from the initial concept to the final creation. Cosplay involves the designing or purchasing of costumes and the application of makeup so that one resembles a known character from a digital game, a popular television series or film, an anime series or manga or cartoon, or other media (Lamerichs, 2011; Rahman et al., 2012). Much like esports, cosplay long had an existence outside of Twitch (and YouTube), but both sites have done much in recent years to accelerate and grow this subculture through enabling both the sharing of finishing products *and* sharing of the creative process and effort that goes into a cosplay's creation (Taylor,

2018: 6; Lamerichs, 2021: 183). This connects closely with the idea of the 'art stream' on Twitch, in which one can tune in to watch streamers creating physical or digital art across a wide range of media and topics. Like cosplay there is a strong overlap here with gaming, given that gaming fan art and gaming-related drawing is a central part of these streams, but it also expands beyond gaming (Lamerichs, 2021). Music streams (Pereira & Ricci, 2023), another creative aspect of the site, demonstrate similar trends.

Other creative streams similarly riff off gaming and geek culture through showing the creation of gaming-related media that will go on to have lives beyond Twitch itself. One example of this is the recent trend of some podcast shows being recorded live on Twitch – before then being edited and put out, separately, as a podcast – through which viewers experience a behind-the-scenes look at these audio productions. Given all the previous discussions in this work about the power of *liveness* and hence perceived realness on Twitch, it is easy to see how these streams appeal to existing podcast fans by giving a stronger sense of intimacy and connection with broadcasters. As Ryan Stanton and I have argued, this is an important part of what many gaming podcast listeners seem to be seeking (Stanton & Johnson, 2023). Some other creative streams show the streamer programming computer software, and sometimes even programming games specifically (Consalvo & Phelps, 2019). In these channels the viewer gets to see the code as it's produced, and to talk in most cases with the streamer about their specific project or about coding in general. Some are even more unusual and distinctive – one channel I found was dedicated to the making of real-world metal armour using traditional techniques. These examples show how Twitch facilitates and supports intersections between different aspects of geek and nerd culture as well as gaming culture, while also introducing users to more niche aspects of these cultures that they are perhaps unaware of.

In art creation streams we start to see the contestation

between Twitch's 'established' purposes and the purposes
that innovative and inventive streamers put it to. They are
creative in the way that Twitch means it – artistic, aesthetic,
and so on – but in a deeper sense they are also *creative* in
the sense that the other types of streams I discuss below
are creative, which is to say innovating and sometimes also
pushing the boundaries of the site in clever and novel ways.
They create a new niche and a new area in which people
can create content that is interesting and compelling for a
substantial number of viewers, even if this is itself surprising
and one might never have otherwise believed people would
gather to spectate such an activity. Each one fits into Twitch's
rules while nevertheless going potentially against what a large
portion of Twitch's wider culture think the platform is for.
There has been little in the way of backlash against creative
streams – especially when compared to the gambling streams
and Hot Tub streams I discuss shortly – but they nevertheless
still represent a challenge to the gaming hegemony of Twitch.
Discussing chess on Twitch, Johansson (2021: ii) demonstrates how the site can shift gaming fan interest *away* from
'game proficiency' and towards 'spectacle and entertainment';
creative streams show how this interest can be successfully
moved further to the creation of games or the creation of
game-related content, or even towards things which have
little or nothing to do with games and gaming. The appeal
of watching others on Twitch doesn't have to be limited to
gaming or esports. Just as the ancient *agora* was also diverse
in its functions – one day 'a market', the next 'an election, a
dramatic performance' or 'an athletic competition' (Camp,
1986: 6) – the contemporary *agora* on Twitch can comfortably
accommodate this same multiplicity.

Gaming or gambling?

The second interesting form of non-gaming content I want to
explore is the rise of real-money gambling on Twitch. 'Twitch

gambling' essentially began with 'Twitch poker' streams in the early 2010s, with large amounts of money – often in the thousands, sometimes in the tens of thousands of dollars or more – being wagered live on online poker sites while being broadcast on Twitch. Yet what truly caused Twitch gambling content to explode was not poker, but slots. Unlike poker, online slot machines require no skill or previous experience, no degree of deep strategy, and the rules are extremely simple for anyone to understand. Slots can also lead to exciting moments far more often than poker, and online slots sites are vastly more common than online poker sites. These channels have since, however, become a highly controversial element of the platform. Some of the site's most successful streamers transitioned into slots streams while others built their profile solely from slots. Some of them were later 'outed', or outed themselves, as having or having developed gambling problems and being sometimes hundreds of thousands of dollars in debt, with the already engrossing nature of online gambling being apparently further psychologically cemented by having potentially tens of thousands of people constantly cheering you on while placing online wagers. What was particularly notable here was the fact that before the site's stricter regulation of these channels, some of Twitch's most popular streamers were subsidized by gambling companies in order to support their ability to live stream slots at very high stakes. Twitch gambling does not at present seem to have acquired much of an *agora*-like function within the *gambling* world – but that is not what interests us here. Its mere presence on Twitch instead can be used to shed light on controversies around Twitch's regulation, on the behaviour of its most visible and highly successful streamers, and on the extent to which 'people power' can overcome the wishes and actions of the site's elites.

In the first case Twitch gambling tells us even more than we have already seen about the platform's hands-off approach to regulation. Gambling broadcasts were an entirely new form of Twitch stream that rapidly gained popularity. Those who created slot streams discovered a form of broadcast that turned out to be massively compelling. Despite widespread dislike of these broadcasts, their immediate success in terms of viewer numbers meant that Twitch appeared loath to step in until the degree of public pressure become too significant. What we see here is Twitch once again using its hands-off approach as a *strategic* measure. Framed (as previously noted) as encouragement to users to personalize their channels, here it also means that users are always creating new ways to use and make money on Twitch – and make money for Twitch – *without the platform itself having to do much*. The idea that Twitch as a company is somewhat 'absent' from the platform – while nevertheless collecting half of all the subscription money that comes to streamers and at least some portion of their donations – circulates commonly among Twitch users, often with resentment. It is one that re-surfaces when we consider gambling streams on a site that nominally presents itself as being focused on digital gaming. Just as Justin.tv transformed into Twitch.tv without any specific intention for gaming to come to dominate the site – simply the openness and possibilities of the platform enabling the growth and success of gaming content – so Twitch became by far the leading website for the live spectatorship of real-money gambling content almost without anybody noticing. Twitch's overseers are sufficiently hands-off and sufficiently keen to prioritize innovation and income generation over community management that slots streams expanded and grew with alarming speed and without any corporate intervention.

Twitch gambling can also shed light on the roles and behaviours of Twitch's most famous, influential and well-viewed streamers; which is to say, its celebrities (Catá, 2019; Johnson et al., 2019b; Speed et al., 2023). Although there are gambling streams of all different sizes, the largest such channels – despite being few in number – were some of the most-viewed channels of any sort on Twitch until recent restrictions. While the platform happily turned a blind eye to gambling content, Twitch's *streamers* – ever innovative and responsive – had their fingers on the pulse to a far greater extent. When Twitch made a few initial moves to finally limit some of the more obviously egregious aspects of gambling streams such as direct referral links to gambling websites, streamers quickly deployed a new set of discourses to continue to justify their broadcasting of gambling content. For example, in a channel where hundreds of thousands of dollars were seemingly wagered in real-money online slots play, I noted the phrase 'gambling is for stupid rich people' in the streamer's broadcast title. Similar articulations could be found in other channels – though generally played a little straighter and with a little less appar-ently self-deprecating humour (cf. Johnson, 2022) – such as admonitions that gambling is dangerous, gambling should only be done if you can afford it, and even links to gambling support websites or telephone lines. These statements were largely absent until Twitch's first steps against slots streams in 2021 and clearly represented an attempt to acknowledge the changing political climate on Twitch gambling. This is our second observation from Twitch gambling: that streamers are not just innovative in finding new forms of content but also innovative in striking balances between the platform and its larger groups of users, and keeping a keen sense of what is considered acceptable (or not).

Finally Twitch gambling shows us important things about the power of Twitch's community to create change – or, at least, to take credit for change when it happens at the same time as a popular groundswell of interest. In 2022 the degree of resentment and opposition to gambling streams among many Twitch streamers had reached fever pitch. Twitch announced major changes to gambling streams – not their total removal but a significant reduction in what could be broadcast on gambling channels, and major new rules to limit the possibility of gambling sites being advertised (Gerken, 2022; Wynne, 2023). The response on

Twitter to this change was unparalleled. Massive numbers of Twitch streamers and Twitch viewers were united in their approval of these restrictions, and many took this moment as an opportunity to emphasize the perceived potential of community influence – the collective voice – on shaping Twitch. Many superstar celebrity streamers had been pursuing the constant excitement and big-money lifestyle of high-stakes slots, while Twitch's owners pursued a hands-off strategy for the website that involved not stepping in to do anything about or around gambling streams until, it seems, the controversy reached a point where they felt they had no alternative. As we have discussed previously, the goals and interests of a platform's users do not necessarily align, and here we can helpfully look at how O'Kelly and Dubnick (2014: 1) describe the ancient *agora* as an 'accountability space' that was 'founded on an unending cascade of social situations and the relationships that these situations inform' (ibid.: 9). Twitch's community claimed that because of some streamers and the platform having created on-site situations and relationships (e.g., between celebrity streamers and multi-million-dollar gambling companies) that were widely seen as undesirable, they had been held to account and forced to change. Gambling streams and the involvement of gambling companies appeared to undermine streamers' brands – friendliness, approachability and *authenticity* – and hence had to be resisted.

Twitch gambling therefore tells us little specifically about the Twitch *agora* for *gaming* – yet it tells us much about Twitch as a platform on which this *agora* exists, and on the extent to which its *agora*-like functions are not limited to gaming. It tells us about priorities in the infrastructure and governance of Twitch for those in charge of it; about the individuals with the loudest voices and who have accumulated the most success on Twitch; and about another way that Twitch is coming to demonstrate a potential emerging divide between the masses and these two sorts of elites (Twitch's owners, Twitch celebrity streamers) when it comes to what the platform 'should' be all about. Celebrities clearly have tremendous power to push new forms of content on a site like Twitch that remains relatively lax on regulation – and even pushes this laxness as a key point of interest for its users – yet large numbers of users banded together to push back against what they perceive as activities and influences outside the collective norms of the site as a whole. Twitch's owners, meanwhile, demonstrate a focus on securing profit and exploiting new niches rather than the maintenance of a community so many have come to rely on. As with art and creative streams, the *creativity* of streamers in creating new kinds of Twitch content is again on display here, but in a far more contentious manner. These factors are all therefore important if we are to understand not the actual use of Twitch as a forum for debating the nature and importance of events in gaming, but rather if we are to understand how the forum *itself* is being contested and fought over. Twitch remains contested, and open to change.

Hot Tub streams

The third interesting development in Twitch's non-gaming content in recent years is the rise of the so-called 'Hot Tub' stream. Pioneered although not directly invented by one of the most famous women Twitch streamers, these broadcasts generally involve women live streaming from inflatable pools in bikinis or other swimwear. The streamers who now go live within this genre alternate 'between multiple activities dressed in a bikini' while 'in a blow-up pool', many of which are designed to enable the streamer to turn, look in different directions, show their body from different angles, and so forth (Kejser, 2021). This streamer and others since have used their existing extreme popularity on the site to create in effect an entirely new genre of Twitch channel (Jackson, 2023a: 214), and one that was immediately contentious due to its foregrounding of female bodies (Kejser, 2021; Jackson, 2023a) on a site already uncomfortable with them (Ruberg et al., 2019). The Hot Tub streams were praised and lambasted in equal measure, with the cleverness and entrepreneurial spirit of these initial streamers and those who followed being widely acknowledged, while many of the site's always-simmering resentments around women as gamers and the place of women on a site 'for' gaming (Partin, 2019: 154; Ruberg et al., 2019) also came back to the fore. Examining Hot Tub streams allows us to further interrogate the role of money on Twitch, the discomfort felt by many of the site's users about anything framed as even quasi-adult, but *also* the appeal of this same content, and the discourses deployed to argue various sides in the fundamental and seemingly now endless debate about what Twitch is actually *for*.

One of the most important aspects of these channels' contentiousness is how they complicate a key part of the relationships between streamers and viewers on Twitch – the role of money. As noted throughout this work, streamers generally offer rewards to their viewers for donating, such as access to special emotes, access to private forums (see chapter 4) and so on. A streamer might also make it clear that donating a certain amount will allow the donor to choose the next song playing in the channel's background; donating more might allow the donor to select the next game; and even more might allow the donor to play alongside the streamer in a multiplayer match. These are different because they are ways for the viewer to exert a small amount of control over the stream and the streamer. Much like donating or subscribing and gaining their attendant in-chat badges, rewards give the viewer a feeling of presence and impact in the stream and the channel that they might not otherwise have. Yet such rewards both in Hot Tub streams and elsewhere are also sometimes body-related, which highlights another context where there can be overlap between Twitch and forms of adult live streaming. Rewards might include a streamer changing their clothes (off-camera), performing a certain exercise, performing a dance move (Uszkoreit, 2018: 172), or even writing on their body in pen (generally the username of the donor).

What is interesting here is that on Twitch the *physicality* of the reward that one might get on an adult live streaming site is present – the viewer donates money for a physical action and gets the streamer to perform that physical action – but the unambiguous sexuality of the reward (e.g., nudity or a sexual act) is omitted. Yet the eroticism remains as evidenced by how actively Twitch's viewers are engaging in this practice – Hot Tub streams are now one of the most popular non-gaming genres of content on the site. Even without explicit nudity there appears to still be something strangely compelling about having another human perform a physical action, even a harmless one, at one's whim (cf. Chesher, 2024). The appeal of offering donation rewards such as writing on the body, or the appeal of body painting streams (with no nudity**), show us that much of the appeal of live streamed adult content lies not solely in the sexuality of naked or partly-naked bodies, but rather in the power dynamic of apparent control – albeit 'playfully' given and, one hopes, without any coercion – over the streamer's body. The fact that such streams are so popular on Twitch when there is no nudity involved makes this point very well, especially when coupled with chapter 1's discussions of streamer and viewer motivations. Welch (2022: 526) describes it perfectly by asserting that although live streaming on Twitch is certainly not 'erotic *per se*', it nevertheless has some of the 'same kinds of authentic embodied performances' that adult live streamers engage in when doing their broadcasts on other sites. These, it seems, can be every bit as compelling as gaming mastery or other kinds of content.

** The 'punishments' for transgressing Twitch's rules range from temporary bans to permanent bans, although it is widely felt among Twitch users that these are unevenly handed out.

The backlash against Hot Tub streams, however, was rapid and strong. Two distinct articulations against rapidly emerged – that Twitch *is* for gaming, and Twitch is *not* for this kind of quasi-adult content. Although they reach the same point, the perspectives are distinct. The first one involved many streamers and viewers both on Twitch and elsewhere (Twitter, gaming news websites, Reddit, etc.) expressing a strong feeling that Twitch is essentially a website for gaming. These stressed the important and substantial things that Twitch had done for gaming, the extent to which it was a site for people who shared this key leisure and creative interest, and that one of its strengths was its focus on gaming, the gaming community and gaming culture. From this point of view there was something important to be preserved in keeping Twitch solely for gaming – although even this definition is of course a simplification (Siutila, 2018; Taylor, 2018: 22; Ask et al., 2019; Cabeza-Ramírez et al., 2021: 4) – and not allowing any other content, whether this kind of quasi-adult content or anything else. Some of these articulations emphasized that they didn't object to the Hot Tub streamers specifically, but rather that any non-gaming content should be limited on the site to maintain a clear sense of a single community and purpose. The speed with which Twitch as a platform and Twitch's users have traditionally responded to regulating (female) bodies on the platform, and the slowness with which the former responded to the meteoric rise of real-money gambling channels, are telling.

The other side was the articulation that Twitch may well be for many things – not just gaming – but that it is definitely *not* a site for this. This perspective tended to emphasize that pornography and adult-related content more broadly represent a tremendous amount of internet content, and do not need another outlet. Some comments of this sort discussed the fact previously mentioned that these streams were clearly attempts to slide around Twitch's rules – following their letter, not so much their intent – with content that skirted the definition of adult live streams while maintaining nominal compliance with the platform's rules. This is indeed a reasonably accurate assertion, since like gambling streams, Hot Tub streams represent another example of streamer-driven innovation on Twitch, finding new and highly compelling forms of broadcast and then developing them at pace while Twitch the company, and Twitch's viewers, are still 'catching up' and deciding how they actually feel about this. Yet this articulation was most often entangled with the routine (Ruvalcaba et al., 2018: 307) negativity and hostility towards women streamers – for many these streams seemed to confirm already-held beliefs that women are often not 'real' gamers, or are only on Twitch to make money. Ruberg et al. (2019: 478) have demonstrated how any visible presence of female breasts on the site is seen by reactionary gamers as unfairly taking attention away from true gamers on the site. Twitch's recent salary leaks demonstrate the highest paid streamers are almost exclusively men, showing that being a culturally legitimate (male) gamer (cf. Cullen, 2022b) *and* someone financially self-interested actually go together very comfortably. Much like Twitch's policies and community guidelines (Ruberg, 2021: 1681), these debates thus 'reflect anxieties about the relationship between live streaming and webcam-based sex work' that are seemingly shared not just by Twitch, but also by a large portion of its users (cf. Ruberg & Brewer, 2022; Tran, 2022).

Even more than gambling streams it is Hot Tub streams that represent, in a sense, the apex of the creativity shown by live streamers in attempting to find new ways to produce compelling and highly-watched channels. Just as the *creative* streams such as art and podcasting emerged organically before then being accepted and embraced by the platform, the same can be said of Hot Tub streams. They now also represent their own category on the site, signalling Twitch's tacit acceptance of the genre, while still being contained *within* that category and hence kept somewhat separate from the rest of the site. As with gambling streams Twitch has again demonstrated relatively little concern over what many viewers object to, and has been keen to continue a new and highly profitable form of streaming on the site. These streams also show that Twitch's *agora*, even if most users understand it to be essentially one for gaming, *can* indeed be changed by users who develop new forms of content. But the *agora* is also the place for reflection, for interrogating or even resisting these new developments, and for asserting what Twitch is and what it is for. This is important to understand because it highlights a difference between a widespread audience perception of the site, and the company's intentions and motivations. As with gambling streams and Hot Tub streams and many others, there is rarely any objection to the emergence of new content so long as it minimally meets Twitch's requirements and rules and brings in viewers and income. We might therefore propose that what Twitch's gaming viewers think the platform is – essentially a gaming one with, maybe, some other bits thrown in – appears quite different from what the company understands the site to be. Its focus on gaming live streams has allowed Twitch to reach its current extraordinary height, but the company does not appear *committed* to this status in the way that many viewers are. Twitch appears keen to pursue content that is compelling, draws viewers and yields income; Twitch's users are generally eager to police the boundaries of what can and cannot be on the site, even while some are more than happy with the blurring of lines that so many others object to in such strident terms.

Webcams, private homes, live-streamed lives

As we have seen, Twitch's content consists primarily of, and in the minds of most remains wholly associated with, gaming. Other forms of content – artistic, gambling, Hot Tubs and so on – challenge these connections and, when taken together, represent an impressive degree of *creativity* on the part of Twitch's (aspirational) broadcasters. Yet in all channels there is one vital element that still needs addressing a little more fully: the role of the webcam, and perhaps more centrally the role of what the webcam *shows* to the viewer. This is most obviously relevant in the Hot Tub stream, but extends far beyond this, and is an essential, rather than side, element of what Twitch content consists of. Not all Twitch channels offer a webcam alongside a game or other activity, but it is a clear norm on Twitch for a webcam to be included. This generally means that the webcam captures not only the streamer's face (Dargonaki, 2018: 105; London et al., 2019: 53, Uttarapong et al., 2021: 7, 13) but also sometimes body or at least upper body. This might seem too obvious to mention, but compared with many other leading platforms there is something distinctive here. Sites like Reddit and Twitter make no expectations of showing face or body. On Twitter this is often an effective engagement tool for certain Twitter users or certain accounts but is far from essential; on Reddit showing faces and bodies is generally associated with the over-18 parts of the site, although not exclusively. On YouTube gaming videos are far less likely to show a Let's Player's face than is the case on Twitch, even though the content – gaming – is the same. Yet on Twitch showing one's face is considered the norm, and even after almost a decade of research on Twitch I am still sometimes surprised when I go onto a channel and find no webcam present. Guides that recommend strategies for growing one's channel and engaging with one's viewers regularly mention the importance of showing one's face, and the 'higher' up the listings of Twitch channels one goes (according to viewer numbers), the less and less common it becomes for someone to not show their face on stream.

Twitch also, compared with Instagram or Facebook for example, offers less potential for the obvious *curation* of one's physical appearance due to the inherent liveness of the site. Instagram, in particular, has become notorious for the use of 'filters' that transform users' appearance, as well as for the suite of techniques – camera angles, the use of lighting, certain poses, etc. – that users can deploy to make themselves appear more attractive, taller, physically fitter and so on (Garcia et al., 2021; Savolainen et al., 2022). Twitch does give one control over the lighting of one's face or body, the position of the camera and so forth, but unless explicitly broadcasting as a VTuber (Lawson, 2023: 22) – in which case the transformation of the image of one's physical self is immediately obvious – Twitch streamers are not able to deploy filters to consistently alter their appearance on the fly. In contrast to other major platforms, Twitch appears to show an unfiltered, un-curated real person in a real setting. Social media celebrates 'connectedness, accessibility and intimacy' and thus 'performances of a private, authentic self' (Jerslev, 2016: 5246) are highly valued. On sites like Twitch 'authenticity itself becomes a platform' (Tran, 2022: 513) and the liveness and immediacy of the platform, coupled with the ability to see into homes and see the streamer in a seemingly unplanned way, facilitate a sense of 'authenticity and genuineness' in broadcasters (Speed et al., 2023: 2; cf. Persaud & Perks, 2022). This is an important part of what makes a speaker on Twitch compelling, especially if they are a 'top' streamer who is inevitably also fully engaged with money, metrics, career considerations and the like.

The second aspect of private lives we see on Twitch is the *background* behind a streamer. Some broadcasters on Twitch deploy 'green screens' to integrate their webcam video more fully with the game or other content being played, but it is not hard to imagine that for some this also serves a privacy function by masking whatever might be on the wall or in the room behind them. For those without green screens, however, the viewer is free to see whatever lies behind the streamer when a webcam is pointed at them, easily blurring the boundaries between home and work (Lark, 2022). Some streamers clearly select carefully what should appear behind them – this is often a sign that a streamer is beginning to take Twitch a little more 'seriously' than they perhaps were before (cf. Phelps et al., 2021b) – and these backgrounds might show shelves of books, geek merchandise or games; lighting and artworks selected to evoke or suggest particular moods; or some combination of these. A de facto low-level curation of environment does therefore take place. Recent research during the Covid-19 pandemic has studied the backgrounds people select when using internet conferencing software such as Zoom, confirming that such functionality easily becomes a site of active curation with the intention of creating particular affective states and atmospheres, and controlling one's presentation to others (Marsden, 2022). Similar trends can be seen on Twitch, where the curation of backgrounds is designed to make the stream more of a *place* – see the next chapter's discussion of this aspect – and to humanize the streamer, and allow them to display traits or items which are imagined to connect to the audience and the intended tone of the channel.

In other channels the viewer will see someone else occupying the same home as the streamer. Younger streamers who are adults but living at home are often highly reluctant for family members to appear on their broadcasts, and the times when this nevertheless happens are often recorded and teasingly reposted around the internet by their more subversive viewers (cf. Johnson, 2022). Other channels sometimes show a flatmate or a friend coming onto the channel, either by design or simply because they share the same dwelling. These perhaps unsurprisingly yield a less embarrassed response in most streamers and are often quite friendly, with streamers sometimes taking a second to greet a flatmate passing by in the background. Some channels can also briefly include romantic partners of the streamer, again either by intention or by accident. There is a wide spectrum of potential responses and objectives here from streamers, ranging from those who try to keep any hint of their private lives entirely off-camera and try to prevent anyone else in their home coming on-screen, up to those streamers who regularly invite a partner to game or do some other activity with them. There are even now examples of so-called 'streamer couples' where both members of the pairing are Twitch broadcasters and appear in, or regularly recommend, the other person's channel. Pets are also regular visitors on many channels, either wandering in and out of the background or sometimes interacting with the streamer. Viewers will sometimes request additional webcams – 'cat cam', 'rabbit cam' and so forth – to be set up so that they can watch the pet in question alongside the streamer, and pets often find their way into the channel-specific emotes for a particular stream.

It is interesting to examine the presence of these individuals, planned or unplanned (and human or nonhuman), when we think about the *agora* dynamics of Twitch. As noted in previous chapters, Twitch presents – and streamers reinforce – a sense of the live streamer as an *independent* figure, someone whose channel is very much their own and who is solely responsible for what they have to say. This connects to the idea of the liveness and hence realness of the site, and also connects to the more entrepreneurial discourses that circulate among more aspirational streamers. It is also reflected in some of the tension of the Twitch *we* and ambiguity over what aspects a streamer allows viewers to claim some degree of ownership over, and what aspects remain their own. Streamers are also of course in a relationship that inevitably marks them out from viewers, with a *single* streamer broadcasting to thousands or even tens of thousands of viewers simultaneously; this fundamental asymmetry reinforces this idea of the streamer as a sole and independent actor. Yet these interruptions into their real-world streaming spaces – somewhat like the roles of moderators – complicate the picture. Streamers do not exist in isolated bubbles but are humans who occupy a distinct physical space (Ruberg & Lark, 2021), one which might also include others, and who have relationships, pets, social interactions, and all the things their viewers might also have. Streamers' lives are messy as most lives are, no matter the attempts to control and curate. It also inevitably humanizes the streamer to some extent, furthering the 'friend' side of the celebrity–friend relationship. Even while someone's space for gaming might be carefully maintained and planned, it defies a curatorial totality – there is always the possibility for the image to be broken or altered. For all of Twitch's metrics and all the aspirational discourse around streamers, Twitch's broadcasters – its speakers in its gaming *agora* – are every bit as present in the material specifics of their lives as the rest of us are.

Utterances and arguments in the agora

In the first chapter we explored Twitch as a platform, and in the second we looked at its users. In this chapter I've built on these foundations to examine what these people are broadcasting and watching when on Twitch – which is to say, the 'content' on the site. Having explored the various sorts of channels Twitch offers, a key takeaway here is how *anticipation* is central to both 'focused' channels and 'variety' channels, which formed the core of this chapter. Focused channels are specifically and discursively constructed around a particular game or a game genre or the games of a particular company. The content that comes out of these channels is thus less focused on high achievement (though there can be overlap here) and much more about the *depth* of engagement with a particular sort of gaming, and hence the degree of knowledge, skills, expertise and experience that go into the statements these channels make. These are channels on which streamers put forward highly informed opinions, and these channels are framed as speaking gaming expertise (Toft-Nielsen & Nørgård, 2015; cf. Ruvalcaba et al., 2018: 299) to expert viewers. This in turn is what the viewer comes to expect in these broadcasts, feeling comfortable and familiar when the relevant game-focus is displayed, and potentially disconcerted and confused when it is not. What we therefore see is how the *expectations* on streamers in Twitch's gaming *agora* are placed on them through the relationships between the streamers and the viewers, who mutually constitute what the channel entails and what the stream is, in some sense, supposed to entail. Focused streamers define their streams to appeal to particular viewers but can find those same definitions becoming constricting and limiting, while viewers flock to focused channels precisely for that *focus*, and collectively demonstrate their displeasure when the stream changes its orientation.

Twitch has also, however, emerged as a platform with an essential relationship with gaming news and the always-changing up-to-the-minute aspects of gaming culture, which we see most strongly in *variety* streams. This has a two-part dynamic: Twitch has become usable both as a clear metric of what games are considered interesting and important among those which are newly released, and also as an actor that itself shapes the conversation around what is currently important. In the first case Twitch's gaming *agora* often foregrounds new releases which feature in many streams – primarily by variety streamers – and demonstrate both in their broadcast by many streamers, *and* their watching by many viewers, the interest that gaming culture has in a new release. The ability for the most popular channels to sometimes feature games earlier than their overall release dates, or to play sections of games not accessible to most players just yet, demonstrates how Twitch streamers are taking on some of the roles traditionally assigned to game reviewers (Johnson & Woodcock, 2019b) – the ability to articulate ideas of what gaming *news* matters and is of consequence, and what recently released games do and don't deserve our attention (Nieborg & Foxman, 2023). In turn, however, Twitch as an actor has become large and influential enough that the site itself can shape the conversation around the gaming as well as giving us a way to measure ideas of interest in games. The case of *Among Us* (2018) is an ideal example of this, with the game's immense rise to success – and significant length of time 'at the top' – during the Covid-19 pandemic being almost exclusively driven by Twitch (e.g., Grayson, 2020; Matthews, 2020; Rodriguez, 2020). The ability of the site to offer a platform on which the wider gaming community can identify *and* shape ongoing matters in gaming in such a highly public and social way is one of Twitch's key appeals, and one of the things that has made it such an important actor in gaming. Anticipation is thus once again key here, but in the opposite manner – these streams emphasize the anticipation of the new, and the antici-pation that one stream will *not* be like the stream one watched a week ago.

The final key point to make here is in the idea of *creativity* on Twitch. At one point – a little over a decade ago – live streaming anything whatsoever was automatically a creative and innovative act, with the emergence of lifecasting (Taylor, 2018; Ask et al., 2019; Ruberg & Lark, 2021) demonstrating the interest in seeing an individual live streaming themselves over the web, and having the ability to directly interact with that person through a chat window. Broadcasting live gaming was in turn a creative and innovative act – and as a Twitch researcher I would note that many people are *still* surprised upon learning the size of Twitch and how many people enjoy watching others playing games – but so, too, are some of the alternative forms of content we now see emerging on the site. Twitch might indeed be 'primarily focused on video game content' (Condis, 2023: 968) but this is a boundary that is becoming ever more permeable, simultaneously allowing streamers to innovate and create new forms of broadcast, allowing Twitch to secure new revenue streams, and allowing viewers to both enjoy a greater diversity of content and rally against it.

A decade ago Walker (2014: 438) identified that existing 'power structures and systems of broadcasting' in place for the better part of a century are being challenged by Twitch's ability to give 'new voices' access to 'platforms which grant them a broad audience'. This is certainly true, but alongside those new voices – and often being championed *by* those new voices – are these new forms of broadcast material. They are sometimes among the most appealing and well-viewed forms of content when they come into being, but also can easily be the most contentious. Runco and Jaeger (2012) note that there are many definitions of creativity, but the element of 'surprise' is often evoked – and this helps us to see one of the most important elements of creativity on Twitch, which is often most effective when some unexpected or unanticipated new kind of stream emerges. All of this sits in turn within a culture that has come to see innovation and creativity in content creation as a way to make oneself stand out alongside other broadcasters. In a recent conversation I had with a non-academic partner on a Twitch-related project, they were intensely surprised to learn quite how *many* active Twitch channels exist (several million). It is this size and scale of Twitch that innovation and *creativity* of a new form of stream can harness with remarkable efficacy – figure out the next big thing and the rest of the platform's infrastructure, culture, existing userbase and monetization systems can swing into action and lead to striking outcomes for those who leap into the new trend. Walker was therefore completely right in his observation, but given Twitch's development of such a strong profile specifically for gaming voices, the presence and possibility of non-gaming channels are likely to remain a complex and contested part of the site for the foreseeable future.

CHAPTER 4
Community and Culture

Introduction

Twitch as a platform, Twitch's streamers and viewers, and Twitch's content are three of the four main parts of understanding *Twitch* and making sense of its emergence as an *agora* for debate, discussion, contestation and proposition about what *matters* in gaming. One component now remains: the community and the culture, or rather the communities and the cultures, of *Twitch*. How might ideas of community on Twitch and the site's relationship to gaming communities shape its functioning as a gaming *agora*? In turn, is Twitch simply an extension of gaming culture, a site where we see the emergence of new cultural norms, or some combination – and how might Twitch's cultural norms (irrespective of their origin) affect how statements are made and consumed in the gaming *agora*?

To answer these questions I start this chapter by analysing how streamers and viewers alike treat channels as distinct virtual 'places' with marked differences from those around them, and how this sense of place is quite distinct to Twitch and sheds new light on how community functions on the site. I then examine Twitch channels as *hubs*, rather than hermetically sealed places, by looking at the relationship between Twitch and other platforms such as Twitter, Reddit, YouTube and especially Discord. After these examinations of community I switch to culture, addressing some of the key elements of Twitch culture that are not found on other platforms. The first and the one I focus most on is the heavy use of 'emotes' to convey meaning, play with shared cultural touchstones, craft histories and archaeologies of shared events within a channel, and develop apparent *characters* through whom viewers communicate with surprising ease and fluidity. The second and third then further develop some of the ideas around Twitch-based communication, beginning with an examination of the use of 'raiding' to both strengthen relationships between streamers but also potentially bully and threaten other streamers, and then moving to the role of 'copypasta' messages through which ideas about Twitch, streamers, viewers, and games culture more generally, circulate. I conclude by coming back to Twitch's 'one of us' branding, and what the dynamics of community and culture on the site can tell us about its in-groups, out-groups, inclusivity, exclusivity, and the possibilities of true debate in this digital *agora*.

Channel communities

In the introductory chapter I noted how Twitch's motto – 'you're already one of us' – was designed to evoke a sense of a single pre-existing community which one is already a part of before coming to Twitch. Although that claim is rather dubious and highly contingent on particular notions of imagined 'Gamer'-hood, the existence of what appear to be communities in *individual* channels rather than stretching across the entire platform's *agora* is a far more readily identifiable phenomenon. Looking at these channel-specific communities will allow us to unravel more about how each channel functions as a speaking platform for its streamer, and how each channel gains a sense of being a distinctive digital place in which a community is formed and maintained. We have already discussed the importance of this sense of community on Twitch from several perspectives – it is something streamers look to generate, viewers look to enjoy and be a part of, and moderators seek to maintain and construct. However, here I want to propose a further under-standing of Twitch communities, and one focused around an idea that has been present throughout the book but now deserves closer attention – the idea of *place*. This is not simply a spatial metaphor that helpfully connects to some of the ideas of the *agora* I have been deploying throughout this book, but rather appears to be a quite important force in how individual Twitch channels are framed and understood. This sense of place is something that I will show live streamers actively try to create, and is therefore also in turn a useful analytic tool for us in trying to understand how people behave on Twitch.

The *place*-ness of a Twitch channel is first evident in the language used to invite viewers into one's channel. A popular Instagram user or Twitter user, for example, might encourage potential fans to 'follow' them (to sign up to see regular updates) or encourage existing fans to 'like' (express a metri-cized approval of) or 'share' (spread around to *their* networks) something the creator has shared. Twitch streamers, however, will often encourage their existing viewers and any other potential new viewers to 'come and hang out', or 'come and join us', or 'come and chill', or 'come and play [game]', or other similar constructions. Rather than directing the viewer or potential viewer to a specific piece of content or requesting a fairly simple initial interaction (e.g., following someone's Twitter account), the Twitch streamer offers something that is far more relaxed, open-ended and expansive in its scope. It is more relaxed because the would-be viewer here is not being encouraged to perform what might feel like a fairly transactional and soulless exchange (clicking a follow button). Instead the implicit suggestion is that nothing is wanted from the viewer except their *company*, and that the streamer is encouraging open-ended friendship, interaction and sociality, rather than the advancement of a metric (Phelps et al., 2021a; cf. Beer, 2016; Pellicone & Ahn, 2017) of follows, likes or subscriptions. In turn, it is far more expansive because it is not simply a shuffling of a few bytes of internet data to turn someone's following status from *off* to *on*, but rather implies that by *hanging out* in a streamer's particular corner of the wider Twitch *agora* the viewer might be doing something bigger and better – getting to know people, relaxing, enjoying themselves, and perhaps forming friendships or relationships that might last and grow beyond this initial stream.

Another component of this picture lies in the practice of naming one's Twitch community. This is an entirely emergent practice with no specific infrastructure or affordance to support it on the platform, but something that streamers took to doing quite early on. A community name is generally a collective noun referring to the totality of one's viewers. The name of a channel could therefore be something like 'The Pack' or 'The Freaks' or 'The No-Hopers' – terms chosen because they in some way relate to the streamer or their content or some long-running in-joke for a channel. Sometimes they take the form of relatively assertive or positive terms, as in the first example I gave here, while other times they can be a little more self-referential and dependent on a shared understanding of what is an in-joke and what is an insult (Johnson, 2022; cf. Lo, 2018: 19; Taylor, 2018: 81). Sometimes there will be no definite article and subscribers or fans might instead be categorized as simply belonging to a category of person. An example of this I saw in one channel was a streamer referring to their fans as 'simps', a contentious term usually used to denote 'men who seem desperate for a woman's attention' (Kastrenakes, 2020) but used, in this case, as a tongue-in-cheek name for the channel's community (cf. Jackson, 2020: 79–82). What is important here is that these shared identities are only realized in the *place* of the channel and (as I discuss in this chapter) other associated online settings. Outside those contexts they hold no particular meaning. A comparison with other social media sites is again fruitful, as people who follow a particular person on Twitter would rarely if ever use a collective noun to describe themselves, precisely because the sense of place-ness in a Twitter feed is far below that of a Twitch stream.

This aspect of a Twitch channel and the tightly-knit nature of its associated community is further reinforced by in-jokes or references that only those in that community fully understand the history or meaning of. For example, we might imagine a streamer playing a game with a detailed character creation system electing to create an in-game character whose face is deemed particularly unusual or hideous. This might then in turn become a source of amusement for their chat, and consequently that face might be later installed as an official emote (more on this later) in that person's channel. Such an emote then enables viewers to refer to this previous moment in a way that reminds the streamer and the viewers of it, but unavoidably excludes – until they learn the reference – new people who join the channel. What is particularly interesting here is that each custom emote has a unique meaning. To keep with the example of an unusual or unpleasant-looking character, an emote of this character might then become used by a channel's viewers whenever the streamer is in a character creation screen to hark back to a past 'classic' and amusing character creation experience. On other occasions, the same emote could instead be used whenever the player encounters a non-player character whom the channel's viewers perhaps deem to be ugly. It could even become associated with viewers exerting a kind of pressure on a streamer, using the emote to encourage a streamer to create another character with similar or equally objectionable looks, or it might become associated with the behaviour a player exhibited with that character rather than necessarily the specifics of their looks. What happens in this process is that both a channel develops its own unique set of references and shared moments, *and* all of these jokes only work in *that* channel, and immediately lose their meaning anywhere else on Twitch.

Community is an essential part of the appeal of Twitch for streamers (Kersting et al., 2021; Phelps et al., 2021b; Young

& Wiedenfeld, 2022), viewers (Sjöblom & Hamari, 2017; Hilvert-Bruce et al., 2018; Taylor, 2018; Wu et al., 2022) and moderators (Lo, 2018; London et al., 2019; Seering & Kairam, 2023) alike. Scholars have interrogated many aspects of this, yet individual Twitch channels are able to go further than most sites and, through a variety of means, generate a deep sense of distinctiveness and *place*. A Twitch channel is presented as somewhere one *goes*, as a viewer, to spend time with a community of likeminded individuals – a particular corner of the overall *agora* where one is welcome, familiar and established. While Twitch's idea of a single vast community inevitably reflects the company's advertising strategies to bring 'gamers' from around the world onto the site, each channel *does* indeed function as a distinct place for a distinct community, separate from all the others on the site and with their own codes, expectations and behaviours, yet also displaying some commonalities alongside the differences. Streamers have a tremendous amount of control and freedom over the presentation of their channel, their content, and the persona they show to viewers which encourages or discourages particular norms of behaving, and these things all build the sense of each channel as a distinct place viewers might spend their time in. The use of specific sorts of language around inviting people into channels is one part of this, along with the practice of naming channel communities, the creation of in-jokes that circulate in and are specific to a single channel, and the broader idea that someone's channel is something you *go to* or *visit*. These all help to further the distinctiveness of each channel and to emphasize how unlike other channels any given channel is, and the extent to which a full and distinct social experience can be found there. This place, this soapbox on which the streamer speaks and around which the viewers gather to listen and contribute, is thus not solely defined by the content being streamed but also by the wider accumulation of norms, practices and assumptions that are distinct to each and every channel, shaped by the streamer's will in part (what is 'allowed', for example) but also shaped by the viewers' response to the streamer, their content, and their achievements and failures.

Twitch and other platforms

A second piece of Twitch's community dynamics now merits attention – the spread of this community to other platforms, particularly Discord, although also YouTube, Twitter, Reddit and others. Not just (as above) does a Twitch channel serve as a place, but it also serves as a *hub*, like the centre of a wheel that connects also to numerous distinct, but secondary, spokes. Many scholars have already noted the diverse range of non-Twitch platforms which are increasingly involved in the experiences of Twitch's users, both streamers and viewers alike. Taylor (2018: 20), for example, describes how a successful Twitch channel can 'also require attention to other forms of social media' to grow and maintain one's audience (ibid.: 69). The use of these other platforms can 'accelerate and accentuate the means by which users' generate their Twitch-related brand (Khamis et al., 2017: 199–200) and, if they are so inclined, grow their channel within the aspirational framing discussed earlier. Spilker and Colbjørnsen (2020: 1220) describe this as 'navigat[ing] across platforms', using each one for a different but related purpose and contributing collectively to Twitch-related discussions (cf. Ruiz-Bravo et al., 2022: 3170). As examples, some streamers have dedicated 'subreddits' on mega-forum Reddit (Cullen, 2022a: 108; cf. Küper & Krämer, 2021: 5) and, in a related vein, some Twitch moderators also use other sites, such as co-working environment Slack and internet conferencing software Skype (Lo, 2018: 38).

We therefore see that Twitch's communities of viewers stretch far beyond the single platform and find various manifestations on other sites, most of which are also major internet platforms. Two sites stand out in particular: YouTube and Twitter. Many Twitch streamers put their streams (Ruberg & Cullen, 2019: 90–1) or the highlights of their streams (Speed et al., 2023: 6) onto YouTube (Sixto-García & Losada-Fernández, 2023: 718; cf. Taylor, 2018: 20, 69). This tends to be streamers who are more on the aspirational end of the spectrum (Woodhouse, 2021: 22) but this is not always the case. Uploads made by the streamers themselves and 'compilations' of video clips showing 'streamers receiving large donations' have also become popular on the site (Partin, 2019: 156), again highlighting the centrality of money to Twitch and to how people talk and think about Twitch. Although the liveness of Twitch is one of its strongest features, viewer access via YouTube demonstrates both that many who might be interested in a streamer's content are not necessarily watching on Twitch, and that streamers are aware of this and the more aspirational are making appropriate strategic choices to reach this demographic through recorded, rather than live, video. Twitter also plays a part. Many streamers use Twitter to keep in touch with their fans (Guarriello, 2019: 1759), with many choosing to 'leverage' Twitter for 'public facing modes of interaction with viewers, other streamers, and even sponsors' (Cullen, 2022a: 108). Although at time of writing the future of Twitter is uncertain and unpredictable, it would still be unusual for any larger or aspirational streamer to lack a Twitter presence, and the same is true of many microstreamers as well (cf. Taylor, 2018: 16, 20; Küper & Krämer, 2021: 5; Uttarapong et al., 2021: 8).

Discord, however, is the site most closely associated with Twitch. Discord is 'used by many Twitch streamers' (Sheng & Kairam, 2020: 12) and it is 'common for streamers to set up private or semi-private Discord spaces for their communities' (Cullen, 2022a: 108). Discord has increasingly overtaken YouTube and Twitter for the position of the most important non-Twitch platform that Twitch streamers are utilizing. It is a site that enables streamers or anyone else to create a custom server which can be built around the requirements of its creator and enables people to communicate asynchronously and synchronously by both text and voice. A Discord server – often confusingly known as 'a Discord', as in the sentence 'you can chat to me in my Discord' – can have different forums in which people can talk. This might include one about the Twitch stream itself, one about games the streamer has recently played, one about recommendations for other games, or whatever it might be. Discord had an explicitly 'gamer-oriented branding' (Lo, 2018: 39) from its very first days by presenting itself as a 'home for online gaming communities' (Garcia, 2022: 1), and is recognized as being a 'popular platform for gamers' (Guarriello, 2019: 1756; Gerber, 2022: 3; Robinson, 2023: 82), marketed as having 'especial utility for gaming groups' (Baguley, 2019: 29). Discord servers allow viewers of a Twitch channel and its streamer to communicate beyond Twitch chat itself during a broadcast, and to communicate outside broadcasting times as well. It is this latter point that is especially crucial.

Discords are hence important for our understanding of Twitch's *agora* in several ways. First and foremost, Discord is a way for a Twitch channel's culture, or rather the viewer consumption of that culture, to become ever more central to a viewer's overall online cultural life. Cullen (2022a: 42) notes that the more aspirational live streamer is expected to be 'available to viewers outside of stream time', such as by constructing Discord communities. When a Discord does not exist, a viewer of a given Twitch channel might indeed tune in to view that stream's content during the times it is live, and might perhaps look at recordings of missed streams, but other aspects of their online social life likely take place far away from Twitch. Their interactions with the live streamer and that community are then, unsurprisingly, focused only on when the live streamer is actually conducting a live stream. A viewer interacting with a Discord server, however, means that a larger portion of their online lives then comes to revolve *around the streamer* and their Twitch channel, with the unifying aspect of the Discord – its association with a given Twitch streamer – being a constant presence in all sociality and interaction on that Discord server. This makes Discord an 'auxiliary' method of 'reaching out and communicating' with one's viewers (Brown & Moberly, 2020: 57; Cai et al., 2023: 7) and one which occurs when the streamer is not streaming, and even when the streamer is doing something else, or asleep, or in any other non-streaming situation. Uttarapong et al. (2021: 8) describe how Discord thus 'reside[s] within the ecology of a streamer's community' when streamers are not broadcasting, allowing them to transcend the 'time constraint' of real-time streaming to continue to reach their viewers at other times as well.

This is unsurprisingly likely to keep viewers engaged with, thinking about (even if only subconsciously) and connected to the streamer and their content and their community even when the streamer is not actually live. A Twitch-related Discord server can 'help keep conversation around a channel going, even when the channel isn't streaming' (Sheng & Kairam, 2020: 24). The term 'platform capture' is used in media studies to describe the process of attempting to 'create value by extending the capabilities of a platform' (Partin, 2020: 10), and here we might propose the idea of 'streamer capture' – that Discord servers are a method by which a streamer expands their online influence into a wider part of their viewers' lives and online behaviours. Streamers with successful Discords keep viewers interested in and circulating within their community even when they aren't broadcasting, which is especially noteworthy in the light of my (Johnson, 2021) and others' research showing the pressure streamers feel to be always live and always producing content (Guarriello, 2019; Wulf et al., 2020). The presence of a Discord is a way to address the 'always-on' drive whilst achieving comparable objectives during periods the channel is not active. As I discussed in a previous publication, Discord shows how 'creating a broader ecosystem of media content and online community', with the aspirational streamer at its centre, is an important ambition for many broadcasters (Johnson, 2021: 1010).

Not for the first time in this book we are therefore faced with a question about the extent to which an innovation should be best understood as a strategy – which in this case taps into streamers' desires for channel growth or user loyalty – or as a manifestation of generosity and a desire for sociality, which just happens to also have strategic benefit for the streamer. These questions are central to understanding Twitch communities and cannot be overlooked given the platform's interweaving of play and leisure, celebrity and visibility, and profit and income. Suggesting *all* live streamers are rational and calculating strategists seeking to maximize profit and pursue Twitch as a full-time job is certainly not supported by research data. It would nevertheless be naive to overlook how deeply metrics are built into the streaming experience; the psychological effect these have on encouraging particular 'optimized' behaviours and thought processes among streamers; the compelling nature of live streaming and the pleasures of visibility and attention; the lure of (game) live streaming as a profitable pursuit in an ever-harsher job market for young people and a wider global cultural context where paradigm breakers are praised; and more broadly the widespread cultural ideas around Twitch that emphasize anyone can 'make it'. All these factors take their toll. Like so many other activities on Twitch, a streamer's creation of a Discord server might be an entirely altruistic and positive gesture intended to help like-minded viewers find a place to talk about topics of mutual interest; it might be a wholly strategic and cynical gesture pursued with the goal of further tethering viewers into their channel; it might be a combination, or the latter disguised as the former. Discord is often mentioned by streamers as 'essential' for the offline maintenance of one's live Twitch community (Cullen, 2022a: 184) but that does not allow us to identify motive – simply to acknowledge a widespread practice. Many aspects of Twitch community and culture are unplanned and emergent, yet most – such as the use of Discord – can also achieve particular objectives when deployed by a broadcaster.

Discord also touches on the idea of in-group associations on Twitch. Throughout the book I've discussed some of the methods by which ranking and hierarchies of social status and prestige in Twitch channels are shaped, such as taking on a role as a moderator or through the visibility of subscriber or donation badges (Lo, 2018; Johnson & Woodcock, 2019a; Wohn, 2019). Having a streamer remember one's username is also another way in which a certain user can be seen to stand above others – and given the conflation of *celebrity* and *friend* viewers see when it comes to Twitch streamers, viewers' pursuits of these distinguishing elements are unsurprising (and also strongly encouraged by the platform's design). Discord servers slot neatly into this story, with many streamers making their Discords available only to those who have subscribed to their Twitch channel. This gives subscribers 'greater access to streamers off [Twitch]' (Cullen, 2022a: 32) and such spaces are 'often deliberately made to be a private space for a particular community' (ibid.: 113). Subscribing or otherwise giving money to a Twitch streamer is a way to deepen one's community engagement with that streamer, or the sense of one's place within that community – not just through icons of prestige in the channel itself but also through gaining access to a more private and elite community of people, all of whom have financially demonstrated their interest in the streamer and who stand out from the others watching that channel.

We have therefore seen that Twitch is absolutely replete with both platform systems and cultural practices that reinforce a sense of belonging and a sense of being distinct from those who are not, as the site puts it, 'one of us'. These range from the site's displaying of the length of one's subscription to the detailed codes of emotes (see next section), and from the understanding of in-jokes to the creation and offering of private Discords for the most elite viewers. Twitch is tremendously open to the casual viewer given that it doesn't require a username to view channels and so many channels are shown to the new visitor, yet *also* filled with so many different ways for viewers to separate themselves from others, develop their personal connections to a streamer and a channel and compete, whether implicitly or explicitly, with other viewers for status and ranking within a channel and the community around that channel. The expansion of Twitch communities beyond Twitch itself is emblematic of this, whether through YouTube, Twitter, Reddit or, most frequently, Discord. The last of these does not have the same impact on gaming (yet) that Twitch enjoys, but is growing each year. These additional locations for sociality and belonging serve to connect a viewer more fully into the streamer and the channel, and to reinforce the central role of a Twitch community in their lives – even when they aren't, actually, on Twitch itself.

Twitch culture: emotes

With these ideas of community established, what can therefore be said about Twitch *culture*? One of the most distinctive elements of Twitch culture – and one that has seen its fair share of scholarship and popular commentary – is the use of small pictures in Twitch chat for a wide range of social and personal purposes. On most sites such small icons are known as 'emoticons' or 'emojis' and generally entail an image of a face pulling a particular expression, an animal, some kind of vehicle, a symbol, and other things that are easily recognizable in a small size and few pixels. Emojis written as text – :), :(and the like – were some of the earliest and most iconic examples of internet-based communication. On Twitch, however, only a small number of default emojis are present – such as smiley faces and sad faces – and the overwhelming majority of emojis ('emotes' in Twitch parlance) are unique (Nematzadeh et al., 2019; Dolin et al., 2021; Kim et al., 2022). They do not just serve as additions to viewers' messages but can be the entirety of a viewer's message, and have even accumulated such linguistic complexity around them (Evans & Llano, 2023: 4) that some act as modifiers of tone or meaning and can even do so in many layers (Jackson, 2023a: 103–13), relying on the expertise and in-group knowledge of the reader to fully decode and translate them (Diwanji et al., 2020: 7; Dolin et al., 2021). To understand 'the secret language of Twitch emoticons' (Uszkoreit, 2018: 170) is to understand key aspects of 'meaning within game streaming culture' (Lin et al., 2019: 4) and how this meaning circulates and is constructed by Twitch viewers (and streamers).

Perhaps the most iconic Twitch emote is known as 'Kappa'. This depicts the face of former Twitch and Justin.tv employee Josh DeSeno, whose 'smirking' (Uszkoreit, 2018: 170) visage in the emote appears to be on the verge of breaking out into a smile, yet could also be seen as a little tense or even a little frustrated yet trying to keep a brave or positive face on things. Gaming news and commentary site Polygon suggests that Kappa is the 'starting point' (Alexander, 2018b) for trying to understand Twitch culture and the role that emotes play within it. Although it was originally added to the site as simply one default emote among many, like most of the highly used Twitch emotes it has taken on an entire set of additional meanings and modifiers, and a full understanding of the Kappa emote is of surprising importance for a new visitor to Twitch looking to understand Twitch chat inter-actions. To begin with, the primary meaning of Kappa is sarcasm (Uszkoreit, 2018: 170). On other sites the characters '/s' are sometimes used to denote that what the writer just wrote was intended to be sarcastic – this is often used on Reddit, for example – while in many cases contextual cues and the like are relied on to convey this, as in the physical world. On Twitch, however, the norm has become to use the Kappa emote to denote sarcasm (Payne, 2018: 293) – a viewer will post a message and by including a Kappa in that message, it is universally understood that whatever the viewer said should not be taken entirely seriously. It is a truism that it is challenging to convey *tone* over internet communication (e.g., Reid, 1993; Kalra & Karahalios, 2005) due to the lack of vocal tone, body language, facial expressions and so forth, and here we see emotes serving as an extra mediator that shapes the meaning of the statement being made.

Yet Kappa has also developed many other meanings, some of which are far more subtle and require a user to spend time on the platform to really appreciate, *and* to distinguish from the more common sarcastic use. The degree of cultural understanding that is required here is significant, and usefully compared to identifying homophones and homonyms in one's second language – knowledge of context and how these words are used in everyday speech are often required to distinguish between them. In the case of Kappa, one of these is that the emote can be used to denote irony (Haak, 2021: 283) rather than sarcasm. The emote can be used as part of a viewer offering an ironic riff or comment on something that just happened in-stream, instead of sarcastic praise or a sarcastic insult directed at the streamer. As part of this the Kappa emote, when associated with a message that might be seen as trolling, serves to signal that an otherwise hostile or unpleasant message should not be interpreted through its surface content. This meaning requires the streamer, if they do not wish to be unnecessarily offended, to know Kappa can be used in this way, and to understand whatever message archetype on Twitch the Kappa emote is being used to send up or make fun of. The Kappa emote can in turn *also* be used to denote that the viewer is unimpressed by something – if the streamer performs a failure in their gaming in an amusing or distinctive way, for example, merely posting Kappa by itself (cf. Ford et al., 2017: 859; Catá, 2019: 136) and without any associated words is seen as a humorous way to express disappointment in the streamer's gaming skills. The emote has therefore shifted beyond simply denoting a different register of text, to being used in an entirely contextual manner alongside whatever is happening on the streamed video itself. This constant relationship between the emotes being used – and the challenge of translating and understanding them fully without *also* having the streamed video content to which they relate – is one of the defining features of emote use on Twitch.

Two other key Twitch emotes with many, layered, and less than obvious meanings are 'PogChamp' and 'Kreygasm'. The former originally displayed a picture of a young man pulling an exaggeratedly excited or surprised expression (Johansson, 2021: 50), though more recently has been replaced (Jackson, 2023b) by the head of a Komodo dragon pulling what was deemed by a site-wide poll to be a comparable expression. The latter depicts Justin.tv streamer 'Kreyg' in a pose that is seen as being one of deep pleasure. Both are generally used to denote amazement, surprise, hype or excitement (Barbieri et al., 2017), although much like all emotes on Twitch (and the wider style of humour on Twitch more generally) they can be used sarcastically to make fun of a streamer's excitement over something banal, or to make a tongue-in-cheek suggestion that the streamer should be excited about something mundane. Both of these emotes can be used to show intrigue or interest, such as when a streamer in a game might unlock a new area or make some new discovery – in this regard they can be used as a genuine expression of intrigue, or used by someone to suggest that there is intrigue and interest in something that might be, in fact, mundane. Comparing them to the Kappa emote we see how both can be used in various registers, the serious and the non-serious, but with different kinds of text required alongside to denote these meanings. Messages like 'oh wow you got the powerup [Kappa]' and 'the item!!! [PogChamp]' can convey similar meanings of sarcasm or fake excitement, although only the latter can *also* be read as a genuine expression of joy.

Another emote worth distinct consideration is the 'TriHard' emote, which depicts the face of streamer TriHex expressing happiness or pleasure (as an aside we might note that most of Twitch's leading emotes, not just those listed here, depict male rather than female figures). It is again one of the most well-used emotes on the platform and, again, we see the overlap with the other emotes already covered in this section. However, TriHard is perhaps the most controversial in the history of the platform – PogChamp's face change was relatively well accepted – due to its use as a form of racist harassment (Lo, 2018: 75–6; Evans & Llano, 2023: 4). The streamer Mychal Jefferson whose face TriHard features is black, and the emote has become regularly spammed in Twitch chat in several ways which emphasize this in abusive and negative ways. At the 'milder' end of the spectrum, viewers of a channel might post the emote simply when someone who is black – a streamer, a friend of a streamer, someone else the streamer is watching, a character in a game, someone in an esports tournament, etc. – appears on stream. At the far more overtly hostile end of the spectrum, the emote might be spammed whenever fried chicken, bananas or watermelons are mentioned, or when monkeys or apes might be on stream within a game. Integrating here with the previous discussions of moderation, we see that the use of emotes in this way allows people to express 'offensive sentiments' in 'ways that are harder for filters to handle' (Lo, 2018: 75–6) because emotes allow hostile users on Twitch to readily and easily 'encrypt text metaphorically' (Kim et al., 2022: 1). The use of emotes like TriHard in this way enables one to 'tell a person's politics at a glance on Twitch' (Cullen, 2022a: 193) – at least in a high-level sense – and to make judgements about a viewer that can then lead to moderation decisions (Cai & Wohn, 2021; Li et al., 2023).

The perhaps obvious solution – regular calls exist to ban this emote (Taylor, 2018: 113) – is itself problematic, however, because it suggests the emote in some sense '*has* the racist meaning' and hence 'forecloses the possibility' of alternative ways to use it (Evans & Llano, 2023: 5). The banning of a black face from Twitch's suite of default emotes, especially when few of the default emotes represent marginalized demographics, is very far from ideal. Leaving the emote in, especially since it was originally meant to denote excitement and entertainment and is indeed still used in that way by many (Taylor, 2018: 113), means that it serves to highlight not just the complexity of Twitch's emote system but also the importance of understanding context and setting in the use of any emote. TriHard's unexpected uses for racial harassment are far more toxic than those of most other emotes, but identifying the different meanings is again contingent on understanding the language of the site and situating a specific use in the broader contexts of what the speaker is doing or saying, what's happening in the stream's content, what viewers are doing or discussing at the moment, and so forth.

Emotes are therefore now well acknowledged as a key part of understanding Twitch. However, in keeping with this work's focus on Twitch as a gaming *agora*, I wish to now propose a new understanding of the Twitch emote – as representing a kind of *character* whose culturally accepted behaviours and ways of speaking are adopted and taken on board by a viewer whenever they frame a textual statement within the context of a Twitch emote. Using Twitch emotes is therefore often a kind of roleplaying, except that characters are constructed by all users on Twitch or in a channel rather than by a single person, *and* they can be simultaneously occupied and played by a massive number of people at the same time. This idea is closest to that of Ford et al. (2017), which seems to have prompted comparatively little engagement from the wider Twitch research community despite its value. Ford et al. (2017: 860) describe an approach based on 'voices' that represent 'shared viewpoints or stances', enabling 'several individuals [to] join into a single voice' or one individual to 'adopt multiple voices, switching positions

and roles as the conversation unfolds'. Doing this entails
adhering to 'a consistent viewpoint, syntax, or style of speech'.
To illustrate these ideas they give an example of the 'SMOrc'
emote which depicts an archetypal fantasy 'orc' character,
and is used as a means for viewers to humorously 'shun
advanced game tactics and tactful expression' (ibid.: 866)
and whose shared meaning achieves 'coherence only because
participants and viewers are in the know about gameplay,
the streamer, and the semantics of the emote'. Here I look to
build on these foundations, and in the process convert them
to a more fully ludic framework appropriate to the nature
of Twitch's audience, as well as considering what and how
emotes contribute to conversation in the Twitch *agora*.

Firstly, by using the above ideas we can immediately
appraise what sorts of character each of the emotes represents, and hence how Twitch's viewers are roleplaying when
they adopt that particular stance. The Kappa 'character' is
essentially one whose statements generally represent the
opposite of what they mean. Kappa is a character who
is perennially sarcastic, unimpressed, and who actually by
definition cannot utter a genuine or unironic statement.
Transitioning into this character as easily as simply posting
a common emote (Heikkinen, 2021) allows Twitch viewers –
who are often, of course, trying to post in rapidly moving chat
windows – to explore these sorts of registers which have been
explicitly noted as being *difficult* to ordinarily convey using just
text without physical, body, and tonal information (Reid, 1993;
Kalra & Karahalios, 2005). By putting the lines into the mouths
of characters whose forms of speaking have become well
known and well accepted across the platform, this challenge
is entirely avoided – but only for the knowledgeable user. The
new user faces not the task of structuring their messages in
a way to convey their intended meaning, but rather the task
of understanding what each of these emote characters represents. A statement uttered 'by' Kappa is unlike that very same
statement uttered 'by' another character or a viewer's 'real'

self, just as the same can be said for PogChamp, Kreygasm, and many of the other leading emotes on the platform.

What is also interesting to consider here – especially given the platform's issues with toxicity and harassment discussed previously (and shortly again in the following sections) – is what the use of these characters means for the *responsibility* of users and how they behave on the site. It is one thing to express something unpleasant or disagreeable as oneself, but perhaps another to utilize a site-wide character – especially one of the many who have become coded with ample potential for sarcasm and hostility – to express the same statement. Above I showed how certain emotes can function as ways to potentially transmit abusive and unpleasant messages. Users doing so are not just able to evade automatic detection but are also able to dodge at least some degree of responsibility for their statements via the use of emotes, maintaining – sometimes – the ability to say, if pressed, that they meant nothing hostile by their use of a given emote. In turn the act of expressing through the evoked *characters* also separates the user from their statement, *and* adds a degree of acceptability in statements precisely because all users (streamers and viewers alike) understand these characters and accept the sort of behaviour they normalize and enable as being par for the course and acceptable on Twitch. They simultaneously add a great deal of ease to the sorts of communication that are often difficult over text alone for the reasons discussed above, but they also present a sort of defence for viewers wishing to pursue more hostile behaviours on the platform. With so much of Twitch interaction focused around what I've previously called stream-humour (Johnson, 2022), otherwise nasty things can be readily reframed as being funny, and a streamer can easily be characterized as a spoilsport if they do not explicitly acknowledge such messages as being, supposedly, intended to be amusing.

Yet these characters also allow viewers and streamers who might not know each other well to achieve a startling complexity of language. In more conventional circumstances, meaning, subtlety and truth normally require interlocutors to be familiar with each other's mannerisms and norms, and consequently able to pick out unique traits that indicate the mood of the person sending a message, and therefore how to decode or receive it. Twitch's emotes bypass this lengthy process, requiring viewers to learn nothing about each other – but merely to learn about these characters. Twitch's *agora* is therefore an interesting one where viewers readily switch between roles and characters to convey their responses to events taking place, simultaneously offering something of their self and their own opinions, and a further mutual co-construction of these characters whose existences shape so much of the behaviour on the site. In this way the gaming *agora* of Twitch is actually not quite as open to opinion, perspective and dissension as it might first seem, precisely because so many statements and responses take place *within* the context of these well-established character-like modes of communication. The possibility of using these characters in one's messages and the smooth interaction they facilitate is not the same thing as facilitating *meaningful* or honest interactions. Although the emotes do much to enable faster communication without the risks that other text-based communication suffers, they also constrain and limit the space for possible discourse on the site, as well as putting large amounts of communication within particular, and familiar, boundaries.

This is further complicated when we consider the relationships between emotes and specific channel cultures. Not all emotes are universal and 'global' (Evans & Llano, 2023: 4) across Twitch (London et al., 2019: 56; Cullen, 2022a). Kappa, PogChamp, Kreygasm and TriHard are all available in every channel on the site, but streamers whose channels are above a certain size can create and codify into the Twitch platform their own custom emotes (Nematzadeh et al., 2019; Gerber, 2022: 15; Wolff & Shen, 2022: 9). These take many forms – just as other aspects of a Twitch channel can be heavily customized, a custom emote can feature essentially anything if it doesn't transgress Twitch's norms and guidelines. Nevertheless, despite this potentially immense variety, a number of common custom emote 'categories' can be identified. One category is the custom emote that reflects on a default emote – it might feature the streamer's face doing an impression of a famous site-wide emote, for example. By riffing off 'emote templates' (Jackson, 2023a: 106) these custom emotes then often come to replace the default (Kappa, Kreygasm, etc.) in that one channel. Another category seen in many streams is emotes that denote certain emotions which are *not* generally coded to existing emotes. A common example would be emotes that are designed to evoke some sense of comfort, or relaxation, or a 'cosy' aesthetic. As Youngblood (2022) has noted, a 'cosy' aesthetic is becoming an ever-more popular one on the platform (cf. Ruberg & Lark, 2021), often in stark contrast to both the default assumptions of gamer–gamer interactions being often hostile and combative (cf. Johnson, 2022) and in contrast to many of the behaviours and forms of self-presentation pursued by many of the largest and most influential streamers on the platform. These emotes might therefore contain little figures – people, animals, game characters – hugging each other, or offering a heart, or being curled up in a blanket, and so on. Twitch itself does not really have many default emotes of this sort, but the sheer volume of channels which have comparable emotes shows us how the cultural norms of riffing off *existing* emotes has also led to the idea of riffing off the emotes owned by other channels, with entirely new types of emotes coming into being.

While emotes that clearly reference existing emotes are generally used in the exact same way as the existing ones – so a channel-specific version of Kappa is almost always entirely interchangeable with the usual form of Kappa, although this relationship is strongest in the channel it comes from

– entirely new emotes can lead to the emergence of *new*, channel-specific characters, whose roleplaying possibilities are determined by the nature of the emote. An emote within a given channel whose image entirely references known and accepted cultural touchstones specific to that channel can thus take on any potential characteristics. It might be a character whose use in Twitch chat is intended to denote stupidity, for example, or confusion, or disappointment, or (normally humorous) anger. These then join the existing emotes as offering new forms of speech and new possibilities for leaving comments in Twitch chat, with new registers of comment available to all users through the custom emotes. Yet these *characters* associated with new emotes are, of course, generally only available in the channel they came from (cf. London et al., 2019: 56). A 'generic' custom emote will have some meaning in all channels, such as an emote showing a cute animal and a heart, but a far more obscure custom emote – such as perhaps the custom-made face of a game character that particular streamer made in a particular game, and which caused amusement to their viewers – might be simply confusing in another person's stream. Character-based emote roleplaying on Twitch is therefore further complicated by the place-ness of Twitch streams and the diversity of the site's content, with some characters only functioning in certain streams – or, if you will, in certain stories being constructed by streamers and viewers alike.

To conclude this section, Twitch therefore takes the idea of the emote or emoji further than arguably any other major platform, simultaneously transforming it into an absolutely central and hugely polymorphic tool for communication, and a method for the inscribing and recording of cultural moments and shared ideas and sources of amusement. Emojis outside of Twitch of course also take on new cultural meanings, but when it comes to emotes, this process is both accelerated by Twitch and exhibits a number of additional dynamics on the platform that are not readily seen elsewhere.

Some of these are desirable and facilitate conversation, while others are arguably less desirable and either limit conversation, or enable the sorts of conversations that one doesn't want to enable. Twitch's emote dynamics make it unusually easy to convey meaning and intent across the otherwise very basic facilities of the text- and picture-based chat window, but also delimit what *can* be transmitted due to the finite set of recognized characters and the centrality of those characters to communication. They prevent misunderstanding by giving methods to convey and make sense of sarcasm, irony and related registers, but have to be learned and understood if one is to get a full appreciation of what is taking place here on Twitch. Just as an effectively infinite number of people can potentially sign up to Twitch and begin streaming, there is similarly no obvious upper limit on the number of characters who can be created on the site through the ability to create customized emotes, and the practices and norms through which these become imbued with character-like meaning.

Twitch culture: raiding and copypasta

Emotes are a central element of Twitch culture and a vehicle for the expression of cultural specificity and particularity within a given channel. They can perhaps best be understood as *characters* for Twitch viewers wishing to engage with other viewers or with streamers, and hence present a set of commonly understood speakers (responders?) in the gaming *agora* through which viewers roleplay when they act and interact. They are hence absolutely central to the site, but are not the only cultural aspect of the platform to shape and define how the site functions as an *agora*. Another cultural phenomenon on Twitch with a somewhat comparable role is the practice of *raiding*. Outside of Twitch the term refers generally, in gaming, to a 'collective project' (Golub, 2010: 18) in massively-multiplayer online games involving large numbers of players working together to overcome a shared challenge such as a difficult in-game area or boss. On Twitch, however, raiding refers to both directing one's viewers into another channel, and more recently hosting that channel on one's own channel, a pair of actions that 'significantly increases the numbers of current and potential future viewers' (Jodén & Strandell, 2022: 1982) for the receiving streamer. Raiding is seen as supportive of one's fellow streamers (Wohn & Freeman, 2020) and a way, often, for more successful streamers to support smaller channels that broadcast similar or related content. It is primarily an aspect of Twitch culture designed to bolster connections between streamers, and between different but potentially related groups of viewers, but it also serves several novel communicative purposes. Like raiding in gaming, it is a collective action, but with a different set of objectives in mind.

A raid takes place when one streamer is finishing up a broadcast but still has viewers in their channel. Rather than ending the stream and the viewers dispersing – some going to other channels, some leaving Twitch for the time being, and so on – some streamers will instead choose to 'raid' another streamer (Jodén, 2020: 3). This involves the streamer first giving their viewers a 'raid message', which is something that they are all expected to post (Wohn & Freeman, 2020: 109) in the other streamer's chat once they arrive in the other channel. This might just be something like '[streamer name] raid!', or simply some emotes, but can also be far more involved and convoluted. Once the message has been agreed on, the streamer will then direct their viewers to a channel they have selected to be the recipient of the raid, at which point some percentage of those viewers will move into that new channel and paste the raid message into that channel's chat window. Upon noticing a raid the receiving streamer will generally express appreciation to the sending streamer for directing viewers into their channel – the degree of the praise and appreciation exhibiting a rough correlation with the number of users in the raid, much like on-stream verbal appreciation scaling to the size of donations – and will respond to the raid message, often expressing amusement or appreciation for the wit and cleverness it displays. This sort of behaviour on Twitch generates 'momentary spikes of emotional energy' (Jodén, 2020: 33) and leads to 'excited reactions from viewers' (Jodén & Strandell, 2022: 1982), both those who are transmitting the raid message in going from one channel to another, and the viewers in the channel receiving the raid.

Raiding is thus another quite novel form of communication on Twitch, making the practice worth exploring. A raid message might, for example, be sent from one speedrunning streamer to another speedrunning streamer with a message like 'World record pace!!' alongside some associated emotes. This message might be designed to playfully rib the receiving streamer by both making light fun of a phrase regularly used by speedrunners – denoting that their current speedrun attempt is 'on pace', i.e. currently good enough, to potentially be a world record time – and poking fun at the fact that most speedrun attempts are not of that high calibre. This could be further intensified by the sending streamer perhaps being the one who currently holds the record on the speedrun the receiving streamer is currently attempting, or could be congratulatory and positive if the *receiving* streamer currently holds the world record. Context is the most important thing here – like so much on Twitch (and in gaming culture more broadly), otherwise hostile or aggressive messages are easily seen as neutral or amusing, or even endearing or strengthening to online friendships, in the right settings. Mihailova (2020: 1842) similarly talks about a moment in their study of Twitch when a streamer was assailed by a statement that might ordinarily appear 'mean', but instead yields a 'friendly' response, and one that makes it clear it was received in good humour (Johnson, 2022).

The ability to decode these contexts, much like in the context of emotes, consists of a complex set of understandings around different channels, the sorts of messages sent on Twitch, the relationships (if any) between the sending and receiving streamer, and so forth. What makes raids interesting is therefore the fact that in a raid a streamer's viewers are used to *communicate* something to another streamer, and to do so in a way that is highly public and highly structured by the norms of the site and the relationship between the two individuals. This communication's meaning and import is largely constructed through the fact it is done in a raid rather than by some other means, and by the fact it is a public act rather than a private one. The raid establishes relationships between streamers and between ideas in the large public forum of Twitch, rather than in private messages or personal communication. A streamer could have simply sent a private message to another streamer, but instead a meaning is conveyed through the medium of dozens, hundreds, or even thousands of viewers. A raid is performative and says the same thing as a private message but in a way that might more fully affect a broadcast and the relationship between two streamers' communities, as well as the streamers themselves. In this way viewers become enrolled into the streamer's communicative act, ceasing to be just the receivers of the streamer's statements (and the creation of their own statements in the chat window) but constituents in *what* the streamer has to say to others in their wider Twitch circle, and *how* the streamer says it. This consequently shapes how a streamer is seen by other streamers – as a fun and playful contributor, or someone who perhaps behaves unpleasantly to their contemporaries.

Much like emotes, however, raiding can also be a vehicle for harassment and toxicity on Twitch. This involves the practice now known as 'hate raiding', which is unlike the mutually amusing trolling and provocation described above and instead entails a set of practices specifically designed to bully and intimidate other streamers. Somewhat similar to the harassment directed towards women during the 'Gamergate' campaign in the mid-2010s (Salter, 2018), a hate raid involves multiple viewer accounts, often anonymous, being used to swarm into a streamer's channel and send unpleasant messages into their Twitch chat window. The goal is to launch an attack which 'overwhelms a streamer's chatroom with hateful messages' (Han et al., 2023: 1). In smaller channels this influx of messaging will absolutely swamp the streamer's chat window and overwhelm any 'legitimate' messages, while even in the largest channels it will still be highly noticeable, visible, and disruptive to the channel's normal functioning. At the milder end of things such messages might, on the surface, look not too different from other forms of raiding – the milder hate raids could in the right context even be seen as an edgy and provocative, but ultimately acceptable, kind of playful competition or playful ribbing between streamers who know each other well. These are rare, however, and the overwhelming majority of hate raids are so obviously hostile that they could not possibly be seen in any other way, hurling sexist, homophobic or racist abuse at the streamer and flooding their channel's chat with such messages (Evans & Llano, 2023; Han et al., 2023; Meisner, 2023).

These have become a major issue on Twitch in recent years, with numerous streamers finding themselves harassed by large numbers of attackers, and without an easy recourse when it happens. In 2021 bots on Twitch were 'flooding chats with racist statements, slurs, and offensive words' (Evans & Llano, 2023). Some of these comments were surprisingly close to 'specific forms of subcultural trolling', while others were more overtly 'highly-targeted, hate-driven attacks' (Han et al., 2023: 1) targeted towards queer or ethnic minority streamers (ibid.: 2, 11). Hate raids were and are unfortunately effective at being able to 'circumvent proactive moderation tools' and 'overwhel[m] human labor' (Cai et al., 2023: 16). By the end of 2021 Twitch stated that around fifteen *million* bots participating in hate raiding had been banned, and they had implemented new features to reduce the ability of such bots to successfully function (Evans & Llano, 2023: 4). Yet these alterations to the site's infrastructure and the site's overall response to the problem, especially since the hate raids were targeted almost exclusively at marginalized streamers, were seen as inadequate. This led to significant dissatisfaction with Twitch's 'handling of rate raids' and its 'poor treatment of marginalized-identity streamers' (Han et al., 2023: 2), and the community rallied together, shared 'strategies for managing audiences during attacks' and 'emotional support for peer creators' (Meisner, 2023: 1), staged major protests, and presented 'their views of the platform as unprepared and detached from the community's suffering' (Han et al., 2023: 20).

Both ordinary raids and hate raids therefore use, as described above, particular messages repeatedly typed by the viewers (or bots) moving into a new chat window as a means of conveying an amusing or hostile message. There is also another related practice on Twitch that is nevertheless distinct, and which again shows us how ideas of playful or antagonistic humour circulate on the platform, as well as how this *agora*'s particular functionality and set of possibilities, and constraints, is understood and used by viewers. This is the use of so-called 'copypasta' messages by viewers. Copypastas (as they are known) have seen only the slightest academic study. They are mentioned in passing in two early Twitch publications, with Churchill and Xu (2016) presenting copypastas as 'blocks of text repeated by participants' using the *copy* and *paste* functions on a computer – hence the name – and Seering et al. (2017a: 114) calling them 'long, often nonsensical messages' which viewers 'copy and paste into a chat repeatedly', on Twitch and elsewhere. More recently and in more focused studies of copypastas, they have been defined as 'meme text regularly copied and pasted into forums or chat' (Chamberlain, 2022: 8) and as 'a meaningless block of text' that can only be interpreted by 'the already-initiated' (Topinka, 2022: 392). Like emotes and hate raids they represent another form of communication on Twitch, another way both for streamers and viewers to trade and exchange messages and ideas, but also to step outside the normal forms of communication – streamers saying original things, viewers typing original messages – to reflect on the norms and standards of communication on Twitch. Just as emote-facilitated characters have become standardized forms of Twitch dialogue, copypastas also take on a similar role, with their repetition becoming a key part of communicating on Twitch.

The first thing to note is that when a streamer sees a copypasta turning up in their chat, it is rarely taken 'seriously'. This is a commonality with emote usage and raid messages, both of which demonstrate how stream-humour is 'playful and subversive' (Johnson, 2022: 12) but also sometimes 'chaotic' and 'sarcastic' (ibid.: 16). Instead, the message becomes a topic of discussion. A streamer might therefore say 'that's a really good copypasta!' or 'not that one again!' in the manner and tone of what could almost be called a connoisseur. The streamer presents themselves as arbiters of taste across the full range of copypastas that circulate on Twitch, and the copypasta is thus 'recognized' but 'not read' (Topinka, 2022: 412). Some copypastas are part of a streamer's personal reper-toire or canon and often elicit clear enjoyment and a wry smile when they resurface after time away; others, new, are graded and rated on their amusement value and often on their ability to iterate on and be in conversation with other copypastas. Some others are direct copies of messages that were originally sent with serious intent by their creator, but are now deemed by the community to be so ridiculous or laughable in their attempts to make a stupid point seriously that they have been reframed as a source of amusement. Others can be hostile in nature, such as a copypasta which perhaps attempts to make a negative comment about women gamers, but simply ends up being embarrassing and laughable. Yet other copypastas are written by generally unknown or anonymous authors as deliberate parodies (Topinka, 2022: 396) of such laughable messages, generally involving complaints about a streamer or their gaming ability or their behaviour or the things they say on Twitch.

Such messages – whether 'real' and repurposed, or written in a parody of the real – therefore connect strongly to the kinds of criticism and critique that streamers, especially from more marginalized demographics, are used to receiving. The repositioning of these into a humorous copypasta enables the streamer to shift into a position of (relative) power vis-à-vis such messages (when sent seriously) and to undermine the seriousness of these messages through making them a source of laughter. Chamberlain (2022: 9) notes the 'strong remix tradition in copypasta' with users often 'iterat[ing] on content within the basic structure' and this is also the case on Twitch, with minor changes or alterations to established copypastas often eliciting even greater amusement. Just as emotes are often used to fake seriousness or even fake sarcasm, and raiding is often used to playfully jab at other streamers, copypasta messages are *again* a way for Twitch users to redefine what is serious and what is not. In my previous publication on Twitch's humour dynamics I noted how its cultural norm of transforming seriousness into humour can lead to some quite negative outcomes for many streamers (Johnson, 2022), but here we see the opposite in play, with the reframing into humour being a form of defence and *support* for live streamers as a whole. Given the serious issues of harassment and toxicity on Twitch, the possibility of such psychological defences through humour merits further research.

With emotes I showed how they require readers to be in the know and can facilitate communication between those who are, but also the risk of repetition and iteration due to the limitations of the established characters who dominate the use of emotes in Twitch chat. Similar dynamics can be observed in the context of copypasta. These repeated blocks of text represent a 'repetitive, performative anti-discourse that discharges affect through *contribution* rather than *content*' (Topinka, 2022: 395, emphasis mine) – or to put it another way, the information in a copypasta is not meant to be read as text which is primarily about its apparent semantic content, but rather should be seen as a single unit, a single item, like a page from a book or a few clips from a film which have been removed from their 'intended' context to the point that they no longer contain any of that original sense. In emphasizing the historical antecedents of the practice, Topinka (2022: 394) calls the copypasta 'a bizarre, overlooked, and yet foundational digital form' and although a study of the practice going back decades is beyond the scope of this book, it is certainly all of these things in the context of Twitch, let alone in the context of the wider internet. Just as emotes facilitate rapid communication and amusement on the site while also shaping the potentials of conversation, copypastas adopt a similar role of simultaneously making easier, and perhaps making more constrained, the possibilities of discussion on Twitch.

To summarize, in these cultural practices – emote characters, raids and copypasta – we have seen that humour is a central part of Twitch culture, alongside and as a vehicle for the communication of affect and the display of in-group membership. Understanding how humour (Johnson, 2022) manifests on Twitch, what forms it takes and how it is deployed, and to what *purposes* it is put, are all essential for making sense of the platform's dominant practices and how the site functions as a gaming *agora*. Many of the dynamics that form the core of wit, comedy and amusement on Twitch can be potentially quite hostile and even exclusionary, reinforcing existing power dynamics and often attacking marginalized streamers. The humour that many streamers deploy is often antagonistic and can play off serious moments in games by transforming them into jokes, as well as riffing off the idea of 'toxic' behaviour where the riffing and the self-referential nature of these jokes itself becomes a form of humour. Streamers are highly adept at finding ways to capture critiques and transform them into humour, as well as seemingly possessing a deep understanding of the ability for comedy to grow their channels. Yet humour can also be a source of power for streamers who feel ground down by spam or hostility, allowing broadcasters to step outside the potential intensity of those discourses to instead see many of these messages as laughable or even pitiable. It serves also as a means of communication between streamers and within specific channels, with humour facilitating much of the social behaviour on Twitch both for good and for ill. Humour therefore serves as a valuable site for us to study the contestation of cultures on Twitch and to understand the different ideas of being a gamer that are being fought out on the site.

Tones and norms of the agora

In this chapter my goal was to build on the pieces laid in the previous three chapters to explore the communities of Twitch and the cultures that have emerged on the platform. I hope to have shown that both are crucial for understanding what takes place on Twitch, but also for appreciating the idea of Twitch as a gaming *agora*. One of the key insights here, building on my previous publication on Twitch humour (Johnson, 2022), is the central role played by viewers' speech acts which do not mean what they appear to on the surface. One might quite reasonably think that for an *agora* this would be an issue. Many scholars – not to mention many users – perennially note the difficulty in conveying meaning and tone through online communication when the tone required is anything other than the most surface or direct understanding of a word or sentence (Reid, 1993; Kalra & Karahalios, 2005). People with shared histories learn the tones of one another, and other options – such as the '/s' phrase to denote sarcasm unambiguously – have been trialled, and of course some common emoticons such as the raised eyebrow or the laughing face can be used to similar effect. On Twitch, however, a range of different norms and practices has emerged for stepping outside the apparent surface content of a message, and instead stating or playing with the idea of stating something very different instead. Many of the most used emotes convey similar transitions of language from serious to joking, and other practices on Twitch do similar. Twitch thus exhibits what is almost a consistent background noise of sarcasm, irony, light-hearted trolling (cf. Phillips, 2015), and statements whose true and generally not unpleasant meanings require a strong working knowledge of the site or specific channels, and a situational awareness around tone, event and circumstance (Jackson, 2020). Some of these apply across the entire site while others apply within specific channels or communities, but all display complex understandings of the different layers of meaning which take place on Twitch, as well as the central role of non-seriousness.

I have thus tried to illustrate in this chapter the *new forms of communication* on Twitch by which the various members of the *agora* communicate with each other and express their views. Twitch scholarship has to date tended to focus on how streamers talk to their viewers and present their streams, and the textual comments that viewers leave in chat. All of these are essential components, but although a handful of papers have touched on the roles and use of emotes in chat, the further development I propose in this chapter – to identify emotes as representing characters that Twitch viewers elect to roleplay – has not until now been fully elucidated. In this chapter I hope to have therefore shown how these emotes are used to immediately transition a viewer's writing into the character depicted by a given emote, and in doing so enables much faster communication than is otherwise the case on many other online text platforms, *and* communication that can achieve a surprising degree of depth and nuance. In turn we must actually regard these emote-transmitted characters as being, in a certain sense, speakers in their own right.

These are ethereal speakers collectively constructed by all of Twitch's users as well as the site's affordances, and although they enable viewers to speak in many different ways to streamers and to each other, the fact that so much written discourse on Twitch takes place through them must, itself, be at least some cause for concern. The use of emote characters does *limit* what can be said on Twitch to statements that make sense for the character being used, in some cases with the limits being specifically tethered to individual channels. Channel-specific characters – like much else – do work to define what makes one channel a distinct place compared to another, but also to potentially exclude outsiders. Again, we would be right to worry about what such limitations mean for speech and the exchange of ideas in an *agora*, especially one where these dynamics can often reinforce existing issues of marginalization.

This observation and the final point to be made here brings us full circle from the very first paragraphs of the first chapter of this book – the sense of Twitch as an in-group, and the idea of the user as being already 'one of us' through their gaming experience before they ever start spending time on the platform. The communities and cultures described here are sometimes vast in size, reaching across the entire platform, and sometimes much smaller and focused on a particular stream – yet all come with a distinct set of norms and private knowledge which the outsider cannot easily gain access to, but whose understanding and manipulation marks out someone on the inside from someone on the outside. A knowledge of gaming *is* on one level sufficient to engage with Twitch, but the site has seen the birth or the refinement of many different forms of communication, simultaneously promoting the ability to rapidly and easily interact in potentially complex ways with relatively little effort, while also potentially undermining the variety and depth of what is actually being said. I therefore conclude that we should see Twitch as a space that is tremendously inclusive to those who already have the prerequisite cultural knowledge – many are, indeed, already 'one of us' – but just as exclusive to outsiders as other aspects of gaming already are. While Twitch does allow a viewer without gaming expertise to quietly spectate and learn about the culture, something far less possible in the actual *play* of games, this is counterbalanced by the extra set of norms and behaviours and practices which are distinct to Twitch and build on top of the already complex terminologies and behaviours associated with gaming more generally. Twitch's *agora* is a strange and challenging one, both very open and very closed, very flexible and very unyielding, and both very broad and very narrow in its scope and focus.

Conclusion

Twitch as the agora

In writing this work I had two key objectives.

The first was to update our understanding of Twitch, an internet platform of significant size and reach which is changing at a sufficiently rapid pace to merit an updated overall account of its nature and functions. Much of Twitch has remained largely unchanged since Taylor's (2018) monograph on the platform, yet much *has* changed. Twitch's ideology of 'one of us' remains attractive to game streamers and game viewers alike. The relationship between these users has instrumental aspects but also affective aspects – viewers want closeness and proximity, to feel part of a community, to be interacting with a friend (the streamer) and a celebrity (again, the streamer). Live streaming has emerged as a viable and in some cases very lucrative career (provided the time and effort are put in), financed through both the altruism of massed online spectators and comparatively rare but sometimes quite profitable commercial sponsorships. Gaming streams on Twitch have moved further and further away from a focus on esports and further towards being personality-driven, massively diverse in terms of the games played, and ever more focused on the formation of communities and the emergence of channel-specific cultures, forms of communication, in-group norms and styles. The nature of the platform – with relatively low-key governance and regulation and an emphasis on self-moderation – promotes a more personalized, permissive and freewheeling style than most other contemporary platforms, but also exhibits relatively little concern at the less acceptable ways some people use its functionality. As the platform has become far more integrated into flows of online currency, streamers securing and displaying financial support through donations, subscriptions and sponsorships becomes a key and highly visible part of essentially all of the largest channels.

Yet game live streaming is no longer the whole story. In recent years non-gaming streams have exploded in popularity on the site, showing the pleasure that viewers can get from watching creative practices, chatting and conversations, trips to real-world locations, quasi-erotic body-oriented streams, or even watching others playing real-money gambling. Several of these developments have generated significant controversies and resentment among Twitch gaming users, demonstrating both that understanding the platform as being solely for *game* live streaming is no longer an exhaustive definition, and that understanding Twitch actually helps us understand broader dynamics in gaming culture relating to gender and race and sexuality, the politics of games and gaming, competitive and non-competitive gaming, the sociality and communities surrounding gaming, the monetization of play, the possibility of gameplay careers and, most centrally of all, the ever-growing role that *spectating* plays in digital gaming. Spectating has always been part of gaming but has surely never been so central and so fundamental as it is today, in large part because of Twitch (and, also, YouTube). In looking at these various pieces of the jigsaw I hope to have given a full picture, drawn from contemporary scholarship, of what Twitch is today, what happens there, who does it, how they do it, what it is as an internet platform, and how it is evolving.

The second primary objective was to propose that Twitch should now be understood as perhaps the most important gaming *agora* we have. This perspective opens up our ability to understand Twitch's ability to identify, debate, moderate and shape matters of consequence and importance in gaming, and our ability to understand how speakers, different modes of speech and different topics – to continue the metaphor – co-exist and compete on the site. The concept of the *agora* in ancient Greece related to a town square in which debates were held and matters of importance were settled. Throughout the work I have tried to both demonstrate the striking degree to which Twitch now occupies and offers an *agora*-like role within the wider gaming community, but also how this *agora* is complex, contested, far from neutral, exists on a platform with specific infrastructural and technical decisions, and is shaped by the power of money and metrics on Twitch, and numerous social and cultural elements of the broader world of the internet and gaming. Yet the *agora* comparison is a sound one – as Camp (2016: 304) notes, the creation of the ancient *agora* was a 'process rather than an event' and this is once again reflected in Twitch's unplanned emergence from Justin.tv, without any deliberate, top-down, strategic measure or decision. In turn, just as those who 'spoke well and effec-tively' in the ancient *agora* 'gained power' (Eble & Breault, 2002: 317), the same can be said of the striking number of highly influential gaming celebrities we see now at the very 'top' of Twitch, exerting influence not just on the site but throughout a wider web of connections into other internet platforms, and even into games companies themselves.

Collectively Twitch's streamers, viewers and moderators now tell us what is happening in gaming: what's up, what's down, and what *matters*. Competitive gaming broadcasts have always done this to some extent, but this practice and this impact have now expanded massively across the other sorts of gaming channels to be found on the site. Where Taylor's (2018) work focused on the blurring of public and private play through individual esports streamers, I have instead sought to take a step 'back and out' to look at the *collective* effects of these millions of (mostly game) streamers and these hundreds of millions of viewers. What effects are they exerting on gaming culture and what role has Twitch now come to find itself occupying within the digital gaming world? Gaming has established itself comfortably as one of the pre-eminent media formats of the twenty-first century, and Twitch has taken on a number of roles within this context. All these public streams and public displays of gaming activity are not simply important and intellectually intriguing when thinking about how games are played or the experiences of the streamers and viewers assembled in a given channel, but *also* represent a much larger transformation in how important matters in gaming are created, displayed, resolved, understood, consumed and contested. Twitch has come to the fore in an era where internet celebrities are taking on more importance and prominence than ever before – most obviously in the context of the so-called 'influencer' emerging as a new category of online figure – and influencer dynamics are emerging not just in 'top' streams but also in the channels of microstreamers as well.

What we therefore see is that Twitch has led to an unprecedented degree of game spectating and an unprecedented *position* for game spectatorship within gaming culture as a whole. Framing Twitch as an *agora* allows this position to be understood in terms of the functions the site now increasingly serves for gaming and for 'gamers' – particular modalities of visibility for players and games, the shaping and reflection of matters of importance, a place for debate and discussion, and so forth. Thanks largely to Twitch's *agora*, game spectatorship is no longer something comparatively private and small scale, but now something massive and public enough to exert an influence on other aspects of gaming ranging from game design and the games industry, to the emergence of gaming celebrities and the pursuit of gaming careers. The site has become a major player in the world of computer gaming, and one whose effects are arguably only growing with each passing year. Yet although Twitch is first and foremost a platform for live streaming gaming, and has transformed our understanding of game spectatorship, it is not only that. In recent years a wider variety of live streamed activities has become available – artistic and creative streams, gambling channels, Hot Tub broadcasts, chatting, visiting and eating at restaurants, and more – raising questions about what Twitch is for. Two clear components can be identified here. As a company Twitch wants to continue recruiting game streamers and banking the attendant income, but it is also more than happy to accommodate other forms of live streaming, especially when they too bring in large numbers of viewers and healthy income.

Although many gamers are less than enthusiastic about this, this is in fact wholly consistent with Twitch's evolution as a gaming platform. There was no grand plan and no mission statement to achieve its current position – this all happened organically as a function of the growth in popularity of game spectatorship. We now see other forms of stream also achieving popularity, but in this case only *after* Twitch has risen to global prominence on the back of its gaming channels, and the hundred million or so people using the site for that specific purpose. *Defining* the nature of a website at the time of its creation is not the same thing as seemingly *changing* the nature of that website after norms and expectations have been established – although I would argue that little has in fact changed, even while it clearly appears that way to many users – and the tension here over what Twitch's *agora* is for helps to explain much of the frustration that users seem to feel. In the same way the increasing displeasure many users feel over Twitch's monetization schemes – and how much it seems to be focused on profit rather than community – suggests a tension between visions of Twitch as a platform *for gaming* (in which some people make money), and as a platform for *making money* (which some people do via gaming).

Throughout the work I have highlighted the central role of money to Twitch, and here in this final chapter another valuable point can be made. All these astonishing volumes of donations, subscriptions, sponsorships and the like – what do they add up to? The answer is that the parts of these financial contributions taken by Twitch, rather than its streamers collectively, make Twitch a valuable window for understanding the major economic and strategic roles that gaming properties now play in digital business more broadly. It is always surprising to remind oneself that the digital gaming industry now makes more profit each year than the music industry and the film industry *combined*, and the largest games companies producing the most financially successful blockbuster or mobile games make huge profits and pay corporate CEO salaries to rival most banks or hedge funds. Much of the gaming world has consequently long seen takeovers, mergers and acquisitions, and gaming companies are increasingly sought after by non-gaming tech companies. Most visible in the last few years has been the ongoing attempted purchase of games company Activision-Blizzard – itself obviously the result of a merger evidenced in its double-barrelled name – by Microsoft. Twitch itself was taken over by Amazon in 2014 and its nature as a primarily gaming site, and the immense amount of money that flows through it, show us that gaming has reached a point where even the largest tech giants on the planet can enhance their portfolios of companies through seizing some of these gaming-led profits. For an industry that famously began with bedroom coders posting floppy disks in Ziploc bags to gamers who mailed them a cheque, this is an extraordinary transformation for the gaming sector.

What does it therefore mean for perhaps the foremost gaming *agora* to be owned and controlled by a vast corporate edifice? Twitch shows us what the tech giants are really looking for in the acquisition of new platforms and profit streams, and the strategies being pursued in trying to expand into the gaming sphere. Twitch's disappointed streamers and viewers are not 'wrong' to express discontent at the platform's consistent decisions to take an unusually large portion of streamer revenue and to enable forms of content – like gambling channels – that many find objectionable, but it does perhaps suggest that there is no widespread clarity about where and how Twitch fits into the wider platform ecosystem, how profit is made for investors and shareholders in this ecosystem, and where the actual users of a platform – even those who make their living on it – really fit in. I do not mean to suggest Twitch's users are naive about the business dimensions of the website, given that it is very publicly and visibly owned by one of the largest companies and richest men on the planet, but there does seem to remain on the site a degree of wistful optimism that, each time the site does something objectionable, *this* will be the last time before it wakes up and realizes how much these decisions are frustrating its users. The fact that Twitch has transformed many elements of gaming and facilitated the creation of perhaps millions of gaming micro-communities, as well as tens of thousands of jobs and uncountable billions of hours of entertainment, does not change the bottom line: Twitch is a property in a larger portfolio, in a context of a massively more corporatized gaming industry, and all involved would do well to keep this in mind.

Where is Twitch going?

Despite some dubious decisions in recent years Twitch is arguably the dominant *agora* in contemporary digital gaming – a place where matters of importance are discussed, where even the nature of importance is decided, and where gaming celebrities find an unparalleled amount of visibility, influence, and closeness to their fans. We should therefore think about the future of Twitch, and the future of game live streaming. Where is all of this *going*?

One of the most important elements when we consider the future of Twitch is the question of whether Twitch will remain the (essentially) monopolistic actor in game live streaming, at least in most countries. There are many other ways to stream live game content and platforms like Facebook, YouTube,

TikTok, Steam and others have functionalities comparable with Twitch. Other major internet platforms, especially in China, allow and sometimes centre on the live streaming of gaming – Douyu being the primary and most-researched example (e.g., Zhang & Hjorth, 2019). These are not the focus of this work, nor do some have much reach outside of their home country and their native language group. Most other platforms lack the intricate user-retaining ecosystem that we have described on Twitch (ranking, badges, emotes, links to private Discords, etc.) throughout this work when it comes to attracting people and keeping their interest in game live streaming, and also do not attempt to discursively position themselves in a primarily or exclusively *game* streaming context. They also lack the wider global impact Twitch can confidently claim to have enjoyed, as well as often having administrative or even legal requirements – such as the registering of a real name and ID to stream – that would seem over-the-top on Twitch or elsewhere. For most of the planet the idea of *game streaming* is ultimately synonymous with Twitch, and it is therefore useful to ask whether or not this state of affairs will continue; if it does, what this means for gaming and for Twitch; if it doesn't, what *that* would mean for gaming and for Twitch; and whether or not the gaming *agora* described in this book is one that could only appear on Twitch with its specific infrastructures and cultures, or whether it perhaps instead represents the first iteration of something that could eventually mutate, elsewhere, into other forms.

Firstly, YouTube would appear to be the primary competitor to Twitch. This is the case in two main ways, each of which is interesting and worth a brief consideration. The first and most obvious challenge is the fact that YouTube is already the primary website for the sharing of recorded (i.e., not live) gaming video. I have already noted that Twitch and YouTube currently complement each other – the latter being a repository for recorded broadcasts and interesting moments from the former – but we also currently see more direct forms of competition. Whereas early sharing of gaming videos took place across a wide range of contexts and sites, YouTube is essentially now the *sine qua non* for sharing one's *recorded* gaming content with others, or watching whatever other people have shared. There is as ever some overlap here with sites like Facebook and TikTok on which one can readily find gaming videos, but YouTube's position for recorded gaming videos is presently as strong as Twitch's position for their live-streamed equivalents. This makes YouTube an obvious and key site for those wanting to consume video gaming content of any type, and could make it easy for people to notice and transition into live gaming streams on YouTube. Yet YouTube's comments sections do not come even close to the degree of community construction – whether culturally or in terms of infrastructure – that is provided on Twitch, and nor does YouTube show much indication of developing these, even in its current live gaming offering. Elements that have been fundamental to the growth of Twitch, the growth of live streaming in all its manifestations, the career and life opportunities available to streamers, and the emergence of Twitch's *agora* qualities, have yet to appear on YouTube in any significant fashion. YouTube has also, as I finish writing this book, made clear their intention to heavily promote adverts on the site going forward, a decision presently creating (much like on Twitch) a great deal of backlash.

The second aspect that makes YouTube a potential competitor to Twitch lies in the politics surrounding both platforms, particularly the negative press that Twitch has received in recent years and how YouTube has consequently come to be discursively positioned by many Twitch users as a possibly valuable and viable alternative. One of the most visible of Twitch's unpopular decisions was the change to the amount of revenue that streamers can generate. This was taken down to half of subscriptions for even the most successful streamers (Pequeño, 2023), a revenue share for creators that remains small compared to almost any other similar platform. It was later partly raised for some streamers who consistently meet certain targets – metrics, again – and this appeared to be a measure looking to partly downplay the negativity generated by the previous choice. Another was Twitch's sudden change to sponsorship rules on the platform which would have severely limited how many successful streamers earn income (Hatmaker, 2023). The platform again rolled these back within days, but the same hard-to-dismiss discourse on Twitter and other social media platforms – that Twitch is ever more concerned solely with short-term profit rather than the long-term sustainability of the site or the lives of those who use it – was again extremely visible. During both controversies streamers moved over to YouTube, often for one stream a week or something equivalent, to protest (compare this against the Hitbox incident described below). The existence of YouTube's game live streaming functionality seems to offer streamers a way to express displeasure and frustration with Twitch, but at the time of writing it appears that most of these protests have fizzled out, and users have returned to Twitch for all rather than just most of their streams. Nevertheless, increasing negativity towards Twitch is a potentially important trend in how users view the platform – many users seem to see the site's monetization focus and practices to be a threat to its longer-term cultural and communal viability.

YouTube is not, however, the only other live streaming platform that might challenge Twitch in the future. 'Kick' launched in 2022 via funding associated with Stake.com, a major online casino site notable for its widespread use of cryptocurrency. The site appears to be in part driven by a desire to escape Twitch's (hardly restrictive) rules and guidelines (D'Anastasio, 2023). Within days real-money gambling content became extremely popular on Kick, but of consequence is the fact that this was coupled with a highly publicized change to the revenue share that streamers collect. On Twitch only around half of all money paid to a streamer actually reaches the streamer, whereas Kick proudly noted that almost all direct financial support goes straight to the streamer. Twitch has also been increasingly pushing advertising income and it remains to be seen what Kick will do in this regard, or the extent to which Kick's owners will continue to foot the bill for running the site. Much of the other discussion surrounding Kick also emphasized the value of so-called 'free speech' – as imagined by the growing numbers of internet users who think more consequence-free hatred in popular discourse is a desirable thing – and a desire to construct a live streaming platform that was not as risqué as an adult content site, for instance, but certainly more comfortable with potentially controversial content than Twitch. During the writing of this book Kick has recruited world-famous streamers to its site in highly touted multi-million-dollar deals, seemingly copying the failed strategy of now-defunct Twitch challenger Mixer (2016–2020). The future of Kick remains uncertain, but its combination of gambling streams and edgier gaming streams, combined with the apparent political interests of some of its streamers and viewers along lines of libertarianism, NFTs,*** cryptocurrency and 'free speech' absolutism, makes it a site that could potentially cleave off a portion of Twitch's userbase who feel themselves constrained even by the site's already lax enforcement policies.

Yet YouTube and Kick are not the first time that another site with game live streaming capability has seen keen interest from streamers becoming disheartened or disillusioned with Twitch. In 2013 one of Twitch's first major 'incidents' occurred when a staff member and site-wide moderator known as 'Horror' rose to sudden controversial prominence after removing a number of custom emotes from a streamer. Users later discovered that a different

*** NFTs are so-called 'non-fungible tokens', which are blockchain-recorded identifiers of what adherents claim is the uniqueness and even the ownership of digital items.

site-wide emote had been implemented as a 'personal favour' (Hernandez, 2013) to Horror despite breaking the exact same rules Horror had removed other emotes for apparently violating. There is here an interesting echo of the 'Gamergate' harassment campaign against women in games, infamously spawned by the claim that female game developers received unfairly positive reviews from male games journalists. Just as Gamergaters perceive(d) gaming as being an idealized 'meritocracy free of cultural bias' (Dowling et al., 2020: 993) where nobody should get 'special treatment' (Easpaig, 2018: 128), the backlash against Horror demonstrates a surface similarity that highlights gamer resentment of anything seen as *unearned* or *unfair*. Given the meritocracy of gaming (Paul, 2018) and the continued emphasis for many gamers on high skill and high ability, this is perhaps unsurprising. In this case such apparent favouritism soon spiralled to the point where many streamers made harassing and abusive comments towards Horror and were swiftly banned for this, but then even users making harmless comments, merely asking about the controversy or suggesting that Horror was abusing their powers, were likewise banned by this moderator, who Twitch later said 'should have recused himself' for being too close to the situation (Hernandez, 2013). During this period many popular streamers moved onto Twitch's then-competitor 'Hitbox' for a couple of days as a protest, with that site almost buckling under the sudden influx of streamer and viewer traffic. In the end, once Horror had been removed from their staff, streamers – especially those whose accounts had been banned and were now unbanned – returned to Twitch.

I know at present of no study specifically addressing the Hitbox incident – though it would make for a valuable piece of live streaming scholarship – but the most important point here is what the incident can tell us about the dynamics of Twitch users in the context of a highly dominant platform that does, nevertheless, exist in a space with other potential competitors. The initial shift *towards* Hitbox (much like towards YouTube more recently) must be understood as primarily a discursive move and an expression of community power and ability to shape the changes they wanted to see on Twitch. Doing so articulated the idea that users did not have to put up with Twitch's behaviour and the seemingly significant and unwarranted power given to an individual who evidently could not be 'trusted' with it, and the idea that Twitch *needs* users and that collective action is a way to elicit changes in the platform's management and governance. The shift to Hitbox was highly effective due to both the number of streamers who moved but also, crucially, the number of *famous* streamers who made the shift and the number of users who followed them, seemingly wrapped up in the excitement of it all and being part of a major – if temporary – movement of resistance to a major internet platform. The anti-Twitch comments made by viewers throughout this period were startling in how rapidly they appeared, how common they were, and how quickly they faded after the brief sojourn was over.

The rapid *return* to Twitch, however, was primarily a practical and instrumental move, even though the rebellion itself found its roots in the political and the discursive. The return was an acknowledgement not so much that Twitch had addressed the problem but more to do with the fact that Hitbox lacked much of the infrastructure of Twitch as well as lacking equivalents of the Twitch metrics of time and achievement (donations, subscription icons, etc). Had Hitbox had some of this infrastructure already in place it is possible, although still not likely, that the event would have played out differently. Without this infrastructure Hitbox was doomed to simply be a receptacle for the frustrations and resentments of Twitch streamers and Twitch viewers at that exact moment, but never really a serious competitor. These two facets – the ideological resistance to a monopoly platform demonstrated in the move to Hitbox, and the pragmatic acceptance demonstrated in the rapid return to Twitch – speak volumes about how difficult it is for another platform to mount a serious resistance against a dominant and well-established competitor. Twitch is not just synonymous with game streaming but has, as we have noted, a range of techniques for connecting its streamers and viewers closely to the platform through the scope for person-alization of channels, the conception of channels as places and communities, the affective styles of streamer and viewer interactions, the techniques for channel- and site-specific communication, the ubiquity of compelling metrics, the ability for viewers to signal their commitment to a channel, techniques for streamers to easily monetize their broadcasts, the capacities and functionalities of the *agora* including its ability to accommodate innovation, and a lot of cultural cachet in gaming constructed over a decade.

Even if a full move to another platform for Twitch's community seems unlikely in the near future, the blurring *between* platforms is also an important factor to consider here when we wonder about the future of Twitch. When attempting to describe to my students the difference between the internets of our respective youths, one of my go-to sentences is to suggest that the internet I grew up with had 'a thousand sites with one purpose each', whereas their internet features 'a few dozen sites which each do a hundred different things'. These numbers are not intended to be precise, of course, but readily get across one of the major trends we have witnessed in the past few decades – that of platform envelopment (Eisenmann et al., 2011), or as it has also been called, platform capture (Partin, 2020). This is a phenomenon through which an existing internet platform expands the total services it offers to its users, in the process both brushing up against and sometimes pushing out of the market other sites which only offer a given service. One of the key appeals to the user in this context is the ability to do more on a single platform than before, thereby reducing the amount of time spent changing sites, remembering multiple passwords, inputting payment details over and over, and so forth – it becomes a 'one-stop shop'. There are many examples but one of the most obvious is Twitch's owner. Amazon began as an internet bookseller, and now sells almost any legal good one might imagine, creates artificial intelligences and home security systems and billion-dollar television shows, and sends people into space on specialized rocket ships. This is the most extreme example, of course, but far from unique.

In the context of Twitch we can see the possibility of platform envelopment in recent hints that Twitch itself might be looking to expand into other areas. A leak from a few years ago suggested that Twitch was in the process of developing its own gaming platform, not just game streaming platform, which would envelop some of the functionality of a major market-leading platform like Steam. Twitch naturally intend(ed?) this to boost and further cement their market share and market position by having people do more of their gaming activities on Twitch rather than elsewhere, but it also carries a risk. In the reduction of the *distinctiveness* of Twitch – framed as a site for (game) live streaming and almost nothing else – such envelopment procedures also carry a possibility of reducing the site's *focus* on streaming. Right now Twitch is the only place for live streaming and nothing else; if that blurs, who is to say that its central selling point might not become obscured, allowing for greater competition in that market? Twitch's expansion or return into non-gaming content is already contested enough by broadening the question of what the site is 'for', and an expansion into the buying and downloading of games as well as their broadcast might well have a similar effect. What we therefore see across these factors is that Twitch's current position and status in the gaming world are not guaranteed to continue indefinitely. Like past internet giants, Twitch's status is powerful but not unassailable. Continuing to emphasize company profit over community support as it has in recent years will do little to strengthen the site against growing competition. What seems certain, however, is that now gaming has experienced such a live *agora* for shaping and reflecting matters of importance, that *agora* will not be going away. For the foreseeable future at least, that *agora* remains Twitch. Only time will tell whether Twitch will strengthen its lead position, or in fact unintentionally lay the groundwork for a diverse range of similar platforms to follow in its wake, building on the distinctiveness and uniqueness of such a vast (gaming) *agora*.

The future of Twitch research

When I first started looking into Twitch the better part of a decade ago, fewer than half a dozen academic articles could be found. Writing now in 2023 there are many hundreds from a variety of disciplines, a substantial and I hope representative portion of which can be found in this book's bibliography. Twitch research has come remarkably far, yet the hundreds of publications on Twitch pale in comparison with the thousands we see examining platforms like Twitter, YouTube or Facebook. These platforms are indeed a little more popular, but such numbers tell us less about the relative importance of one platform or another, and more about the sheer immensity of the task involved in researching *any* of them. We are forced to contend with the fact that modern internet platforms with hundreds of millions of users are entire universes for research unto themselves. So much of online social life is taking place on fewer and fewer sites with more and more users or consumers on them, and this means that these sites are acquiring greater importance in our understanding of the internet with every passing year. Important major themes of Twitch have been identified and pinned down but the sheer size of the site means that so much of Twitch remains unexamined – and the site and its users are always mutating and changing with every passing month. Nevertheless, a near-decade of studying the site as almost my sole academic research concern does suggest a number of obvious key research directions for the future of understanding Twitch; three in particular seem clear omissions in the present body of academic understanding.

Perhaps the most glaring and understudied – almost unstudied – aspect of Twitch that merits our attention is the role of specific games on Twitch. The reader might pause at this moment and note that I've talked about games, gaming and gamers on Twitch in every chapter of this book, and you would not be wrong – but the actual games *themselves* being played on Twitch, and how they shape what goes on in a stream, remain curiously understudied. How are streams shaped by games in which one dies a lot (or rarely), or games that are fast (or slow?), or games which are easy or hard for a viewer to understand, or games which are niche or popular, or games with particular themes, or games that are old or new, games which are controversial or well loved, games which are clear or confusing, or games which are innovative or predictable? I suspect that simply in reading the previous sentence the reader immediately begins to develop some hypotheses in answer to these questions, yet essentially none of this has been studied. It is as if the games themselves on Twitch have been so completely taken for granted as the unquestioned or assumed raw material for everything *else* – the sociality, the community and culture, the flow of money, the experiences of streamers and viewers, the wider politics of the platform – that they have been almost entirely overlooked. Only a handful of publications have really engaged with this topic through esports, speedrunning and challenge runs (Scully-Blaker et al., 2017; Carter & Egliston, 2021; Jackson, 2023a: 319–37), but such gaming is comparatively rare on modern Twitch. In our rush to understand the platform, a part of its very core has been omitted from research – so compelling are the platform's other complexities – yet a full understanding of the contributions that different sorts of games make to the Twitch experience seems certain to yield vital new insights.

The second key research direction I would expect to see

expanding in the coming years is further study of non-gaming
behaviours on Twitch. The relationship between gaming and
non-gaming on Twitch has been one of the questions I have
addressed in my exploration of the politics of Twitch and
contestations over what the site should really be 'for'. On the
one hand, gaming remains the central part of Twitch in terms
of user numbers and wider cultural associations about what
Twitch really entails, yet on the other, non-gaming streams
have become increasingly popular and influential – and
controversial – on the site, complicating our ideas about the
site and the relationship between gaming and other cultural
practices. Despite the rise of these non-gaming streams and
the increasing influence they exert on the site, these channels
have seen relatively little study to date, although some initial
engagements exist (e.g., Faas et al., 2018; Ruberg & Lark, 2021).
These non-gaming streams should be studied not just in their
own right as interesting and novel new media phenomena,
but as I've shown in this book, they also merit study for what
they tell us about gaming and gaming practices on Twitch,
and Twitch's position within wider gaming culture. Studying
them does not distract from studying gaming on Twitch but
actually *helps* us to understand how gaming intersects and
interfaces with other cultural practices and concerns; some of
gaming's more problematic and gate-keeping behaviours; and
the more general appeal of live streaming in our particular
political, internet and wider media moment.

   The third key research direction will involve expanding
our understanding of Twitch outside of the English-speaking
portions of the site, and developing a more comprehensive
sense of how nationality, culture, language and even time
zone shape the experiences of its users and the flows and
creations of metrics, money and attention so integral to
Twitch's success. Initial publications in this area have begun
to appear (e.g., Sixto-García & Losada-Fernández, 2023) and
much of my own research in the past couple of years has
focused on this topic. Channels may well be often conceived

of as digital *places* with distinctive feels and distinctive communities, but this does not mean that the physical places from which streamers stream – and from which viewers view – do not matter. Some of my early findings demonstrate that variation in Twitch streams has a significant cultural and linguistic component, with Japanese streamers (for example) having a far lower incidence of webcam usage than native English-speaking broadcasters or those streaming in other European languages. In the Japanese case this stems from cultural norms regarding a sense of potential embarrassment were one's streaming to be 'discovered' – contrast this with the ardent self-promotion of English-speaking streamers, even from those with the smallest of channels – and different perceptions of online safety. This is only one example but highlights some of the potential complexity to be uncovered here. In turn, non-English streamers are likely to be a significant source of growth for Twitch as the English-speaking audience becomes increasingly saturated, again pointing to the importance of studying these users.

Across these three directions and others, therefore, I am confident that Twitch researchers will be kept busy for the foreseeable future, and that new and wholly unanticipated domains of study will emerge with the next innovation, the next spark of creativity, or the next controversy, to come to our attention via the world's leading gaming *agora*. Such enquiries will also still have significant value even if Twitch ceases to have much of the influence it currently enjoys, or even perhaps fades from view altogether – although in an era where it is rare for major internet platforms to fizzle away in the manner Yahoo and Bebo once did, I think this day is unlikely, and quite distant if it does come to pass. I have noted a couple of times in this book some of the controversies which have dogged the website in recent years, and all of these have elicited hostile feedback from viewers. Yet the site remains the go-to for game live streaming in most countries and a site of constant change, including growth in the streaming of non-game activities. In turn, just as YouTube demonstrated there is a massive market for recorded online video content, Twitch has done the same for *live* video content, and the practice – even if, perhaps, not the website – is not going anywhere. Researching Twitch therefore offers lessons that extend far beyond the boundaries of the platform itself, and that cut across a range of different fields. Like other internet platforms Twitch can be a subject of study in its own right, but also a lens through which to address a large number of other concerns in our understanding of the internet, online life and digital culture(s).

'You're still one of us'

As I write this last section I have a Twitch stream open in the background. I am someone who sometimes works best with a little bit of background noise and the channel I've chosen for today is that of a former esports player in what is probably the only competitive game I really 'follow' (and even that, far less than I used to). While I write my scholarly book and only pay a little attention to the channel's streamed content, I know that at this same moment thousands around the world are glued to the channel and watching every moment; some significant portion of those are talking to others in the chat window, sometimes posting silly memes and emote-driven comments, but other times perhaps interacting with fellow viewers they've known for months or even years; money is flowing towards the streamer and towards Twitch itself from these viewers and, potentially, from sponsors and partners who have committed some level of support to the streamer; the discourse and discussion around a popular game is being incrementally shaped and adjusted by what goes on in this broadcast and what the streamer, and their viewers, have to say about it both on Twitch and beyond; and a skilled, enterprising and hard-working – though likely also quite lucky – young person is performing a job and indulging in the success of a career path they have likely worked years to achieve. Entire universes of social, communal and economic life are manifesting and playing out in this channel and this is just *one* of Twitch's millions of channels, a substantial portion of which are also running as I type this, unseen by me but not unseen by others, while I half-watch the channel I've selected for my day's audiovisual static. There's something beguiling yet also alarming and even daunting about the sheer volume of activity going on here, and the understanding that each one of these channels is, in a certain sense, a complete universe of people and practices and entertainment – most of which I will never even know exist – yet also just one constituent of the Twitch *agora*.

In the first chapter I used Twitch's recent slogan – 'you're already one of us' – to explore how Twitch imagines itself, what demographics of people it's looking to target, and how the site and company frame themselves primarily in terms of gaming but also in terms of the wider social dynamics which the platform enables and supports. The use of this slogan is one that is intended to evoke a particular set of associations and ideas for many avid game players currently in their twenties and thirties – the idea of being part of a noteworthy subculture, one which requires knowledge and competence to associate with, and which to some extent implies some degree of membership in an 'elite'. Twitch has indeed been very successful in establishing 'you're already one of us' as its guiding ideology. That sense of welcome, the membership of a club with shared interests, the significant scope for personalization of channels and autonomy in the construction and conduct of channels, of everyone playing in a looser and almost more 'old school' internet, of being seen and heard in the wider *agora*, all still remain. Of course, comparable formulations are sometimes used by other internet platforms, and an apprehension of greater instrumentality may be creeping into user perceptions of their changing relationship with Twitch. Time – or maybe Amazon – will tell. For the time being, however, nobody is going anywhere. Twitch facilitates practices and behaviours that have long been on the edges of gaming but now finally have found their way to the centre. Spectatorship is now one of the most central parts of modern digital gaming, in large part because of Twitch's existence and its unexpected, and thus far enduring, success.

My last point is therefore a reminder of how strikingly *agora*-like Twitch has become for gaming, and indeed may well be in the process of becoming for other activities and other cultures as well. Eble and Breault (2002: 316) assert that the ancient *agora* was a place for people to 'eat, worship, perform, and argue'. Taking these in reverse, on Twitch streamers and viewers alike endlessly debate the merits and demerits of games new and old, fellow players and esports competitors, game mechanics and the state of the games industry; they perform feats of extraordinary gaming skill and accomplishment both in multiplayer and single-player contests of ability; viewers and even streamers express their admiration for their fellow gamers both on Twitch and beyond, and form into cliques and communities who promote those seen as having the highest degree of gamer capital; and indeed, now, people eat on Twitch, in live 'social eating' streams that demonstrate the platform's increasing return to its not-just-gaming roots. Twitch is indeed the most perfect manifestation of a modern gaming *agora* – with all the strengths and weaknesses that go with such a space – and seems to be in the process of transforming into even more than that. A decade ago nobody predicted that watching *other* people playing games, a medium famed for its interactivity, would be so compelling. Twitch demonstrates the speed with which something that hits a cultural zeitgeist, and slots into so many other existing trends (celebrity influencers, metric-ization, etc.), can rise to sudden and immense prominence. Twitch has become a machine for producing and reinforcing gamer subjects, yet also for renegotiating the norms and wider associations of gaming. It exhibits also tensions between the site's owners and the site's users, and questions of where Twitch the company ends, and where Twitch the *agora* begins, remain contested and in flux. Much is understood on the platform but much remains opaque – not least where Twitch's gaming *agora*, and everything else it seems to represent in this huge and complex package, will be going from here. But for now, our end is our beginning: if you want to know what's happening in gaming, what's important, what the issues are, what's on the horizon – and what non-gaming forms of live online celebrity and broadcast are starting to really grab the populace's attention – Twitch remains the place to go.

References

Abarbanel, B. & Johnson, M.R. (2020). Gambling engagement mechanisms in Twitch live streaming. *International Gambling Studies*, 20(3), 393–413.

Alexander, J. (2018a). Abuse of KFC emote on Twitch leads to more conversations about toxic chat culture. *Polygon*, available at: https://www.polygon.com/2018/3/26/17163582/kfc-emote-twitch-trihex-forsen-trihard-xqc.

Alexander, J. (2018b). A guide to understanding Twitch emotes. *Polygon*, available at: https://www.polygon.com/2018/5/14/17335670/twitch-emotes-meaning-list-kappa-monkas-omegalul-pepe-trihard.

Apperley, T.H. (2006). Genre and game studies: Toward a critical approach to video game genres. *Simulation & Gaming*, 37(1), 6–23.

Ask, K., Spilker, H.S. & Hansen, M. (2019). The politics of user-platform relationships: Co-scripting live-streaming on Twitch.tv. *First Monday*, 24(7).

Auslander, P. (2012). Digital liveness: A historico-philosophical perspective. *PAJ: A Journal of Performance and Art*, 34(3), 3–11.

Auslander, P. (2022). *Liveness: Performance in a Mediatized Culture*, 3rd edn. London: Routledge.

Baguley, J. (2019). *Gates and Channels: An ANT-oriented Approach to Understanding Fan Community Behavior and Identity on a Discord Chat Server*. Honours thesis, University of Sydney.

Baldauf-Quilliatre, H. & de Carvajal, I.C. (2021). Spectating: How non-players participate in videogaming. *Journal für Medienlinguistik*, 4(2), 123–61.

Barbieri, F., Espinosa-Anke, L., Ballesteros, M. & Saggion, H. (2017). Towards the understanding of gaming audiences by modeling Twitch emotes. In: *Third Workshop on Noisy User-generated Text*, Copenhagen: Association for Computational Linguistics, pp. 11–20.

Baym, N.K. (2013). Data not seen: The uses and shortcomings of social media metrics. *First Monday*, 18(10).

Beer, D. (2016). *Metric Power*. London: Palgrave Macmillan.

Bowman, N.D., Rieger, D. & Lin, J.H.T. (2022). Social video gaming and well-being. *Current Opinion in Psychology, 45*, 101316.

Brandis, R. & Bozkurt, C.M. (2021). Player agency in audience gaming. In: B. Beil, G.S. Freyermuth & H. Schmidt (Eds.), *Paratextualizing Games: Investigations on the Paraphernalia and Peripheries of Play.* Bielefeld: transcript Verlag, pp. 165–81.

Brett, N. (2022). Why do we only get anime girl avatars? Collective white heteronormative avatar design in live streams. *Television & New Media, 23*(5), 451–61.

Brock, T. (2021) Counting clicks: Esports, neoliberalism and the affective power of gameplay. In: D.Y. Jin (Ed.), *Global Esports: Transformation of Cultural Perceptions of Competitive Gaming.* New York: Bloomsbury, pp. 132–49.

Brown, A.M. & Moberly, L. (2020). Twitch and participatory cultures. In: R. Kowert & T. Quandt (Eds.), *The Video Game Debate 2: Revisiting the Physical, Social, and Psychological Effects of Video Games.* London: Routledge, pp. 53–65.

Burroughs, B. (2020). Statistics and baseball fandom: Sabermetric infrastructure of expertise. *Games and Culture, 15*(3), 248–65.

Burroughs, B. & Rama, P. (2015). The eSports Trojan Horse: Twitch and streaming futures. *Journal of Virtual Worlds Research, 8*(2), 1–5.

Bussey, Z. (2020). Is twitch profitable? *CreatorHype*, available at: https://creatorhype.com/is-twitch-profitable/.

Cabeza-Ramírez, L.J., Fuentes-García, F.J. & Muñoz-Fernandez, G.A. (2021). Exploring the emerging domain of research on video game live streaming in web of science: State of the art, changes and trends. *International Journal of Environmental Research and Public Health, 18*(6).

Cai, J. & Wohn, D.Y. (2019). What are effective strategies of handling harassment on Twitch?: Users' perspectives. In: *CSCW '19 Companion: Companion Publication of the 2019 Conference on Computer Supported Cooperative Work and Social Computing,* pp. 166–70.

Cai, J. & Wohn, D.Y. (2021). After violation but before sanction: Understanding volunteer moderators' profiling processes toward violators in live streaming communities. *Proceedings of the ACM on Human-Computer Interaction, 5*, pp. 1–25.

Cai, J., Guanlao, C. & Wohn, D.Y. (2021a). Understanding rules in live streaming micro communities on Twitch. In: *Proceedings of the 2021 ACM International Conference on Interactive Media Experiences,* pp. 290–5.

Cai, J., Wohn, D.Y., & Almoqbel, M. (2021b). Moderation visibility: Mapping the strategies of volunteer moderators in live streaming micro communities. In: *ACM International Conference on Interactive Media Experiences*, pp. 61–72.

Cai, J., Chowdhury, S., Zhou, H. & Wohn, D.Y. (2023). Hate raids on Twitch: Understanding real-time human-bot coordinated attacks in live streaming communities. *arXiv preprint*: 2305.16248.

Camp, J.M. (1986). *The Athenian Agora: Excavations in the Heart of Classical Athens*. London: Thames & Hudson.

Camp, J.M. (2016). The Greek Agora. In: M.M. Miles (Ed.), *A Companion to Greek Architecture*. Oxford: Wiley-Blackwell, pp. 300–13.

Carter, M. & Egliston, B. (2021). The work of watching Twitch: Audience labour in livestreaming and esports. *Journal of Gaming & Virtual Worlds*, 13(1), 3–20.

Catá, A.S. (2019). Convergence of rhetoric, labour, and play in the construction of inactive discourses on Twitch. *Digital Culture & Society*, 5(2), 133–48.

Chae, S.W. & Lee, S.H. (2022). Sharing emotion while spectating video game play: Exploring Twitch users' emotional change after the outbreak of the COVID-19 pandemic. *Computers in Human Behavior*, 131, 107211.

Chamberlain, E.F. (2022). 'Our world is worth fighting for': Gas mask agency, copypasta sit-ins, and the material-discursive practices of the Blitzchung controversy. *Computers and Composition*, 65, 102725.

Chan, B. & Gray, K. (2020). Microstreaming, microcelebrity, and marginalized masculinity: Pathways to visibility and self-definition for black men in gaming. *Women's Studies in Communication*, 43(4), 354–62.

Charles, C. (2016). Keeping quiet: Investigating the maintenance and policing of male dominated gaming space. *Electronic Theses and Dissertations*, http://stars.library.ucf.edu/etd/5115.

Chesher, C. (2024). *Invocational Media: Reconceptualising the Computer*. London: Bloomsbury Academic.

Churchill, B.C.B. & Xu, W. (2016). The modem nation: A first study on Twitch.TV social structure and player/game relationships. In: *2016 IEEE International Conferences on Big Data and Cloud Computing (BDCloud), Social Computing and Networking (SocialCom), Sustainable Computing and Communications (SustainCom) (BDCloud-SocialCom-SustainCom)*, Atlanta, GA, pp. 223–8.

Clarke, R.I., Lee, J.H. & Clark, N. (2017). Why video game genres fail: A classificatory analysis. *Games and Culture*, 12(5), 445–65.

Condis, M. (2015). No homosexuals in Star Wars? BioWare, 'gamer' identity, and the politics of privilege in a convergence culture. *Convergence*, *21*(2), 198–212.

Condis, M. (2023). Desert Bus: Abusive game design, the martyrdom effect, and fan activism on Twitch.tv. *Games and Culture*, *18*(7), 959–74.

Consalvo, M. (2007). *Cheating: Gaining Advantage in Videogames*. Cambridge, MA: MIT Press.

Consalvo, M. (2018). Kaceytron and transgressive play on Twitch.tv. In: K. Jorgensen and F. Karlsen (Eds.), *Transgression in Games and Play*. Cambridge, MA: MIT Press, pp. 83–98.

Consalvo, M. & Phelps, A. (2019). Performing game development live on Twitch. In: *Proceedings of the 52nd Hawaii International Conference on System Sciences*.

Consalvo, M., Boudreau, K., Bowman, N. & Phelps, A. (2023). Fame! I wanna stream forever: Analysis and critique of successful streamers' advice to the next generation. In: *56th Annual Hawaii International Conference on System Sciences, HICSS 2023*, pp. 2326–35.

Cook, J. (2014). Twitch founder: We turned a 'terrible idea' into a billion-dollar company. *Business Insider*, available at: https://www.businessinsider.com/the-story-of-video-game-streaming-site-twitch-2014-10.

Cook, L. & Duncan, S. (2016). 'Any% No Sketch Glitch': Speedrunning Final Fantasy VI and expanding 'well played'. *Well Played*, *5*(2), 173–88.

Cote, A.C. (2017). 'I can defend myself': Women's strategies for coping with harassment while gaming online. *Games and Culture*, *12*(2), 136–55.

Cullen, A.L. (2022a). *Playing with the Double Bind: Authenticity, Gender, and Failure in Live Streaming*. PhD thesis, University of California, Irvine.

Cullen, A.L. (2022b). Just on the right side of wrong: (De)legitimizing feminism in video game live streaming. *Television & New Media*, *23*(5), 542–52.

Cullen, A.L. & Ruberg, B. (2019). Necklines and 'naughty bits': Constructing and regulating bodies in live streaming community guidelines. In: *Proceedings of the 14th International Conference on the Foundations of Digital Games*, New York: ACM, pp. 1–8.

D'Anastasio, C. (2023). Twitch's new streaming rival kick tests waters of lighter moderation. *Bloomberg*, available at: https://www.bloomberg.com/news/newsletters/2023-03-03/twitch-s-new-video-game-streaming-rival-kick-goes-light-on-moderation.

Dargonaki, S. (2018). Performing gender on Twitch.tv: Gendered playbour through Butlerian theory. *International Journal of Media and Cultural Politics*, 14(1), 103–10.

Davenport, S. & Leitch, S. (2005). Agoras, ancient and modern, and a framework for science-society debate. *Science and Public Policy*, 32(2), 137–53.

De Grove, F., Courtois, C. & Van Looy, J. (2015). How to be a gamer! Exploring personal and social indicators of gamer identity. *Journal of Computer-Mediated Communication*, 20(3), 346–61.

De Wit, J., Van der Kraan, A. & Theeuwes, J. (2020). Live streams on Twitch help viewers cope with difficult periods in life. *Frontiers in Psychology*, 11, 586975.

Diwanji, V., Reed, A., Ferchaud, A., Seibert, J., Weinbrecht, V. & Sellers, N. (2020). Don't just watch, join in: Exploring information behaviour and copresence on Twitch. *Computers in Human Behavior*, 105, 106221.

Dixon, S. & Weber, S. (2007). Playspaces, childhood, and video games. In: S. Weber & S. Dixon (Eds.), *Growing Up Online: Young People and Digital Technologies*. New York: Palgrave Macmillan, pp. 17–36.

Dolin, P., d'Hauthuille, L. & Vattani, A. (2021). FeelsGoodMan: Inferring semantics of Twitch neologisms. *arXiv preprint*: 2108.08411.

Dowling, D.O., Goetz, C. & Lathrop, D. (2020). One year of #GamerGate: The shared Twitter link as emblem of masculinist gamer identity. *Games and Culture*, 15(8), 982–1003.

Dunlap, K.N., Shanley, M. & Wagner, J. (2023). Mental health live: An ethnographic study of the mental health of Twitch streamers during COVID. In: J. Brewer, B. Ruberg, A.L.L. Cullen & C.J. Persaud (Eds.), *Real Life in Real Time: Live Streaming Culture*. Cambridge, MA: MIT Press, pp. 57–73.

Dynel, M. (2020). On being roasted, toasted and burned: (Meta) pragmatics of Wendy's Twitter humour. *Journal of Pragmatics*, 166, 1–14.

Easpaig, B.N.G. (2018). An exploratory study of sexism in online gaming communities: Mapping contested digital terrain. *Community Psychology in Global Perspective*, 4(2), 119–35.

Eble, M. & Breault, R. (2002). The primetime agora: Knowledge, power, and 'mainstream' resource venues for women online. *Computers and Composition*, 19(3), 315–29.

Eisenmann, T., Parker, G. & Van Alstyne, M. (2011). Platform envelopment. *Strategic Management Journal*, 32(12), 1270–85.

Evans, S. & Llano, S.M. (2023). Tryhard with a vengeance: Meaning making and boundary keeping on Twitch. *Journal of Electronic Gaming and Esports*, 1(1), 1–7.

Faas, T., Dombrowski, L., Young, A. & Miller, A.D. (2018). Watch me code: Programming mentorship communities on twitch.tv. In: *Proceedings of the ACM on Human–Computer Interaction*, 2(CSCW), 1–18.

Flew, T. (2021). *Regulating Platforms*. Cambridge: Polity.

Ford, C., Gardner, D., Horgan, L.E., Liu, C., Tsaasan, A.M., Nardi, B. & Rickman, J. (2017). Chat speed OP PogChamp: Practices of coherence in massive Twitch chat. In: *Proceedings of the 2017 CHI conference extended abstracts on human factors in computing systems*, Denver, CO, 6–11 May. New York: ACM, pp. 858–71.

Fox, J. & Tang, W.Y. (2014). Sexism in online video games: The role of conformity to masculine norms and social dominance orientation. *Computers in Human Behavior*, *33*, 314–20.

Fox, J. & Tang, W.Y. (2017). Women's experiences with general and sexual harassment in online video games: Rumination, organizational responsiveness, withdrawal, and coping strategies. *New Media & Society*, *19*(8), 1290–307.

Freeman, G. & Wohn, D.Y. (2020). Streaming your identity: Navigating the presentation of gender and sexuality through live streaming. *Computer Supported Cooperative Work (CSCW)*, *29*, 795–825.

Fung, A., Ismangil, M., He, W. & Cao, S. (2022). If I'm not Streaming, I'm not earning: Audience relations and platform time on Douyin. *Online Media and Global Communication*, *1*(2), 369–86.

Gandolfi, E. (2018). Enjoying death among gamers, viewers, and users: A network visualization of Dark Souls 3's trends on Twitch.tv and Steam platforms. *Information Visualization*, *17*(3), 218–38.

Garcia, D. (2022). A gamer's paradise? Understanding how Discord allows online gaming servers to develop and maintain communities. *HCI-E MSc Final Project Report*. UCL Interaction Centre, University College London.

Garcia, R.L., Bingham, S. & Liu, S. (2021). The effects of daily Instagram use on state self-objectification, well-being, and mood for young women. *Psychology of Popular Media*, *11*(4), 423–34.

Gault, M. (2019). Watch a Streamer's emotional reaction to beating all 'Soulsborne' games without getting hit. *VICE*, available at: https://www.vice.com/en/article/7xn34x/watch-a-streamers-emotional-reaction-to-beating-all-soulsborne-games-without-getting-hit.

Gerber, H.R. (2022). The literacies of a competitive esports team:

Livestreaming, VODS, and Mods. *L1-Educational Studies in Language and Literature, 22*(2), 1–25.

Gerken, T. (2022). Twitch announces slots and roulette gambling ban. *BBC News*, available at: https://www.bbc.com/news/technology -62982509.

Glickman, S., McKenzie, N., Seering, J., Moeller, R. & Hammer, J. (2018). Design challenges for livestreamed audience participation games. In: *Proceedings of the 2018 Annual Symposium on Computer Human Interaction in Play*. New York: ACM, pp. 187–99.

Goh, Z.H., Tandoc Jr, E.C. & Ng, B. (2021). 'Live' together with you: Livestream views mitigate the effects of loneliness on well-being. *Journal of Broadcasting & Electronic Media, 65*(4), 505–24.

Golub, A. (2010). Being in the World (of Warcraft): Raiding, realism, and knowledge production in a massively multiplayer online game. *Anthropological Quarterly, 83*(1), 17–45.

Gong, M., Bao, X. & Wagner, C. (2023). Why viewers send paid gifts: The role of social influence on massively multiplayer online games live streaming. *Information Processing & Management, 60*(4).

Gottesman, A. (2014). *Politics and the Street in Democratic Athens*. Cambridge: Cambridge University Press.

Graham, T., Jackson, D. & Wright, S. (2015). From everyday conversation to political action: Talking austerity in online 'third spaces'. *European Journal of Communication, 30*(6), 648–65.

Gray, K.L. (2017). 'They're just too urban': Black gamers streaming on Twitch. In: J. Daniels, K. Gregory & T.M. Cottom (Eds.), *Digital Sociologies*. Bristol: Policy Press, pp. 355–68.

Grayson, N. (2020). Among Us' improbable rise to the top of Twitch. *Kotaku*, available at: https://www.kotaku.com.au/2020/09/among -us-improbable-rise-to-the-top-of-twitch/.

Grayson, N. (2023). How Twitch lost its way. *The Washington Post*, 23 March, available at: https://www.washingtonpost.com/video-games /2023/03/23/twitch-subs-ads-layoffs-kai-cenat/.

Groen, M. (2020). Digital governmentality: Toxicity in gaming streams. In: M. Groen, N. Kiel, A. Tillmann & A. Weßel (Eds.), *Games and Ethics: Theoretical and Empirical Approaches to Ethical Questions in Digital Game Cultures*. Wiesbaden: Springer, pp. 97–111.

Guarriello, N.B. (2019). Never give up, never surrender: Game live streaming, neoliberal work, and personalized media economies. *New Media & Society, 21*(8), 1750–69.

Guarriello, N.B. (2021). Not going viral: Amateur livestreamers, volunteerism, and privacy on Discord. *Popular Culture Studies Journal, 9*(2), 142–58.

Haak, F. (2021). Emojis in lexicon-based sentiment analysis: Creating emoji sentiment lexicons from unlabeled corpora. In: *Proceedings of the LWDA 2021 Workshops: FGWM, KDML, FGWI-BIA, and FGIR*, pp. 279–86.

Hamilton, W.A., Garretson, O. & Kerne, A. (2014). Streaming on Twitch: Fostering participatory communities of play within live mixed media. In: *Proceedings of the SIGCHI Conference on Human Factors in Computing Systems*, pp. 1315–24.

Han, C., Seering, J., Kumar, D., Hancock, J.T. & Durumeric, Z. (2023). Hate raids on Twitch: Echoes of the past, new modalities, and implications for platform governance. *arXiv preprint*: 2301.03946.

Harris, B.C., Foxman, M. & Partin, W.C. (2023). 'Don't make me ratio you again': How political influencers encourage platformed political participation. *Social Media + Society*, 9(2), https://doi.org/10.1177/20563051231177944.

Hatmaker, T. (2023). Twitch backtracks on branded content changes after streamer backlash. *TechCrunch*, available at: https://techcrunch.com/2023/06/07/twitch-backtracks-on-changes-to-branded-content-rules-after-streamer-backlash/.

Heikkinen, L. (2021). *A Case Study of the Linguistic Role of Emoji in Twitch Chat Rooms*. Master's thesis, University of Jyväskylä, Finland.

Helmond, A. (2015). The platformization of the web: Making web data platform ready. *Social Media + Society*, 1(2), 2056305115603080.

Henry, M.V. & Farvid, P. (2017). 'Always hot, always live': Computer-mediated sex work in the era of 'camming'. *Women's Studies Journal*, 31(2), 113–28.

Hern, A. (2022). TechScape: Twitch and the dark side of the streaming dream. *The Guardian*, 26 October, available at: https://www.theguardian.com/technology/2022/oct/26/techscape-twitch-amazon-toxic-community-culture.

Hernandez, P. (2013). Twitch apologizes over recent abuse of power by staff. *Kotaku*, available at: https://kotaku.com/twitch-apologizes-over-recent-abuse-of-power-by-staff-1469301896.

Hilvert-Bruce, Z. & Neill, J.T. (2020). I'm just trolling: The role of normative beliefs in aggressive behaviour in online gaming. *Computers in Human Behavior*, 102, 303–11.

Hilvert-Bruce, Z., Neill, J.T., Sjöblom, M. & Hamari, J. (2018). Social motivations of live-streaming viewer engagement on Twitch. *Computers in Human Behavior*, 84, 58–67.

Hope, R. (2023). Games done quick, organizational presence, and speedrunning identity. In: J. Brewer, B. Ruberg, A.L.L. Cullen & C.J. Persaud (Eds.), *Real Life in Real Time: Live Streaming Culture*. Cambridge, MA: MIT Press, pp. 289–303.

Hou, F., Guan, Z., Li, B. & Chong, A.Y.L. (2020). Factors influencing people's continuous watching intention and consumption intention in live streaming: Evidence from China. *Internet Research*, 30(1), 141–63.

Houssard, A., Pilati, F., Tartari, M., Sacco, P.L. & Gallotti, R. (2023). Monetization in online streaming platforms: An exploration of inequalities in Twitch.tv. *Scientific Reports*, 13(1), 1103.

Huang, V.G. & Liu, T. (2022). Gamifying contentious politics: Gaming capital and playful resistance. *Games and Culture*, 17(1), 26–46.

Jackson, N.J. (2020). Understanding memetic media and collective identity through streamer persona on Twitch.tv. *Persona Studies*, 6(2), 69–87.

Jackson, N.J. (2023a). *Persona Play in Videogame Livestreaming: An Ethnography of Performance on Twitch*. PhD thesis, UNSW Sydney.

Jackson, N.J. (2023b). Emoting culture on Twitch.tv: The removal and reinstatement of PogChamp. In: J. Brewer, B. Ruberg, A.L.L. Cullen & C.J. Persaud (Eds.), *Real Life in Real Time: Live Streaming Culture*. Cambridge, MA: MIT Press, pp. 245–61.

Jacob, A. & Tran, C.H. (2023). How we learned to stop SWATing and love the (zoom-)bomb: A (de)predatory history of disrupting the live stream. In: J. Brewer, B. Ruberg, A.L.L. Cullen & C.J. Persaud (Eds.), *Real Life in Real Time: Live Streaming Culture*. Cambridge, MA: MIT Press, pp. 103–17.

Jaramillo, D.L. (2002). The family racket: AOL Time Warner, HBO, The Sopranos, and the construction of a quality brand. *Journal of Communication Inquiry*, 26(1), 59–75.

Järvinen, A. (2007). *Games without Frontiers: Theories and Methods for Game Studies and Design*. PhD thesis, University of Tampere, Finland.

Jerslev, A. (2016). In the time of the microcelebrity: Celebrification and the YouTuber Zoella. *International Journal of Communication*, 10(1), 5233–51.

Jin, D.Y. (2010). *Korea's Online Gaming Empire*. Cambridge, MA: MIT Press.

Jin, D.Y. (2020). Historiography of Korean Esports: Perspectives on spectatorship. *International Journal of Communication*, 14, 3727–45.

Jodén, H. (2020). *Emotional Energy and Group Membership on Twitch. tv*. Student thesis, Faculty of Social Sciences, Uppsala University.

Jodén, H. & Strandell, J. (2022). Building viewer engagement through interaction rituals on Twitch.tv. *Information, Communication & Society*, 25(13), 1969–86.

Johansson, E. (2021). *Chess and Twitch: Cultural Convergence through Digital Platforms*. Student thesis, Media and Communication Studies, School of Culture and Education, Södertörn University.

Johnson, M.R. (2019). Inclusion and exclusion in the digital economy: Disability and mental health as a live streamer on Twitch.tv. *Information, Communication & Society*, 22(4), 506–20.

Johnson, M.R. (2021). Behind the streams: The off-camera labour of game live streaming. *Games and Culture*, 16(8), 1001–20.

Johnson, M.R. (2022). Humour and comedy in digital game live streaming. *New Media & Society*, https://doi.org/10.1177/14614448221095160.

Johnson, M.R. & Baguley, J. (forthcoming). 'I will design emojis in 24 hours': The gig workers of Twitch live streaming.

Johnson, M.R. & Jackson, N.J. (2022). Twitch, Fish, Pokémon and Plumbers: Game live streaming by nonhuman actors. *Convergence*, 28(2), 431–50.

Johnson, M.R. & Woodcock, J. (2017). 'It's like the gold rush': The lives and careers of professional video game streamers on Twitch.tv. *Information, Communication & Society*, 22(3), 336–51.

Johnson, M.R. & Woodcock, J. (2019a). 'And today's top donator is': How live streamers on Twitch.tv monetize and gamify their broadcasts. *Social Media + Society*, 5(4), 1–11.

Johnson, M.R. & Woodcock, J. (2019b). The impacts of live streaming and Twitch.tv on the video game industry. *Media, Culture & Society*, 41(5), 670–88.

Johnson, M.R., Carrigan, M. & Brock, T. (2019). The imperative to be seen: The moral economy of celebrity video game streaming on Twitch.tv. *First Monday*, 24(8).

Jones, S. (2005). MTV: The medium was the message. *Critical Studies in Media Communication*, 22(1), 83–8.

Kalra, A. & Karahalios, K. (2005). TextTone: Expressing emotion through text. In: *IFIP Conference on Human–Computer Interaction*. Heidelberg: Springer, pp. 966–9.

Karhulahti, V.-M. (2011). Mechanic/aesthetic videogame genres: Adventure and adventure. In: *Proceedings of the 15th International Academic MindTrek Conference: Envisioning Future Media Environments*, pp. 71–4.

Karhulahti, V.-M. (2016). Prank, troll, gross and gore: Performance issues in esports live-streaming. In: *Proceedings of 1st International Joint Conference DiGRA and FDG*.

Kastrenakes, J. (2020). People are watching a lot more Twitch during the pandemic. *The Verge*, 23 July, available at: https://www.theverge

.com/2020/7/23/21335559/twitch-pandemic-viewership-increase
-facebook-gaming-live-streaming.

Kejser, K. (2021). *'Pop a Titty for the Boys': A Qualitative Study of Negative Communication towards Female Streamers on Twitch.* Bachelor's thesis, Örebro University, Sweden.

Kersting, E., Malagon, J. & Moulthrop, S. (2021). Before you step into the stream. *Popular Culture Studies Journal, 9*(2), 6–19.

Khamis, S., Ang, L. & Welling, R. (2017). Self-branding, 'micro-celebrity' and the rise of social media influencers. *Celebrity Studies, 8*(2), 191–208.

Kim, J., Wohn, D.Y. & Cha, M. (2022). Understanding and identifying the use of emotes in toxic chat on Twitch. *Online Social Networks and Media, 27*, 100180.

Kirkpatrick, G. (2016). Making games normal: Computer gaming discourse in the 1980s. *New Media & Society, 18*(8), 1439–54.

Kirkpatrick, G. (2017). How gaming became sexist: A study of UK gaming magazines 1981–1995. *Media, Culture & Society, 39*(4), 453–68.

Kneisel, A. & Sternadori, M. (2023). Effects of parasocial affinity and gender on live streaming fans' motivations. *Convergence, 29*(2), 322–41.

Kocurek, C.A. (2015). *Coin-operated Americans: Rebooting Boyhood at the Video Game Arcade.* Minneapolis, MN: University of Minnesota Press.

Kowert, R. & Daniel Jr, E. (2021). The one-and-a-half sided parasocial relationship: The curious case of live streaming. *Computers in Human Behavior Reports, 4*, 100150.

Kreissl, J., Possler, D. & Klimmt, C. (2021). Engagement with the gurus of gaming culture: Parasocial relationships to Let's Players. *Games and Culture, 16*(8), 1021–43.

Küper, A. & Krämer, N.C. (2021). Influencing factors for building social capital on live streaming websites. *Entertainment Computing, 39*, 100444.

Lamerichs, N. (2011). Stranger than fiction: Fan identity in cosplay. *Transformative Works and Cultures, 7.*

Lamerichs, N. (2021). Material culture on Twitch. *Paratextualizing Games, 13*, 181–212.

Lark, D. (2022). How not to be seen: Notes on the gendered intimacy of livestreaming the Covid-19 pandemic. *Television & New Media, 23*(5), 462–74.

Lawson, R. (2023). *Trans* Streamers on Twitch.tv: The Intersections of Gender and Digital Labor.* MSc thesis, Department of Sociology, Virginia Commonwealth University.

Leith, A.P. (2021). Parasocial cues: The ubiquity of parasocial relation-ships on Twitch. *Communication Monographs, 88*(1), 111–29.

Li, J., Gui, X., Kou, Y. & Li, Y. (2019). Live streaming as co-performance: Dynamics between center and periphery in theatrical engagement. In: *Proceedings of the ACM on Human–Computer Interaction 3, CSCW*, pp. 1–22.

Li, N., Cai, J. & Wohn, D.Y. (2023). Ignoring as a moderation strategy for volunteer moderators on Twitch. In: *Extended Abstracts of the 2023 CHI Conference on Human Factors in Computing Systems*, pp. 1–7.

Lin, J.-H.T. (2019). Because Jimmy Kimmel wants to know: Motivations for watching game streaming as predictors of viewing time and enjoyment. *Journal of Information Society, 36*, 39–74.

Lin, J.-H.T., Bowman, N., Lin, S.F. & Chen, Y.S. (2019). Setting the digital stage: Defining game streaming as an entertainment experience. *Entertainment Computing, 31*, 100309.

Lo, C. (2018). *When All You Have Is a Banhammer: The Social and Communicative Work of Volunteer Moderators.* MSc thesis, Massachusetts Institute of Technology.

London, T.M., Crundwell, J., Eastley, M.B., Santiago, N. & Jenkins, J. (2019). Finding effective moderation practices on Twitch. In: J. Reyman & E.M. Sparby (Eds.), *Digital Ethics: Rhetoric and Responsibility in Online Aggression.* New York: Routledge, pp. 51–68.

Lybrand, E. (2019) *Community in the Crowd: Motivations for Commenting on Twitch.tv Live Streams.* Master's Thesis, Clemson University, Clemson, SC.

McLaughlin, C. & Wohn, D.Y. (2021). Predictors of parasocial inter-action and relationships in live streaming. *Convergence, 27*(6), 1714–34.

Major, N.L. (2015). *Online Stars and the New Audience: How YouTube Creators Curate and Maintain Communities.* PhD thesis, University of California, Irvine.

Marsden, S. (2022). 'I take it you've read every book on the shelves?' Demonstrating taste and class through bookshelves in the time of COVID. *English Studies, 103*(5), 660–74.

Marwick, A.E. (2013). *Status Update: Celebrity, Publicity, and Branding in the Social Media Age.* New Haven, CT: Yale University Press.

Massanari, A. (2017). #Gamergate and The Fappening: How Reddit's algorithm, governance, and culture support toxic technocultures. *New Media & Society, 19*(3), 329–46.

Matthews, E. (2020). Why Among Us is the best game to watch on

Twitch right now. *PC Gamer*, available at: https://www.pcgamer.com /why-among-us-is-the-best-game-to-watch-on-twitch-right-now/.

Mau, S. (2019). *The Metric Society: On the Quantification of the Social.* Cambridge: Polity.

Meisner, C. (2023). Networked responses to networked harassment? Creators' coordinated management of 'hate raids' on Twitch. *Social Media + Society*, 9(2), 20563051231179696.

Meisner, C. & Ledbetter, A.M. (2020). Participatory branding on social media: The affordances of live streaming for creative labor. *New Media & Society*, 24(5), 1179–95.

Mendick, H., Allen, K. & Harvey, L. (2015). 'We can get everything we want if we try hard': Young people, celebrity, hard work. *British Journal of Educational Studies*, 63(2), 161–78.

Mihailova, T. (2022). Navigating ambiguous negativity: A case study of Twitch.tv live chats. *New Media & Society*, 24(8), 1830–51.

Miltner, K.M. & Gerrard, Y. (2022). 'Tom had us all doing front-end web development': A nostalgic (re)imagining of Myspace. *Internet Histories*, 6(1–2), 48–67.

Monahan, S. (2021). Video games have replaced music as the most important aspect of youth culture. *The Guardian*, 11 January, available at: https://www.theguardian.com/commentisfree/2021 /jan/11/video-games-music-youth-culture.

Montelli, C. (2021). What is 'Among Us?' The wildly popular social deduction and deception game, explained. *Business Insider*, available at: https://www.businessinsider.com/guides/tech/what-is-among-us.

Moyse, C. (2018). Streamer completes zero hit run of the Dark Souls Trilogy. *Destructoid*, available at: https://www.destructoid.com /streamer-completes-zero-hit-run-of-the-dark-souls-trilogy/.

Nakandala, S.C., Ciampaglia, G.L., Su, N.M. & Ahn, Y.-Y. (2017). Gendered conversation in a social game-streaming platform. *Proceedings of the International AAAI Conference on Web and Social Media*, 11(1), 162–71.

Nematzadeh, A., Ciampaglia, G.L., Ahn, Y.-Y. & Flammini, A. (2019). Information overload in group communication: From conversation to cacophony in the Twitch chat. *Royal Society Open Science*, 6(10), 191412.

Nguyen, T.T., Hui, P.M., Harper, F.M., Terveen, L. & Konstan, J.A. (2014). Exploring the filter bubble: The effect of using recommender systems on content diversity. In: *Proceedings of the 23rd International Conference on World Wide Web*. New York: ACM, pp. 677–86.

Nieborg, D.B. & Foxman, M. (2023). *Mainstreaming and Game Journalism*. Cambridge, MA: MIT Press.

Nieborg, D.B. & Poell, T. (2018). The platformization of cultural production: Theorizing the contingent cultural commodity. *New Media & Society*, 20(11), 4275–92.

Nieborg, D.B. & Sihvonen, T. (2009). The new gatekeepers: The occupational ideology of game journalism. In: *Proceedings of the 2009 DiGRA International Conference: Breaking New Ground: Innovation in Games, Play, Practice and Theory.*

O'Kelly, C. & Dubnick, M. (2014). Accountability and its metaphors – From forum to agora and bazaar. In: *PSG VII: Quality and Integrity of Governance. The European Group of Public Administration*, Speyer, Germany, 10–12 September.

Ogletree, S.M. & Drake, R. (2007). College students' video game participation and perceptions: Gender differences and implications. *Sex Roles, 56,* 537–42.

Olejniczak, J. (2015). A linguistic study of language variety used on Twitch.tv: Descriptive and corpus-based approaches. *Redefining Community in Intercultural Context,* 4(1), 329–34.

Orme, S. (2018). *Growing Up Gamers: Female Leisure in Digital Games Culture.* PhD thesis, Pennsylvania State University.

Orme S. (2021). 'Just watching': A qualitative analysis of non-players' motivations for video game spectatorship. *New Media & Society,* 24(10), 2252–69.

Paaßen, B., Morgenroth, T. & Stratemeyer, M. (2017). What is a true gamer? The male gamer stereotype and the marginalization of women in video game culture. *Sex Roles, 76,* 421–35.

Papacharissi, Z. (2002). The virtual sphere: The internet as a public sphere. *New Media & Society,* 4(1), 9–27.

Park, M. (2023). Tense exchange between a streamer and Twitch director speaks to the state of streamer-platform relationships. *PC Gamer*, available at: https://www.pcgamer.com/tense-exchange -between-a-streamer-and-twitch-director-speaks-to-the-state-of -streamer-platform-relationships/.

Parker, F. & Perks, M.E. (2021). Streaming ambivalence: Livestreaming and indie game development. *Convergence,* 27(6), 1735–52.

Parrish, A. (2022). Twitch will now let partners stream on YouTube and Facebook. *The Verge,* 23 August, available at: https://www.theverge .com/2022/8/23/23317939/twitch-ends-partner-exclusivity-youtube -tiktok-facebook-gaming.

Partin, W.C. (2019). Watch me pay: Twitch and the cultural economy of surveillance. *Surveillance & Society,* 17(1/2), 153–60.

Partin, W.C. (2020). Bit by (Twitch) bit: 'Platform capture' and the evolution of digital platforms. *Social Media + Society,* 6(3), 2056305120933981.

Paul, C.A. (2018). *The Toxic Meritocracy of Video Games: Why Gaming Culture Is the Worst.* Minneapolis, MN: University of Minnesota Press.

Payne, M.T. (2018). Twitch.tv: Tele-visualizing the arcade. In: D. Johnson (Ed.), *From Networks to Netflix: A Guide to Changing Channels.* London: Routledge, pp. 287–96.

Peel, J. (2013). Own3d will shut down 'within the next two weeks' claims League of Legends streamer. *PC Games N*, available at: https://www.pcgamesn.com/dota/own3d-will-shut-down-within -next-two-weeks-claims-league-legends-streamer.

Pellicone, A.J. & Ahn, J. (2017). The game of performing play: Understanding streaming as cultural production. In: *Proceedings of the 2017 CHI Conference on Human Factors in Computing Systems.* New York: ACM, pp. 4863–74.

Pequeño, A. (2023). Twitch introduces 70/30 revenue split for some streamers through new program – with some caveats. *Forbes*, 15 June, available at: https://www.forbes.com/sites/antoniopequenoiv/2023 /06/15/twitch-introduces-7030-revenue-split-for-some-streamers -through-new-program-with-some-caveats/?sh=4448a63f6759.

Pereira, G. & Ricci, B. (2023). 'Calling all the cattle': Music live streams during the COVID-19 pandemic in Brazil. In: J. Brewer, B. Ruberg, A.L.L. Cullen & C.J. Persaud (Eds.), *Real Life in Real Time: Live Streaming Culture.* Cambridge, MA: MIT Press, pp. 41–57.

Perreault, G. & Vos, T. (2020). Metajournalistic discourse on the rise of gaming journalism. *New Media & Society, 22*(1), 159–76.

Persaud, C.J. & Perks, M.E. (2022). Beauty from the waist up: Twitch drag, digital labor, and queer mediated liveness. *Television & New Media, 23*(5), 475–86.

Phelps, A., Consalvo, M. & Bowman, N. (2021a). Streaming into the void: An analysis of microstreaming trends and behaviors utilizing a demand framework. In: *Proceedings of the 54th Hawaii International Conference on System Sciences,* pp. 2863–72.

Phelps, A., Bowman, N., Consalvo, M. & Smyth, M. (2021b). Streaming small shared spaces: Exploring the connectedness of the physical spaces of microstreamers and their audience. *Selected Papers of Internet Research.*

Phillips, A. (2020). Negg(at)ing the game studies subject: An affective history of the field. *Feminist Media Histories, 6*(1), 12–36.

Phillips, W. (2015). *This Is Why We Can't Have Nice Things: Mapping the Relationship between Online Trolling and Mainstream Culture.* Cambridge, MA: MIT Press.

Poell, T. (2020). Three challenges for media studies in the age of platforms. *Television & New Media, 21*(6), 650–7.

Poell, T., Nieborg, D.B. & Duffy, B.E. (2021). *Platforms and Cultural Production*. Cambridge: Polity.

Poeller, S., Steen, A., Baumann, N. & Mandryk, R.L. (2023). Not Tekken seriously? How observers respond to masculine and feminine voices in videogame streamers. In: *Proceedings of the 18th International Conference on the Foundations of Digital Games*. New York: ACM, pp. 1–12.

Popper, B. (2014). Justin.tv, the live video pioneer that birthed Twitch, officially shuts down. *The Verge*, 5 August, available at: https://www.theverge.com/2014/8/5/5971939/justin-tv-the-live-video-pioneer-that-birthed-twitch-officially-shuts.

Postigo, H. (2016). The socio-technical architecture of digital labor: Converting play into YouTube money. *New Media & Society*, 18(2), 332–49.

Purtill, J. (2021). Twitch hack reveals multi-million-dollar sums top streamers earn from playing computer games. *ABC News*, 7 October, available at: https://www.abc.net.au/news/science/2021-10-07/twitch-hack-reveals-how-much-top-streamers-earn-video-games/100520354.

Rahman, O., Wing-Sun, L. & Cheung, B.H.M. (2012). 'Cosplay': Imaginative self and performing identity. *Fashion Theory*, 16(3), 317–41.

Rao, L. (2011). Justin.TV's video gaming portal Twitch.TV is growing fast. *TechCrunch*, available at: https://techcrunch.com/2011/08/11/justin-tvs-video-gaming-portal-twitch-tv-growing-fast/.

Recktenwald, D. (2017). Toward a transcription and analysis of live streaming on Twitch. *Journal of Pragmatics*, 115, 68–81.

Reid, E. (1993). Electronic chat: Social issues on internet relay chat. *Media Information Australia*, 67(1), 62–70.

Reitman, J.G., Anderson-Coto, M.J., Wu, M., Lee, J.S. & Steinkuehler, C. (2020). Esports research: A literature review. *Games and Culture*, 15(1), 32–50.

Robinson, B. (2023). Governance on, with, behind, and beyond the Discord platform: A study of platform practices in an informal learning context. *Learning, Media and Technology*, 48(1), 81–94.

Rodriguez, S. (2020). How Among Us, a social deduction game, became this fall's mega hit. *CNBC*, available at: https://www.cnbc.com/2020/10/14/how-among-us-became-a-mega-hit-thanks-to-amazon-twitch.html.

Ruberg, B. (2021). 'Obscene, pornographic, or otherwise objectionable': Biased definitions of sexual content in video game live streaming. *New Media & Society*, 23(6), 1681–99.

Ruberg, B. (2022). Live play, live sex: The parallel labors of video game live streaming and webcam modeling. *Sexualities*, 25(8), 1021–39.

Ruberg, B. & Brewer, J. (2022). Digital intimacy in real time: Live streaming gender and sexuality. *Television & New Media*, 23(5), 443–50.

Ruberg, B. & Cullen, A.L. (2019). Feeling for an audience: The gendered emotional labor of video game live streaming. *Digital Culture & Society*, 5(2), 85–102.

Ruberg, B. & Lark, D. (2021). Livestreaming from the bedroom: Performing intimacy through domestic space on Twitch. *Convergence*, 27(3), 679–95.

Ruberg, B., Cullen, A.L. & Brewster, K. (2019). Nothing but a 'titty streamer': Legitimacy, labor, and the debate over women's breasts in video game live streaming. *Critical Studies in Media Communication*, 36(5), 466–81.

Ruch, A. (2021). Signifying nothing: The hyperreal politics of 'apolitical' games. *Communication Research and Practice*, 7(2), 128–47.

Ruiz-Bravo, N., Selander, L. & Roshan, M. (2022). The political turn of Twitch – Understanding live chat as an emergent political space. In: *Proceedings of the 55th Hawaii International Conference on System Sciences*.

Runco, M.A. & Jaeger, G.J. (2012). The standard definition of creativity. *Creativity Research Journal*, 24(1), 92–6.

Ruotsalainen, M. (2022). 'Cute goddess is actually an aunty': The evasive middle-aged woman streamer and normative performances of femininity in video game streaming. *Television & New Media*, 23(5), 487–97.

Ruvalcaba, O., Shulze, J., Kim, A., Berzenski, S.R. & Otten, M.P. (2018). Women's experiences in eSports: Gendered differences in peer and spectator feedback during competitive video game play. *Journal of Sport and Social Issues*, 42(4), 295–311.

Salter, A. & Blodgett, B. (2012). Hypermasculinity and dickwolves: The contentious role of women in the new gaming public. *Journal of Broadcasting and Electronic Media*, 56, 401–16.

Salter, M. (2018). From geek masculinity to Gamergate: The techno-logical rationality of online abuse. *Crime, Media, Culture*, 14(2), 247–64.

Savolainen, L., Uitermark, J. & Boy, J.D. (2022). Filtering feminisms: Emergent feminist visibilities on Instagram. *New Media & Society*, 24(3), 557–79.

Schofield, D. & LeDone, R. (2019). The motivations of a video game streamers and their viewers. *Screen Thought*, 3(1), 1–13.

Schott, G.R. & Horrell, K.R. (2000). Girl gamers and their relationship with the gaming culture. *Convergence*, 6(4), 36–53.

Scott, S. (2019). *Fake Geek Girls*. New York: New York University Press.

Scully-Blaker, R. (2014). A practiced practice: Speedrunning through space with de Certeau and Virilio. *Game Studies*, 14(1), 2016.

Scully-Blaker, R., Begy, J., Consalvo, M. & Ganzon, S. (2017). Playing along and playing for on Twitch: Livestreaming from tandem play to performance. In: *Proceedings of the 50th Hawaii International Conference on System Sciences*.

Seering, J. & Kairam, S.R. (2023). Who moderates on Twitch and what do they do?: Quantifying practices in community moderation on Twitch. *Proceedings of the ACM on Human–Computer Interaction, 7*, pp. 1–18.

Seering, J., Kraut, R. & Dabbish, L. (2017a). Shaping pro and anti-social behavior on twitch through moderation and example-setting. In: *Proceedings of the 2017 ACM Conference on Computer Supported Cooperative Work and Social Computing*. New York: ACM, pp. 111–25.

Seering J., Savage, S., Eagle, M., Churchin, J., Moeller, R., Bigham, J.P. & Hammer, J. (2017b). Audience participation games: Blurring the line between player and spectator. In: *Proceedings of the 2017 Conference on Designing Interactive Systems*, pp. 429–40.

Senft, T.M. (2008). *Camgirls: Celebrity and Community in the Age of Social Networks*. New York: Peter Lang.

Sennett, R. (2016). Concentrating minds: How the Greeks designed spaces for public debate. *Democratic Audit UK*, available at: https://www.democraticaudit.com/2016/11/01/concentrating-minds-how-the-greeks-designed-spaces-for-public-debate/.

Shaw, A. (2012). Do you identify as a gamer? Gender, race, sexuality, and gamer identity. *New Media & Society*, 14(1), 28–44.

Sheng, J.T. & Kairam, S.R. (2020). From virtual strangers to IRL friends: Relationship development in livestreaming communities on Twitch. *Proceedings of the ACM on Human–Computer Interaction, 4*, 1–34.

Sherrick, B., Smith, C., Jia, Y., Thomas, B. & Franklin, S.B. (2022). How parasocial phenomena contribute to sense of community on Twitch. *Journal of Broadcasting & Electronic Media*, 67(1), 47–67.

Siuda, P. & Johnson, M.R. (2022). Microtransaction politics in FIFA Ultimate Team: Game fans, Twitch streamers, and Electronic Arts. In: R. Guins, H.E. Lowood & C. Wing (Eds.), *Feeling the Game: Thinking Critically about EA Sport's FIFA Series*. London: Bloomsbury Academic, pp. 87–105.

Siutila, M. (2018). The gamification of gaming streams. In: *GamiFIN Conference 2018, Pori, Finland, 21–23 May*, pp. 131–40.

Sixto-García, J. & Losada-Fernández, D. (2023). Spanish Twitch streamers: Personal influence in a broadcast model akin to television. *Convergence*, 29(3), 713–29.

Sjöblom, M. & Hamari, J. (2017). Why do people watch others play video games? An empirical study on the motivations of Twitch users. *Computers in Human Behavior*, 75, 985–96.

Sjöblom, M., Törhönen, M., Hamari, J. & Macey, J. (2019). The ingredients of Twitch streaming: Affordances of game streams. *Computers in Human Behaviour*, 92, 20–8.

Speed, A., Burnett, A. & Robinson II, T. (2023). Beyond the game: Understanding why people enjoy viewing Twitch. *Entertainment Computing*, 45, 100545.

Spilker, H.S. & Colbjørnsen, T. (2020). The dimensions of streaming: Toward a typology of an evolving concept. *Media, Culture & Society*, 42(7–8), 1210–25.

Spilker, H.S., Ask, K. & Hansen, M. (2020). The new practices and infrastructures of participation: How the popularity of Twitch.tv challenges old and new ideas about television viewing. *Information, Communication & Society*, 23(4), 605–20.

Stanton, R. & Johnson, M.R. (2023). Inclusivity and diversity in 'actual play': Studying 'The Adventure Zone'. *Journal of Gaming and Virtual Worlds*.

Steinkuehler, C.A. & Williams, D. (2006). Where everybody knows your (screen) name: Online games as 'third places'. *Journal of Computer-Mediated Communication*, 11(4), 885–909.

Stenros, J., Paavilainen, J. & Mäyrä, F. (2011). Social interaction in games. *International Journal of Arts and Technology*, 4(3), 342–58.

Stuart, K. (2020). Among Us: The ultimate party game of the paranoid Covid era. *The Guardian*, 29 September, available at: https://www.theguardian.com/games/2020/sep/29/among-us-the-ultimate-party-game-of-the-covid-era.

Sullivan, A. & Smith, G. (2016). Designing craft games. *Interactions*, 24(1), 38–41.

Sun, N., Rau, P.P.L. & Ma, L. (2014). Understanding lurkers in online communities: A literature review. *Computers in Human Behavior*, 38, 110–17.

Sutton, T.A. (2021). *Gendered Rhetoric of Video Game Streaming: Female Agency, Harassment and Cat Girls*. Master's thesis, State University of New York at Albany, New York.

Tassi, P. (2023). Twitch is starting to feel like a failed state. *Forbes*, 16 June, available at: https://www.forbes.com/sites/paultassi/2023/06/16/twitch-is-starting-to-feel-like-a-failed-state/?sh=44cf87c81ff1.

Taylor, N. & Chess, S. (2018). Not so straight shooters: Queering the cyborg body in masculinized gaming. In: N. Taylor & G. Voorhees (Eds.), *Masculinities in Play*. Cham: Palgrave Macmillan, pp. 263–79.

Taylor, T.L. (2012). *Raising the Stakes: E-sports and the Professionalization of Computer Gaming*. Cambridge, MA: MIT Press.

Taylor, T.L. (2018). *Watch Me Play*. Princeton, NJ: Princeton University Press.

Tiidenberg, K., Hendry, N.A. & Abidin, C. (2021). *Tumblr*. Cambridge: Polity.

Toft-Nielsen, C. & Nørgård, R.T. (2015). Expertise as gender performativity and corporeal craftsmanship: Towards a multilayered understanding of gaming expertise. *Convergence*, 21(3), 343–59.

Topinka, R. (2022). The politics of anti-discourse: Copypasta, the Alt-Right, and the rhetoric of form. *Theory & Event*, 25(2), 392–418.

Törhönen, M., Hassan, L., Sjöblom, M. & Hamari, J. (2019). Play, playbour or labour? The relationships between perception of occupational activity and outcomes among streamers and YouTubers. *Proceedings of the 52nd Hawaii International Conference on System Sciences*, 2558–67.

Törhönen, M., Sjöblom, M., Hassan, L. & Hamari, J. (2020). Fame and fortune, or just fun? A study on why people create content on video platforms. *Internet Research*, 30(1), 165–90.

Törhönen, M., Giertz, J., Weiger, W. & Hamari, J. (2021). Streamers: The new wave of digital entrepreneurship? Extant corpus and research agenda. *Electronic Commerce Research and Applications*, 46, 1–13.

Tran, C.H. (2022). 'Never battle alone': Egirls and the gender(ed) war on video game live streaming as 'real' work. *Television & New Media*, 23(5), 509–20.

Turner, A.B. (2022). *Streaming as a Virtual Being: The Complex Relationship between VTubers and Identity*. PhD thesis, Malmö University.

Twitch (2023a). How to use Automod. *Twitch*, available at: https://help.twitch.tv/s/article/how-to-use-automod?language=en_US.

Twitch (2023b). Guide to building a moderation team. *Twitch*, available at: https://help.twitch.tv/s/article/guide-to-building-a-moderation-team?language=en_US.

Twitch (2023c). Analytics overview. *Twitch*, available at: https://help.twitch.tv/s/article/channel-analytics?language=en_US.

Twitch (2023d). Audience. *Twitch*, available at: https://twitchadvertising
.tv/audience/.

Uszkoreit, L. (2018). With great power comes great responsibility:
Video game live streaming and its potential risks and benefits
for female gamers. In: K.L. Gray, G. Voorhees & E. Vossen (Eds.),
Feminism in Play. Cham: Palgrave Macmillan, pp. 163–81.

Uttarapong, J., Cai, J. & Wohn, D.Y. (2021). Harassment experiences of
women and LGBTQ live streamers and how they handled negativity.
In: *ACM International Conference on Interactive Media Experiences*.
New York: ACM, pp. 7–19.

Uttarapong, J., LaMastra, N., Gandhi, R., Lee, Y.-h., Yuan, C.W. &
Wohn, D.Y. (2022). Twitch users' motivations and practices during
community mental health discussions. *Proceedings of the ACM
Human–Computer Interaction*, 6, 1–23.

Van Dijck, J. & Poell, T. (2013). Understanding social media logic.
Media and Communication, 1(1), 2–14.

Vandenberg, F. (2022). Put your 'hand emotes in the air': Twitch
concerts as unsuccessful large-scale interaction rituals. *Symbolic
Interaction*, 45(3), 425–48.

Veale, T. & Cook, M. (2018). *Twitterbots: Making Machines that Make
Meaning*. Cambridge, MA: MIT Press.

Vella, K., Johnson, D., Cheng, V.W.S., Davenport, T., Mitchell, J.,
Klarkowski, M. & Phillips, C. (2019). A sense of belonging: Pokémon
GO and social connectedness. *Games and Culture*, 14(6), 583–603.

Wadley, G., Carter, M. & Gibbs, M. (2015). Voice in virtual worlds: The
design, use, and influence of voice chat in online play. *Human–
Computer Interaction*, 30(3–4), 336–65.

Walker, A. (2014). Watching us play: Postures and platforms of live
streaming. *Surveillance & Society*, 12(3), 437–42.

Welch, T. (2022). 'Love you, bro': Performing homosocial intimacies
on Twitch. *Television & New Media*, 23(5), 521–30.

Whitmer, J.M. (2019). You are your brand: Self-branding and the
marketization of self. *Sociology Compass*, 13(3), e12662.

Whitson, J.R. (2014). Foucault's fitbit: Governance and gamification.
In: S.P. Walz & S. Deterding (Eds.), *The Gameful World: Approaches,
Issues, Applications*, Cambridge, MA: MIT Press, pp. 339–58.

Wingfield, N. (2014). What's Twitch? Gamers know, and Amazon is
spending $1 billion on it. *New York Times*, 26 August, available at:
https://www.nytimes.com/2014/08/26/technology/amazon-nears
-a-deal-for-twitch.html.

Wohn, D.Y. (2019). Volunteer moderators in twitch micro communities: How they get involved, the roles they play, and the emotional

labor they experience. *Proceedings of the 2019 CHI Conference on Human Factors in Computing Systems.* New York: ACM, pp. 1–13.

Wohn, D.Y. & Freeman, G. (2020). Audience management practices of live streamers on Twitch. In: *ACM International Conference on Interactive Media Experiences.* New York: ACM, pp. 106–16.

Wohn, D.Y., Freeman, G. & McLaughlin, C. (2018). Explaining viewers' emotional, instrumental, and financial support provision for live streamers. In: *2018 CHI Conference,* 1–13.

Wohn, D.Y., Jough, P., Eskander, P., Siri, J.S., Shimobayashi, M. & Desai, P. (2019). Understanding digital patronage: Why do people subscribe to streamers on Twitch? In: *Proceedings of the Annual Symposium on Computer–Human Interaction in Play.* New York: ACM, pp. 99–110.

Wolff, G.H. & Shen, C. (2022). Audience size, moderator activity, gender, and content diversity: Exploring user participation and financial commitment on Twitch.tv. *New Media & Society,* https://doi.org/10.1177/14614448211069996.

Woodcock, J. & Johnson, M.R. (2018). Gamification: What it is, and how to fight it. *The Sociological Review, 66*(3), 542–58.

Woodcock, J. & Johnson, M.R. (2019). The affective labor and performance of live streaming on Twitch.tv. *Television & New Media, 20*(8), 813–23.

Woodhouse, T. (2021). Live streaming and archiving the hegemony of play. *Popular Culture Studies Journal, 9*(2), 20–38.

Wu, Y., Li, Y. & Gui, X. (2022). 'I am concerned, but ...': Streamers' privacy concerns and strategies in live streaming information disclosure. *Proceedings of the ACM on Human–Computer Interaction, 6,* pp. 1–31.

Wulf, T., Schneider, F.M. & Beckert, S. (2020). Watching players: An exploration of media enjoyment on Twitch. *Games and Culture, 15*(3), 328–46.

Wulf, T., Schneider, F.M. & Queck, J. (2021). Exploring viewers' experiences of parasocial interactions with videogame streamers on Twitch. *Cyberpsychology, Behavior, and Social Networking, 24*(10), 648–53.

Wynne, L. (2023). Twitch adds Blaze and Gamdom to list of prohibited sites. *Gambling Insider,* available at: https://www.gamblinginsider.com/news/22038/twitch-adds-blaze-and-gamdom-to-list-of-prohibited-sites.

Yoganathan, V., Osburg, V.S. & Stevens, C.J. (2021). Freedom and giving in game streams: A Foucauldian exploration of tips and donations on Twitch. *Psychology & Marketing, 38*(6), 1001–13.

Yosilewitz, A. (2018). StreamElements analysis on Twitch bullying. *Stream Elements*, available at: https://blog.streamelements.com /streamelements-analysis-on-twitch-bullying-c3f2b2240318.

Young, A. & Wiedenfeld, G. (2022). A motivation analysis of video game microstreamers: 'Finding my people and myself' on YouTube and Twitch. *Journal of Broadcasting & Electronic Media*, 66(2), 381–99.

Youngblood, J. (2022). A labor of (queer) love: Maintaining 'cozy wholesomeness' on twitch during COVID-19 and beyond. *Television & New Media*, 23(5), 531–41.

Yu, V., Alvarez, K.P.B. & Chen, V.H.H. (2021). Game streamers' practices on Twitch and management of well-being. *Journal of Communication Technology*, 4(1), 54–77.

Zhang, G. & Hjorth, L. (2019). Live-streaming, games and politics of gender performance: The case of Nüzhubo in China. *Convergence*, 25(5–6), 807–25.

Index